T0301266

Women Entrepreneurs and the Myth of 'Underperformance'

Dedicated to the potential and strength that lie within every woman in the world, including my mother Zeenat and my daughters Nur and Alif Sufi, who helped me to realize mine! – *Shumaila*

To my family and to all women entrepreneurs who contribute towards changing the world for the better – *Alain*

For Victoria and Zazou; no daughters could make a father happier or prouder – *Adam*

To my mum, for bringing me up to be strong and hard-working! – *Colette*

To my mother, for her selfless love and encouragement! – *Saadat*

To my mother who sacrificed her life to make me what I am today! – *Shandana*

Women Entrepreneurs and the Myth of 'Underperformance'

A New Look at Women's Entrepreneurship Research

Edited by

Shumaila Yousafzai

Reader in Entrepreneurship, Cardiff Business School, Cardiff University, UK

Alain Fayolle

Professor of Entrepreneurship and Director, Entrepreneurship Research Centre, EMLYON Business School, Ecully, France

Adam Lindgreen

Professor of Marketing and Head of Department, Copenhagen Business School, Denmark and Research Associate, Gordon Institute of Business Science, University of Pretoria, South Africa

Colette Henry

Head of School of Business and Humanities, Dundalk Institute of Technology, Ireland and Adjunct Professor of Entrepreneurship, UiT– The Arctic University of Norway, Tromsø, Norway

Saadat Saeed

Associate Professor of Entrepreneurship, Durham University Business School, Durham University, UK

Shandana Sheikh

Doctoral Researcher, Cardiff Business School, Cardiff University, UK

Cheltenham, UK • Northampton, MA, USA

© Shumaila Yousafzai, Alain Fayolle, Adam Lindgreen, Colette Henry, Saadat Saeed and Shandana Sheikh 2018

All rights reserved. No part of this publication may be reproduced, stored in a retrieval system or transmitted in any form or by any means, electronic, mechanical or photocopying, recording, or otherwise without the prior permission of the publisher.

Published by
Edward Elgar Publishing Limited
The Lypiatts
15 Lansdown Road
Cheltenham
Glos GL50 2JA
UK

Edward Elgar Publishing, Inc.
William Pratt House
9 Dewey Court
Northampton
Massachusetts 01060
USA

A catalogue record for this book
is available from the British Library

Library of Congress Control Number: 2017959424

This book is available electronically in the **Elgar**online
Business subject collection
DOI 10.4337/9781786434500

ISBN 978 1 78643 449 4 (cased)
ISBN 978 1 78643 450 0 (eBook)

Typeset by Servis Filmsetting Ltd, Stockport, Cheshire
Printed and bound in Great Britain by TJ International Ltd, Padstow

Contents

Figures

Tables

About the editors

Shumaila Yousafzai is an Associate Professor (Reader) in Entrepreneurship at the Cardiff Business School, Cardiff University, UK, where she teaches entrepreneurship, marketing and consumer behaviour. After her undergraduate studies in Physics and Mathematics (University of Balochistan, Pakistan) and an MSc in Electronic Commerce (Coventry University, UK), she finished her PG Diploma in Research Methods from Cardiff University. Shumaila received her doctoral degree in 2005 from Cardiff University. In her research, Shumaila focuses mainly on topics linked to contextual embeddedness of entrepreneurship, firm performance, institutional theory and entrepreneurial orientation. She has published several articles in various international journals, such as *Entrepreneurship: Theory and Practice*, *Journal of Small Business Management*, *Industrial Marketing Management*, *Technovation*, *Journal of Business Ethics*, *Psychology & Marketing*, *Journal of Applied Social Psychology* and *Computers in Human Behavior*. She has also co-edited a special issue on women's entrepreneurship for *Entrepreneurship & Regional Development.*

Alain Fayolle is a Professor of Entrepreneurship and the founder and Director of the Entrepreneurship Research Centre at EMLYON Business School, a leading European institution based in Ecully, France. He has also been a Visiting Professor at the Ecole Hôtelière de Lausanne, Switzerland, and at the Solvay Brussels School of Economics and Management, Belgium, and is regularly invited by international universities and institutions. Alain has several interests and topics in research: entrepreneurial processes, entrepreneurship education, corporate entrepreneurship, social entrepreneurship, necessity entrepreneurship, critical studies in entrepreneurship, and family entrepreneurship. He has published over 30 books and over 100 articles in leading international and French-speaking scientific journals. Among his editorial positions, he is an Associate Editor of *Journal of Small Business Management* and the Editor of *Revue de l'Entrepreneuriat and Entreprendre & Innover*, a leading French-speaking journal in entrepreneurship. Alain is also a board member of eight entrepreneurship and small business journals. He served on the ICSB's (International Council for Small Business and Entrepreneurship) Board of Directors as Director-At-Large for the year 2013–2014. He has also been elected as a member of the Executive Board of the Entrepreneurship Division of the Academy of Management and was Chair of the Entrepreneurship Division during the academic year 2016 2017.

Adam Lindgreen completed an MSc in food science and technology at the Technical University of Denmark following studies in chemistry at Copenhagen University, engineering at the Engineering Academy of Denmark and physics at Copenhagen University. He also finished an MBA at the University of Leicester, UK. Adam received his PhD in marketing from Cranfield University, UK. His first appointments were with the Catholic University of Louvain, Belgium (2000–2001) and Eindhoven University of Technology, the Netherlands (2002–2007). Subsequently, he served as Professor of Marketing at Hull University's Business School, UK (2007–2010), University of Birmingham's Business School, UK (2010), where he also was the research director in the Department of Marketing, and University of Cardiff's Business School, UK (2011–2016). Under his leadership, the Department of Marketing and Strategy at Cardiff Business School ranked first among all marketing departments in Australia, Canada, New Zealand, the United Kingdom and the United States, based upon the hg indices of senior faculty. Since 2016, he has been Professor of Marketing at Copenhagen Business School, Denmark, where he also heads the Department of Marketing. Since 2017, he has also been a research associate with University of Pretoria's Gordon Institute of Business Science.

Adam has been a Visiting Professor with various institutions, including Georgia State University, Groupe HEC in France, and Melbourne University. His publications have appeared in *Business Horizons*, *California Management Review*, *Entrepreneurship and Regional Development*, *Industrial Marketing Management*, *International Journal of Management Reviews*, *Journal of Advertising*, *Journal of Business Ethics*, *European Journal of Marketing*, *Journal of Business and Industrial Marketing*, *Journal of Marketing Management*, *Journal of the Academy of Marketing Science*, *Journal of Product Innovation Management*, *Journal of World Business*, *Psychology & Marketing* and *Supply Chain Management: An International Journal*, among others.

Adam's books include *A Stakeholder Approach to Corporate Social Responsibility* (with Kotler, Vanhamme, and Maon), *Managing Market Relationships* and *Memorable Customer Experiences* (with Vanhamme and Beverland), and *Sustainable Value Chain Management* (with Maon, Vanhamme, and Sen).

The recipient of the 'Outstanding Article 2005' award from *Industrial Marketing Management* and the runner-up for the same award in 2016, Adam serves on the board of several scientific journals; he is co-editor-in-chief of *Industrial Marketing Management* and previously was the joint editor of the *Journal of Business Ethics*' section on corporate responsibility. His research interests include business and industrial marketing management, corporate social responsibility, and sustainability. Adam has been awarded the Dean's Award for Excellence in Executive Teaching.

Adam is a member of the International Scientific Advisory Panel of the New Zealand Food Safety Science and Research Centre (a partnership between government, industry organizations and research institutions), as well as of the Chartered Association of Business Schools' Academic Journal Guide (AJG) Scientific Committee in the field of marketing.

Beyond these academic contributions to marketing, Adam has discovered and excavated settlements from the Stone Age in Denmark, including the only major kitchen midden – Sparregård – in the south-east of Denmark; because of its importance, the kitchen midden was later excavated by the National Museum and then protected as a historical monument for future generations. He is also an avid genealogist, having traced his family back to 1390 and published widely in scientific journals (*Personalhistorisk Tidsskrift, The Genealogist and Slægt & Data*) related to methodological issues in genealogy, accounts of population development, and particular family lineages.

Colette Henry is Head of School of Business and Humanities at Dundalk Institute of Technology, Ireland, and Adjunct Professor of Entrepreneurship at UiT–The Arctic University of Norway, Tromsø, Norway. She is also a Fellow of the Royal Society, and Visiting Fellow at CIMR, Birkbeck, London, UK. In 2015, Colette was awarded the prestigious Diana International Trailblazer award for her research on female entrepreneurship, and in 2017 became the first Irish recipient of the Sten K. Johnson European Entrepreneurship Education Award. She is the founding and current Editor-in-Chief of the *International Journal of Gender and Entrepreneurship*. Her research interests include: women's entrepreneurship, entrepreneurship education and training, the creative industries, social enterprise and veterinary business. Colette has published widely across a range of journals, with her most recent research published in the *International Small Business Journal*, the *Journal of Small Business Management* and *Small Business Economics: An Entrepreneurship Journal.*

Saadat Saeed is an Associate Professor (Senior Lecturer) in Entrepreneurship at the Durham University Business School, Durham University, UK. Previously he has worked for Essex Business School, University of Essex, UK. Saadat received his doctoral degree in Entrepreneurship from University of Padova, Italy, where he is part of the Global Entrepreneurship Monitor Team. Saadat's past research efforts have included, but are not limited to: the global study of supportive institutions and women's entrepreneurship, entrepreneurship in adverse conditions, corporate entrepreneurship and firm performance in a multi-country context, cross-cultural comparison of corporate support programs on employees' innovative behaviour, all targeted at premier and high quality journals, such as *Journal of Product Innovation Management*, *Entrepreneurship Theory and Practice*, *Journal of Small Business Management* and *Industrial Marketing Management*. He has also co-edited a special issue on women's entrepreneurship for *Entrepreneurship & Regional Development.*

Shandana Sheikh is a Doctoral Researcher at Cardiff Business School, Cardiff University, UK. Her research area particularly focuses on women's entrepreneurship and its challenges and public value amidst an entrepreneurial ecosystem. Prior to her Doctoral studies, Shandana received her MBA in Marketing from Lahore School of Economics, Pakistan and an MSc in Marketing and Strategy from Warwick Business School, University of Warwick, UK. Shandana has also worked in the capacity of a Teaching fellow at the Lahore School of Economics, where she was teaching undergraduate- and graduate-level courses.

About the contributors

Ruta Aidis is a Senior Fellow at the Schar School of Policy and Government, George Mason University, USA. She has more than 20 years' experience teaching, researching, consulting and publishing in the area of comparative entrepreneurship development, innovation, gender and diversity, institutions and public policy. She holds a PhD in Economics from the University of Amsterdam, the Netherlands. Dr Aidis is also CEO and Founder of ACG Inc., a global research and consultancy firm.

Aybeniz Akdeniz AR is an Assistant Professor at Onyedi Eylul University, Turkey. She obtained her PhD in Marketing from Uludag University, Turkey and her MBA degree from the University of Balikesir, Turkey. She gives courses at associate, bachelor and graduate levels. She was also a visiting academic at Cardiff University, UK, doing research on women's entrepreneurship. Her research interests include consumer behaviour, brand management, social marketing and women's entrepreneurship.

Harun Baiya is the founding Chief Executive of SITE Enterprise Promotion, Kenya. A Mechanical Engineer with postgraduate training in business management and planning, he has worked in small business development for two and a half decades. His main interests are in technical and vocational skills formation, informal economy, business institutional development, employment, and industrial development.

Shima Barakat is the Director of Entrepreneurial Learning Programmes and Engagement at the Entrepreneurship Centre, Judge Business School, at the University of Cambridge, UK. Currently her work focuses on how and why gender influences the nature, rate, focus, location, activities, team choices, networks and education/training needs of entrepreneurs and their ventures.

Monique Boddington is a Research Associate at the Entrepreneurship Centre, University of Cambridge, UK. Monique's research includes the study of entrepreneurship strategy, entrepreneurial teams, entrepreneurship education, entrepreneurship and gender; and the use of sociological approaches to broaden our understanding of entrepreneurial activity. Monique leads the EVER project, which aims to understand the strategic decision-making of early ventures.

Dallas Brozik is Professor of Finance at the Lewis College of Business, Marshall University, USA. He obtained his PhD from the University of South Carolina, USA, in 1984 and has published articles on derivative pricing theory and tourism in several journals. His research interests include derivative securities prices, simulations development and tourism management.

Julio O. De Castro is a Professor at IE Business School, IE University, Spain. He has been the Lewis Family Distinguished Professor of Global Management at Babson College, USA, and Associate Professor of Strategy and Organization Management at the University of Colorado Boulder, USA. He received his PhD from the University of South Carolina, USA. His research deals with firm strategy and entrepreneurship, and uses a firm's perspective to examine informal businesses, product piracy and knowledge management.

Luisa Delgado-Márquez recently received her PhD in Entrepreneurship from the University of Granada, Spain. She is a research fellow at IE University, Spain. Her research is focused on entrepreneurship at the base of the pyramid. In particular, her research interests examine how public policy may promote entrepreneurship. She is also interested in analysing how pay gaps affect the performance of businesses based on equality, and in the influence of the managerial role of women in community-based enterprises. She has presented papers at top conferences such as BCERC, the SMS Annual Conference and the AoM Annual Conference.

Sunita Dewitt is a lecturer at Coventry University, UK. She obtained her PhD in Economic Geography from the University of Birmingham, UK. Her research interests include: entrepreneurship; firm formation; breaking out, expansion and growth strategies (business); cross-border business expansions (international business); ethnic entrepreneurship (including migration and identity); female entrepreneurship; marketing; travel and tourism business sector and sustainability.

Wojdan Farraj is an instructor at the Faculty of Business and Economics at Birzeit University, Palestine. Upon earning her MBA in 2010, she began teaching courses in management, organization theory, business communication and human resource management. She has also published work in the fields of entrepreneurship and organizational strategy.

Atsede T. Hailemariam is a doctoral candidate at Tilburg University, the Netherlands. She is a senior lecturer at Addis Ababa University College of Economics and Business-School of Commerce, Ethiopia. She has a master's degree in mathematics from Addis Ababa University, Ethiopia, and a master's degree in business administration from the Open University, UK.

Cherisse Hoyte is a Lecturer in Enterprise and Entrepreneurship at the International Centre for Transformational Entrepreneurship (ICTE) at Coventry University, UK. She obtained her PhD in Entrepreneurship from Nottingham University, UK, in 2015 and is the author of *Womenpreneurs: The Shift from Corporate Management to Entrepreneurship*. Her research interests include women in business; entrepreneurial identity; sensemaking; and the opportunity development process.

Bridget Irene is the Dean of the Faculty of Entrepreneurship and Economic Transformation at the Cornerstone Institute, South Africa. She obtained her PhD in Business and Management from Cardiff Metropolitan University, UK, in June 2016. Her research interests contribute to an established discourse within the field of women's entrepreneurship regarding the identification and potential synthesis of personal capabilities, innate cognitive resources, emotional intelligence, and management competencies to produce distinctive formulae for business excellence.

Jeaneth Johansson is a Professor at Luleå University of Technology and Halmstad University, Sweden, working in the field of accounting and financial decision-making in the context of entrepreneurship and innovation. Her research revolves around cognitive, social and organizational aspects of financial decision-making and innovation management contributing to knowledge on social and societal challenges in entrepreneurship and innovation.

Rachida Justo is Professor of Entrepreneurial Management and Social Entrepreneurship at IE Business School, IE University, Spain. She holds a PhD from the Universidad Autónoma de Madrid, Spain. She has been a member of GECES, an expert Group of the European Commission on Social Entrepreneurship, and has also produced several policy reports for the OED and EC. Her research has been published in *Journal of Business Venturing*, and has received several awards such as the 'Best Women's Entrepreneurship Paper Award' from the AoM Conference.

Anne Kamau is a Research Fellow at the University of Nairobi, Kenya. She obtained her PhD from the University of Bielefeld, Germany, in 2006. She is an *ad hoc* committee member for the TDR/WHO Research Capacity Strengthening. Anne has led several research projects and public health evaluations in Kenya and East Africa. Her research interests include health systems, adolescents' sexual and reproductive health, malaria, transport, and socio-cultural dimensions of health.

Paul Kamau is a Senior Research Fellow at the University of Nairobi, Kenya. He has a PhD in Development Economics from the University of Nairobi (2009). He has recently been undertaking research on access to health insurance by the informal sector workers in Kenya as well as on Employment Creation Schemes in Agriculture and Agro Processing Sectors in Kenya in the Context of Inclusive Growth: Political Economy and Political Settlements Analysis.

Grace Khoury is an Associate Professor of Management and the Dean of the Faculty of Business and Economics at Birzeit University, Palestine. She obtained her PhD in Human Resource Management from Bradford University, UK, in 2000 and is an author, co-author and editor of a number of books and journal articles. Dr Khoury is a member of the editorial board of *The Learning Organisation* journal, published by Emerald. Her research interests include entrepreneurship, leadership, organizational behaviour and management.

Brigitte Kroon is senior lecturer and researcher at Tilburg University, the Netherlands. She obtained her PhD on Human Resource Management in Small Organizations in 2013. Her research focuses on decent work in various contexts, including publications on work in agriculture, flexible work arrangements and leadership.

Joan Lockyer is Assistant Director at the International Centre for Transformational Entrepreneurship (ICTE) at Coventry University, UK. She obtained her PhD in Management from Keele University, UK, in 2003. Her research interests embrace entrepreneurship in a range of contexts, but with a focus on the transformative effect of entrepreneurship through education, leadership and innovation. She has successfully led and contributed to a number of European and international projects, many of which have a focus on developing and supporting women entrepreneurs.

Malin Malmström is a Professor in Entrepreneurship and Innovation at Luleå University of Technology, Sweden. Her research interests are related to cognitive foundations and competences in venture's innovation management and in financiers' financial decision-making.

Milka Milliance is the Founder and Chief Executive Officer of We R Artemis Leadership, a women's leadership consulting company in Miami, USA. She obtained her Master's in Business Administration from the F.W. Olin Graduate School of Business, Babson College, USA and her Bachelor of Arts from Columbia University, USA. Her research interests include women in leadership and women entrepreneurs and their journey to entrepreneurship.

Daniel Muia is a Senior Lecturer at Kenyatta University, Kenya. He is currently a co-researcher on a TDR/WHO-supported implementation research project on malaria control in Malindi, Kenya. He has published articles on predictors of food security, and on coping strategies with food insecurity in informal settlements in Kenya. He has also co-edited a book entitled *Introduction to Development Studies in Africa*.

Roshni Narendran serves as a lecturer at the Australian Institute of Business in Adelaide, Australia. She has published across various disciplines: female entrepreneurship, pharmaceutical marketing and economics. She recently had an article published in the *International Journal of Entrepreneurial Behavior & Research* which highlights the importance of social variables, especially the religious composition to be a pertinent predictor of female entrepreneurship.

Jane Ndung'u is a project manager at SITE Enterprise Promotion, Kenya. Her areas of interest are in community development in the informal economy using participatory approaches and enterprise approach. Currently she is the team leader in a four-year *Wezesha Jamii* project being implemented in five informal settlements of Nairobi among women small-scale traders and domestic workers. Jane is also pursuing an MBA in Project Management and Evaluation.

Natalie Sappleton is Senior Lecturer in Manchester Metropolitan University Business School, UK. She obtained her PhD from Manchester Metropolitan University Business School in 2014. She has published widely on gender and entrepreneurship in journals such as *International Journal of Gender and Entrepreneurship*, *Recherches Socioloqiques et Anthropolgiques*, *Gender in Management* and *International Journal of Entrepreneurship and Innovation.* Her research interests include social capital, social networks and crowdfunding in entrepreneurship.

Federica Sist is an Assistant Professor at LUMSA University, Italy. She obtained her PhD in Banking and Finance from Tor Vergata University, Italy, in 2008. Her research interests include banking, internationalization of firms and banks (strategic alliances), ownership structure impact (family business and bank models), gender impact (credit constraints and risk), social entrepreneurship, and sustainable markets (securities bubbles).

Suhail Sultan is the MBA program coordinator at Birzeit University, Palestine. He obtained his PhD in business administration from Maastricht School of Management, the Netherlands, in 2007. He teaches project management and strategic management courses. Dr Sultan has a number of publications and his research interests include clustering, competitiveness and SMEs.

Aija Voitkane is a PhD candidate in Entrepreneurship and Innovation, Luleå University of Technology, Sweden. Her research focuses on gender equality in governmental financiers' decision-making and assessment of entrepreneurial potential and innovation for investment.

Joakim Wincent is a Professor at Luleå University of Technology, Sweden, and Hanken School of Economics, Finland. He currently researches various individual issues such as the role of passion and other related topics. He also has an interest in studying team-level and organizational issues in entrepreneurship.

Alina Zapalska is a Professor at the US Coast Guard Academy, USA. She holds a PhD in Economics from the University of Kentucky, USA. Professor Zapalska's extensive and varied teaching experience spans over 30 years in the US and abroad. Her research is in areas of economics, international business, entrepreneurship and pedagogy.

Introduction

Shumaila Yousafzai, Alain Fayolle, Adam Lindgreen, Colette Henry, Saadat Saeed and Shandana Sheikh

Women entrepreneurs have been identified as the 'rising stars of the economies' (Vossenberg, 2013) and the 'way forward' (World Economic Forum, 2012). While women-owned businesses have increased in number, the *underperformance* of women-owned enterprises compared to the performance of their male-owned counterparts continues to be debated (Ahl, 2006; Eddleston and Powell, 2008; Marlow et al., 2008). The purpose of this book is to provide a fresh perspective on women's entrepreneurship and to co-create knowledge and expertise that can feed joint learning, innovative practices and evidence-based policy-making for the successful promotion of women's entrepreneurship and gender-just inclusive growth around the globe.

Most previous research in entrepreneurship has evaluated the outcomes of an entrepreneurial activity in objective monetary terms, such as financial performance, wealth and job creation, and firm survival. This one-sided analysis limits the contribution of entrepreneurial activity that is initiated by disadvantaged and marginalized groups such as women, ethnic minorities, the disabled, and youth (Welter, 2011), even though these groups often create significant value beyond the purely financial. Such value takes multiple forms and occurs at various levels, so it must be documented if the full contribution that all entrepreneurs make to the economy and society is to be recognized (Sheikh et al., Chapter 2 this volume). The chapters in Part 1 of this book argue that, while women entrepreneurs are often labelled as underperformers in business for low growth and low success rates and are, therefore, under-recognized in the sphere of social value creation, these are criteria that society expects women to meet, and are not necessarily those that women expect or want to meet. Not all entrepreneurs are cut out for or aspire to the standards of high growth and performance as identified by the yardstick of male-owned and/or high-tech enterprises.

Adopting a woman's perspective and using data collected from Ethiopia, Pakistan, the US, Spain and Morocco, the chapters in Part 1 argue that the performance and success of women-owned enterprises should be defined according to women's perceptions. These entrepreneurs may not have high profit margins but may be satisfied with the balance between their businesses and personal lives; they may not have high-tech firms or a physical presence on the high street but may contribute to their families' and households' needs and wants. Hence, one must look beyond standard measures of performance and success and focus on what success and performance mean to the woman entrepreneur.

Accepting that each woman has her own story and offers her own unique value to her entrepreneurial environment will also highlight the importance of women as agents of change for society and the economy, and may direct future researchers to shift the focus of research from questions such as 'what do entrepreneurs do?' to 'how do they do it?' in order to focus on the unique ways in which each woman entrepreneur creates value. In addition, asking 'why do they do it?' helps us to focus on the multiple value outcomes women entrepreneurs create as well as the beneficiaries of that value (Zahra et al., 2009). The implication for policy-makers relates to the benefits of paying more attention to the heterogeneity of women entrepreneurs and to non-financial measures of their performance as they design policy and support programs in pursuit of an entrepreneurial ecosystem that is conducive to women's entrepreneurship.

The chapters in Parts 2 and 3 question the myth of underperformance and suggest that it is not underperformance but the externally constrained performance of women entrepreneurs that differentiates their performance from that of male entrepreneurs (Marlow and McAdam, 2013). Taking insight from the indigenous Māori entrepreneurs of New Zealand, British mumpreneurs, Swedish governmental financiers, Indian officials who are responsible for implementing programmes to facilitate female entrepreneurship in Kerala, small-scale female traders in Kenya, home-based Palestinian female entrepreneurs, and community-based enterprises in Brazil, these chapters suggest that, while traditionally 'successful' entrepreneurs are the driving force behind change and innovation, they alone are not responsible for societal revolution, wealth creation and employment generation in a society. To explain the reasons for underperformance, one must study factors beyond gender differences and pay attention to structural factors that affect women's entrepreneurial activity in a specific context.

Finally, the chapters in Part 4 argue that the so-called underperformance of women-owned enterprises should be understood and treated as a manifestation of entrepreneurial segregation; they highlight that the concept of 'entrepreneur' is limiting to women, and suggest the importance of using a feminist lens in exploring the 'Otherness' of women. In doing so, they suggest that a feminist stance on the field of entrepreneurship would help build new theory and develop a new understanding of the challenges women entrepreneurs face.

PART 1   PERFORMANCE, SUCCESS AND VALUE IN ENTREPRENEURSHIP: A WOMEN'S PERSPECTIVE

In Chapter 1, Atsede T. Hailemariam and Brigitte Kroon explore the meaning of success for female Ethiopian entrepreneurs and challenge the notion of the underperformance of women entrepreneurs. They explain that women entrepreneurs evaluate success in business both in financial and non-financial terms. While some define success as achieving self-fulfilment and in terms of their contribution to society and family, others emphasize communal and religious values. It tends to be the young, educated females and those who have experience and operate more than one business or engage in male-dominated sectors who define their success in terms of profit and growth. The implication for policy-makers relates to the need to pay more attention to the heterogeneity of women entre-preneurs and to non-financial measures of performance as they design policy and support programs to create an entrepreneurial ecosystem that is conducive to entrepreneurship.

In Chapter 2, Shandana Sheikh and her co-authors argue that, although evaluation of entrepreneurial activity in terms of financial performance, wealth creation and firm survival is important, it often results in a one-sided analysis in which entrepreneurship is evaluated and appraised solely in monetary terms, without reference to its social impact and other types of value. They suggest that such approaches limit the contribution of entrepreneurial activity that is initiated by disadvantaged and marginalized groups, even though these groups often create significant value beyond financial value. They argue that, while women entrepreneurs are often labelled as 'underperformers' in business because of their businesses' low rates of growth and success, these criteria are those that society expects women to meet, not those that women expect or want to meet. Hence, one must look beyond standard measures of performance and success and focus on what success and performance mean to the woman entrepreneur. Their study presents narratives from two women entrepreneurs that highlight the unique ways in which they create value and contribute to their economies and societies.

In Chapter 3, Milka Milliance adopts a feminine leadership paradigm to enrich the discussion on redefining performance in entrepreneurship and contributes to the discussion on women's entrepreneurship and its underperformance stereotypes. She highlights the importance of women using their whole selves instead of only their feminism to achieve self-efficacy and drive change. This chapter presents a multi-disciplinary review of the literature across the fields of entrepreneurship, leadership, gender studies and archetypal psychology, and takes a radical feminist point of view to disavow the notion of gender neutrality in entrepreneurial leadership.

PART 2 CHALLENGING THE UNDERPERFORMANCE HYPOTHESIS AND ACKNOWLEDGING THE CONSTRAINED PERFORMANCE OF WOMEN ENTREPRENEURS

Questioning the myth of underperformance in women's entrepreneurship and highlighting the barriers women entrepreneurs face is the focus of Chapter 4. Ruta Aidis explains the influences of gendered stereotypes in entrepreneurship and examines the impact on growth-oriented women entrepreneurs and their ability to access leadership positions. Aidis suggests that, even when women leave the corporate sector to take on entrepreneurial careers and are successful in their ventures, they are limited by the entrepreneurial 'glass ceiling'. Drawing on institutional theory and role congruity theory, Aidis explains that gendered impediments for women constrain their ability to access leadership positions. Aidis further shows that gendered stereotypes that view leadership as a male characteristic make it less socially desirable for women to grow their businesses and affect their ability to acquire the resources they need.

In Chapter 5, Alina Zapalska and Dallas Brozik advance the framework of indigenous entrepreneurship by studying the context of female Māori entrepreneurs who operate in New Zealand's tourism industry. They document that the collective cultural, social and economic value of the Māori female entrepreneurial community has been significant not only for their own communities but also in increasing value for their clients. The authors outline the elements of female entrepreneurial sustainability based on cultural, natural and environmental fundamentals in the context of indigenous entrepreneurship. Their findings suggest that prominent barriers for growth include the lack of financial capital, inadequate human capital and lack of adequate network structures, the availability of which would enable Māori female entrepreneurs to achieve their social, cultural and ecosystem objectives.

In Chapter 6, Bridget Irene analyses the work–life balance issues that impact the success of women entrepreneurs in South Africa. Addressing the need to identify the factors that affect success in SMEs owned and managed by women, she presents an overview of the perceived impact of work–life balance and the perception of success amongst women entrepreneurs. Irene's findings suggest that most South African women entrepreneurs are concerned with achieving a better work–life balance and do not seek financial success at the expense of their family lives, whether their own or those of their employees. Therefore, it is necessary to reconsider women's entrepreneurship as an avenue for social and cultural change, not just a route to financial emancipation.

In Chapter 7, Aija Voitkane, Jeaneth Johansson, Malin Malmström and Joakim Wincent explore the myth of women's underperformance as reflected in Swedish governmental financiers' social interactions when they analyse ventures for investment. Observing governmental financiers' meetings, they consider culture and the discourse that takes place in financiers' performance of entrepreneurial identities and, thus, the construction of the underperformance myth. The authors adopt a symbolic–interpretative lens to explain how men and women financiers interpret and attribute meanings to gender relationships in their assessment work. They also show that such interpretations can influence their interactions both within their organization and with the ventures that apply for financing.

In Chapter 8, Roshni Narendran adopts a social constructionist view to advance the debate on the constrained performance of women entre-preneurs. Narendran highlights the social construction of masculine dominance in entrepreneurship by studying misconceptions and inconsist-encies in the perceptions of officials who are responsible for implementing programmes to facilitate female entrepreneurship in Kerala, India. In doing so, Narendran contributes to the discussion on the myth of women entrepreneurs' underperformance, finding that masculinity overshadows entrepreneurship activity when men are treated better than women. This chapter highlights the constraints that women entrepreneurs in Kerala face in their ecosystem that widen the gender gap and result in low business performance and growth of women-led enterprises.

PART 3   OVERCOMING CONSTRAINED PERFORMANCE: FACILITATING WOMEN ENTREPRENEURS

Enriching the discussion on facilitating women entrepreneurs, in Chapter 9, Monique Boddington and Shima Barakat study the gendered entre-preneurship discourse by challenging the stereotypical characterizations relating to the underperformance of women entrepreneurs within an education setting. They evaluate the impact of a learning intervention (business education tailored to the needs of women in science and engineering) through a women's entrepreneurial programme (EnterpriseWISE) aimed at postdoctoral researchers and PhD researchers at the University of Cambridge, UK. Adopting a qualitative stance, they explore the change facilitated by EnterpriseWISE in increasing women's entrepreneurial self-efficacy and encouraging them to consider entrepreneurship as a viable career choice. Presenting an alternative gendered order of entrepreneurial practice in education, their findings suggest that programmes for women, such as EnterpriseWISE, create a safe working environment that offers them a reflexive space, provides alternative role models, and encourages women to take action towards pursuing an entrepreneurial career.

In Chapter 10, Anne Kamau, Paul Kamau, Daniel Muia, Harun Baiya and Jane Ndung'u contribute to the discussion on the growth and business support of small-scale, informal women entrepreneurs by going beyond economic measures such as financial support. Drawing upon survey data from 398 small-scale women traders in Nairobi, Kenya, the authors outline the importance of investment in social protection for the business support and growth of women entrepreneurs, which may help to increase their business performance. In so doing, they challenge the notion of underperformance that is associated with women entrepreneurs, particularly those in the informal economy, and highlight the role of informal social networks that can provide social protection to women entrepreneurs in the informal sector, easing their financial, psychological and social burden.

Augmenting this discussion, in Chapter 11, Grace Khoury, Wojdan Farraj and Suhail Sultan highlight the challenges and barriers that constrain the performance of home-based women entrepreneurs in Palestine and that prevent them from becoming part of the formal economy. The authors argue that few women attempt to formalize their home-based businesses because of the challenges associated with the legitimization process, leaving the majority to endure constrained performance rather than to pursue the cumbersome alternative. Their findings demonstrate that the most challenging factors are of an institutional nature, both formal (weak institutions, tax policies and support services) and informal (socio-cultural constraints). The chapter also sheds light on the successful initiatives that various institutions have introduced to encourage these women to formalize their home-based businesses.

Advancing the discussion on enabling women entrepreneurs' performance, Chapter 12, by Luisa Delgado-Márquez, Rachida Justo and Julio De Castro, studies gender in social interactions and its impact on implementation of family-friendly policies in the context of community-based enterprises in Brazil. Considering the prevalence of gender egalitarianism in entrepreneurial teams in community-based enterprises, the authors explore the influence of gender on the motivations, outcomes and challenges of these enterprises. Their analyses of the Solidarity Economic database created by the Brazilian government suggests that the presence of women in founding teams in community-based enterprises has a positive impact on the social motivations and achievements of the businesses and on the implementation of family-friendly policies, but not on the businesses' social challenges. The authors highlight the role of gender in influencing business-related decisions, and suggest that studying the role of gender in social interactions helps to determine whether women can influence decision-making and can leverage economic, social, moral or political advantage for themselves, thus negating their image as underperforming entrepreneurs.

PART 4 MOVING FORWARD

Acknowledging the constraints in women entrepreneurs' performance, Chapter 13 by Natalie Sappleton highlights the facilitators of women's entrepreneurship that can overcome constraints on their performance. Sappleton explains the importance of accounting for the role of the industrial sector in analysing the link between gender and performance in entrepreneurship. She calls for consideration of the industry's location and specific types of businesses when comparing male entrepreneurs with female entrepreneurs. Sappleton also contends that the empirical existence of entrepreneurial segregation means that women owner-operators are channelled into business sectors that are riskiest, that attract limited external financing, and that focus on local markets. Thus, the so-called underperformance of women-owned enterprises should be understood and treated as a manifestation and outcome of entrepreneurial segregation.

In Chapter 14, Joan Lockyer, Cherisse Hoyte and Sunita Dewitt put forward an agenda that demands, rather than encourages, parity between the sexes in terms of entrepreneurial performance. Reconceptualizing entrepreneurship, the authors review the discourse on women's entrepreneurship by highlighting key aspects of the discourse, including entrepreneurship, instrumentality and women entrepreneurs as 'Other'. Engaging in this debate, the authors highlight the need to challenge the construction of all three concepts in the field of women's entrepreneurship and illustrate how the concept of the entrepreneur is limiting for women. They suggest the importance of using a feminist lens in exploring the 'Otherness' of women, as a feminist stance on the field of entrepreneurship would help build new theory and clarify the challenges women entrepreneurs face.

ACKNOWLEDGEMENTS

We would like to extend a special thanks to Edward Elgar Publishing and their staff, who have been most helpful throughout the entire process of preparing this book for publication. We also thank all of the authors who sought to share their knowledge and experience with the book's readers, and were willing to put forward their views to be potentially challenged by their peers. We also thank our reviewers, who provided excellent, independent and constructive consideration of the anonymous submissions.

We hope that the chapters in this book contribute to the ongoing debate surrounding the performance evaluation of women-owned enterprises. We hope that the book will help fill some knowledge gaps, while also stimulating further thought and action.

REFERENCES

Ahl, H. (2006). Why research on women entrepreneurs needs new directions. *Entrepreneurship Theory and Practice*, 30(5), 595–621.

Eddleston, K.A. and Powell, G.N. (2008). The role of gender identity in explaining sex differences in business owners' career satisfier preferences. *Journal of Business Venturing*, 23(2), 244–256.

Marlow, S. and McAdam, M. (2013). Gender and entrepreneurship. *International Journal of Entrepreneurial Behavior and Research*, 19(1), 114–124.

Marlow, S., Shaw, E. and Carter, S. (2008). Constructing female entrepreneurship policy in the UK: is the USA a relevant role model? *Environmental Planning C*, 26(1), 335–351.

Vossenberg, S. (2013). Women entrepreneurship promotion in developing countries: what explains the gender gap in entrepreneurship and how to close it? Maastricht School of Management Working Paper Series, pp. 1–27.

Welter, F. (2011). Contextualizing entrepreneurship: conceptual challenges and ways forward. *Entrepreneurship Theory and Practice*, 35(1), 165–184.

World Economic Forum (2012). Women as the way forward. Annual meeting. Online. Available at: http://www.weforum.org/videos/women-way-forward-annual-meeting-2012 (accessed on 10 February 2017).

Zahra, S.A., Gedajlovic, E., Neubaum, D.O. and Shulman, J.M. (2009). A typology of social entrepreneurs: motives, search processes and ethical challenges. *Journal of Business Venturing*, 24(5), 519–532.

PART 1

Performance, success and value in
entrepreneurship: a women's perspective

1. Redefining success beyond economic growth and wealth generation: the case of Ethiopia

Atsede T. Hailemariam and Brigitte Kroon

Entrepreneurship research and policy formulation share a discourse of economic growth and individualism, where female entrepreneurs and their business are seen as underperforming (Marlow and McAdam, 2013). However, such studies neither highlight the complexity of the female entrepreneurship experience in the socio-economic context nor illustrate the influence of specific cultural, legislative, and economic factors on women's entrepreneurial endeavors (Henry et al., 2016). More than half of all women entrepreneurs in Ethiopia often face gender-related challenges in establishing new businesses as well as in operating or expanding existing businesses (Amha and Ademassie, 2004). Their businesses are particularly disadvantaged with regards to access to finance, skills, government support, and the conversion of profit back into investment (Bekele and Worku, 2008; Belwal et al., 2012; Singh and Belwal, 2008).

In particular, challenges that disadvantage women entrepreneurs are found in the culture, religion, and tradition (Bekele and Worku, 2008). Family responsibility, household obligations and lack of support constrain them in confronting these challenges (Belwal et al., 2012). Moreover, in a country like Ethiopia, with no social care system, women play a central role in the extended family. Overall, familial, structural, and cultural constraints have impacts on performance of female-owned businesses. Thus, as Marlow and McAdam (2013) put forward, women-owned businesses demonstrate constrained performance but not underperformance. Hence, a crucial step before concluding that the majority of women entrepreneurs are underperforming is to understand what success in business actually means to the women entrepreneurs themselves within the socio-economic context in which they operate their businesses.

There is some recognition that entrepreneurs' evaluations of success go beyond economic returns (Wach et al., 2016a) and that success in business cannot be equated simply with firm performance or with financial rewards

(Sarasvathy et al., 2013). Moreover, comparing micro and small enterprises' success only along the female-versus-male-owned nexus may generate an impression of 'false universalism' that ignores the heterogeneity of small firms managed by women entrepreneurs (Marlow and Patton, 2005).

Women entrepreneurs are a heterogeneous group differing in where they live, their level of education, their experience, and their networks. Although reports on women's entrepreneurship in sub-Saharan Africa such as Ethiopia indicate that most women-owned businesses operate in the informal sector of the economy based on a necessity to survive (GEM, 2013), a new class of women who are starting their businesses by their own choice rather than out of necessity in the formal sector of the economy is steadily growing in Ethiopia. Despite the financial, cultural, and other disadvantages they face, these women entrepreneurs create significant numbers of employment opportunities for others (ILO, 2003). What distinguishes these women from those operating necessity-motivated ventures is the element of choice: they choose to be an entrepreneur in order to do what they love most or to achieve independence and to fulfill their values, ambitions, and desires in life (Hailemariam et al., 2017). Hence, financial performance measures alone do not capture their perception of success, as their success criteria are tightly related to their motivation to become an entrepreneur in the first place (Buttner and Moore, 1997).

Overall, the motivation and goals for getting into and staying in business, in combination with socio-cultural attributions like family values, influence how this specific group of women entrepreneurs define business success (Toledo-López et al., 2012). The research presented in this chapter explores how women entrepreneurs in the formal sector of Ethiopia's economy define success in their own terms. By attuning the meaning of entrepreneurship to women's experiences, greater credibility and legitimacy can be afforded to their entrepreneurial activities (Ahl and Marlow, 2012). Moreover, when various aspects of success beyond economic growth are known, identification with entrepreneurship may be easier for women and it may become a more socially desirable career to them. An understanding of the diversity of women entrepreneurs' definitions of success and how this is related to their goals and experience are also vital for government and donors offering support for potential or existing women entrepreneurs.

THE CONTEXT FOR WOMEN ENTREPRENEURS IN ETHIOPIA

The revised Micro and Small Enterprise (MSE) development strategy and policy initiated by the Ethiopian government in 2011 has mainly focused on sustainable job opportunities for the unemployed. It includes women entrepreneurs as one of the target groups. The government also initiated a National Policy on Ethiopian Women in 1993, with the aim of eliminating gender and cultural biases that hinder women from participating equally in the economic development of the country. Moreover, the family code policy revised in 2000 aims to eliminate a husband's ability to deny permission for his wife to work outside the home, and requires both spouses to agree in the administration of family property.

Although there is considerable variation within Ethiopia, the global gender gap report 2015 (World Economic Forum, 2015) ranks Ethiopia at number 124 in the list of 145 countries in terms of the magnitude and scope of gender disparities, which shows for example the unbalanced ratio of male to female school attendance. In particular, the patriarchal gender culture in higher-educational institutions exposes female students to sexual harassment and violence and to prejudice and low expectations from male peers (Molla and Gale, 2015).

Overall, the nature of violence against women in Ethiopia is strongly related to cultural beliefs. Women are expected to show the utmost respect and submission to their husbands and to take on the caring and household responsibilities. This tendency also finds justification in religion and has been maintained for centuries (Biseswar, 2008). However, despite all the challenges, the condition of women is not homogeneous in Ethiopia. Many women are able to overcome the structural barriers they face, to actively participate in economic activities. Hence, the way in which a woman entrepreneur in Ethiopia defines her success depends upon her gendered socialization, her motivation, her background, and her value priorities.

THE DEFINITION OF BUSINESS SUCCESS

Motivation and goals for getting and staying in business and socio-cultural attributions such as family values influence how women entrepreneurs define business success (Toledo-López et al., 2012). The importance attached to specific business-success factors varies with the heterogeneity of industry sectors (Wach et al., 2016a) and the age of business owners (Warr, 2008). For example, career prospects and high income are especially valued by younger people who have not yet acquired material goods and related status (Warr, 2008). On the other hand, increasing age is associated with a value shift away from extrinsic towards intrinsic and generous motives, helping other people and contributing to society (Kooij et al., 2011; Lang and Carstensen, 2002).

How small business owners define success also varies greatly depending on the type of business and on the owner's value priorities, including the reason for starting the business. Personal values are found to be drivers behind business owners' choice of success criteria (Gorgievski et al., 2011). Personal values are desirable goals, varying in importance, that serve as guiding principles in people's lives. People pursue qualitatively different types of goals which will lead to considerably different outcomes (Deci and Ryan, 2000). Self-determination theory (SDT) categorizes goals into intrinsic and extrinsic goals. Intrinsic goals include feelings of community, affiliation, health, and self-development, while extrinsic goals include image, financial success, and appearing physically attractive (Kasser and Ryan, 1993, 1996, 2001). SDT also posits that the social context that exists in the family, cultural values, and economic system affects whether people's life goals or aspirations tend to be more intrinsic or more extrinsic, which in turn affects important life outcomes (Deci and Ryan, 2012).

In summary, because entrepreneurs often pursue goals beyond economic gains (Jennings and Brush, 2013), they have their own perceptions of what success means to them. They can regard themselves as successful, even if (looking from the outside with economic growth and profit measures) their businesses have attained different levels of success (Simpson et al., 2004). Hence, entrepreneurial success is a multi-dimensional construct that is best captured by more than financial and economic indicators (Fisher et al., 2014). Entrepreneurial values contain various indicators of success, such as firm performance, workplace relationships, personal fulfillment, community impact, and personal financial rewards (Wach et al., 2016b). Building on this notion of different dimensions of success, the qualitative research presented in this chapter explores how women entrepreneurs in Ethiopia define success in their own terms.

RESEARCH METHODOLOGY

Qualitative case studies, narratives or interpretive studies help to shed light on the actions and efforts in entrepreneurship that are unique to women (Brush and Cooper, 2012). Therefore, we used semi-structured interviews with women entrepreneurs who own small firms and applied a qualitative content analysis method to analyze the data (Hsieh and Shannon, 2005).

The study was conducted in Addis Ababa, the capital city of Ethiopia, because the city is populated with people from different ethnic groups and because various kinds of women-run businesses are found there. Eighteen women entrepreneurs who are owners of their current business in the formal sector of the economy were selected, using a mixed approach of purposive and snowball sampling techniques (Patton, 2002). To identify the first group of participants, four different women's associations in Addis Ababa were contacted. Respondents were then asked at the end of their interview to recommend other women entrepreneurs. The women entrepreneurs included in this study operate in different business sectors, their ages range from 28 to 55 years, and the ages of their businesses range from six months to 21 years.

Data Collection and Analysis

Data collection was conducted using semi-structured face-to-face interviews, with questions developed in advance. The interview protocol was piloted to ensure that the interviewees fully understood the questions and there was a logical progression in the sequence of questions and answers (Patton, 1987). The first author of this chapter and another female researcher on women entrepreneurs from the same institution conducted the interviews at the place where the participants run their businesses. The author conducted the interview and the other researcher took detailed notes without actively participating. All participants were assured that under no circumstances would their personal identity or business name be identified. The interviews lasted between 45 minutes and one hour and 15 minutes. Interviews were audio-recorded, transcribed, and then professionally translated from Amharic (the lingua franca of Ethiopia) into English.

Two of the authors of the study then independently content-analyzed each interview transcript. This was done by initially identifying categories by reading and becoming familiar with the data and using the literature review. Then the authors coded the data independently according to the predetermined categories. After the completion of the coding, both authors compared notes and, when coding differences existed, discussed until a consensus was attained. Some categories were revised, removed, and added during this procedure. Data that could not be coded into one of the predetermined categories was coded with new categories. After the coding process the categories were used to construct a set of thematic charts (Ritchie et al., 2013). The analysis was then conducted through a within and cross-case approach, which is the most appropriate technique for exploring relationships among different cases (Eisenhardt and Graebner, 2007).

Table 1.1   Categories and descriptions

Category	Description[a]
Financial success	● To generate income 　– for a better life and education for children 　– to sustain the business 　– to be financially independent
Growth and profit	● To modernize and grow traditional food processing ● To maximize profit ● To create more employment opportunities ● To grow by expanding the business
Stakeholder satisfaction	● To satisfy employees ● To satisfy customers
Self-fulfillment	● To do what I love to do, to be passionate and creative ● To be proud by introducing culture and tradition or by seeing people using products marked as 'made in Ethiopia' ● To contribute to my country
Social contribution	● To help others ● To contribute to my religion

Note: a. The descriptions are the abbreviated versions of what the participants expressed as definitions of success.

FINDINGS AND DISCUSSION

The interviews with the women entrepreneurs revealed various descriptions of what success meant to them. The data analysis yielded five categories of success criteria that the participants in this study used to define their success in business: (i) financial success, (ii) profit and growth, (iii) stakeholder satisfaction, (iv) self-fulfillment, and (v) societal contribution. Table 1.1 shows the categories with the corresponding descriptions. In this section direct quotes from participants are presented to illustrate each category of success definition. Participants are identified as '(Type of business – Age – Education).'

Financial Success

Financial success was referred to as income generated from the business. Although it frequently appeared as an indicator for success, none of the participants used it as the sole indicator of their success. Rather, they perceived financial success primarily as a vehicle to advance their families and to fulfill their own psychological needs for autonomy and relatedness (Deci and Ryan, 2008; Ryan and Deci, 2000). For example, one of the participants who said 'It's not about the money for me, it's when people love what I do' mentioned the importance of the financial success as follows:

> I want a better life . . . [Ehhh] and to educate my kids, to work hand in hand with my husband and to attain success . . . You see, I say (to spouse), 'We need to have security, money we can rely on in case of an emergency, so let's set some money aside and save it.' (Traditional cloth and accessories designer – 50 – Bachelor's degree)

This quote illustrates that even some women who are motivated to start a business for reasons other than necessity reinvest a big proportion of their earnings from the business in their families. This may be due to the societal expectation that ascribes women to take the role of caring and household responsibility. In most African societies, women are seen to exist not for themselves but for the collective, and are expected to sacrifice their own well-being for that of the community as a whole and the family in particular (Biseswar, 2008).

Similarly, another participant, whose first definition of success was 'doing something that makes people happy also makes me happy,' mentioned the importance of financial success as follows:

> I don't measure my success financially; however, the business has to survive at least to support itself. (Yoga and massage – 37 – Master's degree)

For this participant, the survival of the business was important to fulfill her intrinsic need. On the other hand, some women needed the income generated from the business to become autonomous. By becoming finically independent they could fulfill their needs and help others. Within most Ethiopian households, the head alone (almost always a man) administers key decisions on major expenditures. Women who bargain in overt ways and confront their husbands during household decision-making are often threatened with or face marital dissolution (Fafchamps and Quisumbing, 2005). Consequently, one way of maintaining power in a relationship is to retain control over financial resources. In addition, men's violence can restrict and subordinate women's participation in societal institutions. The following quote from one of the participants illustrates that the financial success of her business is important for the financial freedom it provides her to do what she likes.

> I don't need to ask my husband for anything. If I wanted to help someone in my society or if I went to a funeral in my community, I can do something for them

by my own. If I wanted to fuel my car, I don't need to ask my husband. I can do what I please . . . (Traditional cloth designer – 48 – Diploma)

Overall, the above findings support the view that some women still value financial success (Carter et al., 2003), but rather than reinvesting their profits in their business, they are more likely to spend their income on family and household needs, save cash for emergencies, or both (Klapper and Parker, 2011; Watson, 2002). This may be due to their socialization in a society which associates women with female gender roles such as nurturing children, maintaining the household, supporting their husbands, and caring for others. In particular, in a society such as Ethiopia where households are composed of the nuclear family and extended family and where there is no social care system, some women entrepreneurs' early and ongoing socialization experience influences them to accept and internalize caring and communal goals (Eagly and Wood, 1991). Hence, women who mentioned the financial success of the business as a success criterion did so because they acknowledged its importance for sustaining their business as a source of income for the financial freedom it provides for their children's better education, for unexpected household expenses, and for fulfilling intrinsic values in life.

Profit and Growth

Some participants in the study had clear financial measures in terms of profit and growth targets as primary goals. For example, a participant involved in marketing her company's product in foreign markets had the following to say about profit in her definition of success:

> Success for me is to be on top of my game and to compete with other businesses engaged in the same line of work. In order to do this, I strive to come up with a distinct product and a brand name. I even dream of being competitive in the global market while managing to be profitable every year. That's what success means to me. (Footwear company – 31 – Diploma)

A young, educated participant who introduced a new market for processing and packing traditional food mentioned her growth goal as follows:

> To me, success is a phase. For example, I used to work from home. After passing through many challenges, I acquired this place. This is success and I will use this as a stepping-stone to the next phase. I will say I am very successful when

I get to see this business growing to a larger industry. (Food processing and packing – 28 – Master's degree)

Another young and single participant running a souvenir shop socialized in one of Ethiopia's ethnic groups known as 'Gurage,' who are known for their business culture and who are recognized as mobile and skilled traders in urban settings (Worku, 2000), defined her success in terms of maximizing profit. Moreover, participants who were operating more than one business and had experience in another business defined their success in terms of traditional firm performance-measure criteria. For example, one participant who started her business in the clothing retail sector while she was a university student, and who currently operates two different businesses, expressed her definition of success in terms of creating employment for others:

Of course, your first aim is financial freedom. But success doesn't mean just that. If you have something of your own then being able to employ others is also success. Seeing the reality, there are a lot of capable young people and being able to employ one or two people, for me, is quite satisfactory more than anything else. (Consultant and food supermarket – 36 – Master's degree)

In addition to this participant there were serial entrepreneurs in this study who started their business as micro in the informal sector and who later moved to the formal sector operating other small firms, who defined their success in terms of expansion and profitability. For example, a participant who said, 'I would consider myself successful when everything I dreamt and hoped for happens,' and was then asked what are the things she hopes and dreams of, mentioned:

My future dream is to buy land and start a cattle rearing business. On the same land, I also hope to start chicken farming. (Dairy products and taxi service – 34 – Elementary school)

Overall, this group of women who defined their success in terms of profit and growth differs from the group where a financial success criterion is embedded in societal expectations about the female gender role. The women in this group are either young, at higher-education level, have previous business experience, operate in a male-dominated sector, or belong to an ethnic background that allowed a different kind of socialization. This aligns with previous research that found business owners' goals may vary depending on individual and business demographic factors (Stewart Jr et al., 2003) and the heterogeneity in industry sectors (Wach et al., 2016b). For example, because food and textile businesses are gaining importance, along with the movement to buy local, entrepreneurs engaged in these sectors are better positioned to grow their businesses (Kelly et al., 2015).

Stakeholder Satisfaction

Stakeholder satisfaction (customers, employees) was often mentioned as part of the success definitions. For example, one of the participants defined business success in terms of customers' satisfaction as follows:

> . . . didn't like upsetting them (customers). How can you disappoint people and still love what you do? If you did it for the sake of money, maybe then you wouldn't mind disappointing a customer because there will always be another one. (Traditional cloth designer – 48 – Diploma)

Similarly, the following quote illustrates business success in terms of employee satisfaction:

> Success for me is about fulfilling my responsibilities. Are the workers happy? . . . Am I happy with the work I'm doing, because money alone can't make you feel happy. (Diagnostic center and retail shops – 34 – Bachelor's degree)

As the above two participants mentioned, stakeholder satisfaction is an intrinsic goal that contributes to self-determination (Deci and Ryan, 2000). The participants also defined business success in terms of achieving other intrinsic goals. In particular, self-fulfillment goals and societal contributions were mentioned and will be elaborated upon in the next sections. These success definitions support the view that success in business cannot simply be equated with firm performance or with financial success (Sarasvathy et al., 2013), and that entrepreneurs pursue goals beyond economic gains (Jennings and Brush, 2013).

Self-fulfillment

About 30 percent of the participants mentioned that they are motivated to start a business to do what they love to do. Due to the entwined nature of the business and the owner, the participants viewed their satisfaction in personal life as business success. The following quote is from a participant who mentioned yoga as a hobby and who is involved in the yoga and massage business:

> Passion; to be passionate about what you are doing and being creative. You know, even doing something meaningful for someone, like when I see people coming and getting relief from their pain and stress and becoming happy, makes me feel I am successful. (Yoga and massage – 37 – Master's degree)

Another example of self-fulfillment success criteria comes from Diaspora and repatriate women entrepreneurs. Their life experience in foreign countries helped them develop a sense of their Ethiopian identity which in turn enhanced their love for the different cuisines, cultural ornaments, attire, and the other cultural aspects of their country. They expressed their business success as promoting and contributing to the betterment of their country, as the following quote by a repatriate participant who is engaged in running a guesthouse illustrates:

> Success for me isn't only when people come to stay at my place but also when they learn about the country and its diverse cultures . . .When people leave satisfied and happy, that's a 100 percent success in my eyes. The love for my country is the most important factor. When tourists come to stay at my place, eager to learn about the different cuisines, cultural ornaments, and lifestyles of Ethiopia, it gives me immense satisfaction. I see myself as contributing to my country. (Guesthouse – 51 – Bachelor's degree)

In a similar vein, participants who are engaged in traditional clothes design and art-related businesses stated personal satisfaction as business success, as the following quote illustrates:

> It's not about the money for me, it's when people love what I do . . . money is an end result. A lot of people have stopped buying drinking glasses and plates as a gift . . . so that's a huge success for me. The biggest success for me is to see people buy traditional Ethiopian-made products and hang them on their walls proudly. (Traditional cloth and accessories designer – 50 – Bachelor's degree)

The above three participants found their business to be important to fulfill their childhood dreams or to turn their hobby into a business or to commit to the culture they missed when they lived abroad. Thus, the success criteria they prioritize evolve around achieving intrinsic goals.

Societal Contribution

The other success criteria concern achieving intrinsic goals, phrased as contributions to society and religion. Two of the participants mentioned their contribution to poor people in the community by providing them with a free service. One participant who owns a diagnostic center mentioned that she provides CT scan, MRI, ultrasound, ECG, and ambulance services for free to poor people. The second participant who owns an elementary school said that 'when I opened the school there were children who want to learn but cannot afford . . . So I thought of how many students I can teach for free in a year.' The following quote illustrates her success criteria in terms of both societal contribution and expansion of her business:

For me success is the love of work. First, I love what I do and I have a huge respect for it. Second, the fact that I am helping out not less than 10 to 12 people, those that are in need, considering my capacity, that is for me a great satisfaction . . . And in the future, what I consider to be a success is when I get to build a building and widen my services while helping the students that I need to help. God helped us to reach this stage and the most important thing is working and serving honestly and God is the one who lies in the heart. (Elementary school – 45 – Bachelor's degree)

Notable in this quote is that the respondent refers to serving God as part of her definition of success. Similarly, some of the participants in this study linked their success criteria to their religious beliefs. For example, a participant expressed her success in terms of helping others and her contribution to religion as follows:

When I dreamed about this at first, my goal wasn't to get up to try and become a millionaire; it wasn't making profit. My thoughts were on how I can help out others through what I did. I am a person of the church. My religion and church teach about helping others. And I had the intention of using the money I make to help to spread the word of God. (Jam producer – 53 – Diploma)

This finding supports the view that belief systems in sub-Saharan Africa play a critical role in shaping attitudes toward business and entrepreneurship (Amine and Staub, 2009). The culture, traditions, and values of religious people in Ethiopia are heavily influenced and shaped by their religious beliefs. According to the 2007 population census of Ethiopia the dominant religions, Orthodox Christianity (43.5 percent) and Islam (33.9 percent), each preach about taking care of others and doing good. Consequently, as women in Ethiopia are found to be more religious than men by adhering strictly to their religious obligations (Biseswar, 2008), a profit achieving goal or wealth creation may be of no importance for some religious women entrepreneurs.

In sum, although the interviews revealed that women did mention financial success, profit, and growth, they also attributed success as something to do with other goals, such as stakeholder satisfaction, self-fulfillment, and making a contribution to religion and society. Whereas the language used to express the value of financial success, profitability, and growth success criteria were largely addressing extrinsic goals, the remaining success criteria lay closer to the realization of intrinsic goals (Deci and Ryan, 2000). It is suggested that when people put intrinsic goals first, their performance for the attainment of these goals and the expectation of future goal attainment contribute to their greater health, well-being, and performance (Kasser and Ahuvia, 2002; Vansteenkiste et al., 2006). Thus, those women entrepreneurs in Ethiopia who prioritize intrinsic goals may be more persistent in putting greater effort and energy into the continued existence and success of their business on their own terms.

CONCLUSIONS

This study focused on the question of how women entrepreneurs in Ethiopia define business success in their own terms. Rather than comparing them to men or to women in other countries, the variation in success definitions was sought in a relatively homogeneous group of women entrepreneurs in a single country. Participants defined their success both in terms of financial and non-financial performance measures. The findings indicate that due to their early and ongoing socialization experience as a female in Ethiopia, the majority emphasized family and communal values, stakeholder satisfaction, self-fulfillment, and contributions to society. Even many of those who mentioned their success definitions in terms of financial success emphasized its instrumental value for realizing intrinsic goals. However, some women, who are young, educated, have previous business experience, or who operate more than one business or are engaged in male-dominated sectors defined their success more in terms of financial performance measure criteria as a goal in itself.

Hence, in designing policy and support programs policy-makers should acknowledge that the women entrepreneurs in Ethiopia are not a homogeneous group. Most women use success criteria other than the traditional firm performance criteria that are usually used to assess the success of small firms. When firm performance is conceptualized more in terms of the optimization of personal functioning and well-being, a basic understanding of entrepreneurs' attainment of intrinsic goals should be helpful for policy-makers and donors in facilitating optimal performance and well-being of women entrepreneurs.

Despite the small sample size, the purposive sampling technique proved to be useful in identifying different sub-groups of women entrepreneurs who define their success both in financial and non-financial performance-measure terms. However, further quantitative analysis including male entrepreneurs needs to be conducted to measure between-sex differences and within-sex differences in the socio-economic context of Ethiopia, to further analyze and understand the various definitions of success. In addition, the relation should be sought with start-up motivations of women entrepreneurs, with the type of sector and background characteristics such as education, age, and gender, to further examine whether gender is salient or stronger than other variables in valuing the success definitions as laid out in this chapter.

ACKNOWLEDGEMENT

The authors would like to thank The Netherlands Organization for International Cooperation in Higher Education (Nuffic) for the research grant of NICHE project ETH-020 (Capacity Development of Business and Economics) provided to the first author.

REFERENCES

Ahl, H. and Marlow, S. (2012). Exploring the dynamics of gender, feminism and entrepreneurship: advancing debate to escape a dead end? *Organization*, 19(5), 543–562.

Amha, W. and Ademassie, A. (2004). Rural financial intermediation program and its role in strengthening the rural financial system in Ethiopia. *Journal of Microfinance Development Review*, 3(2), 230–365.

Amine, L.S. and Staub, K.M. (2009). Women entrepreneurs in sub-Saharan Africa: an institutional theory analysis from a social marketing point of view. *Entrepreneurship and Regional Development*, 21(2), 183–211.

Bekele, E. and Worku, Z. (2008). Factors that affect the long-term survival of micro, small and medium enterprises in Ethiopia. *South African Journal of Economics*, 76(3), 548–568.

Belwal, R., Tamiru, M., and Singh, G. (2012). Microfinance and sustained economic improvement: women small-scale entrepreneurs in Ethiopia. *Journal of International Development*, 24(S1), S84–S99.

Biseswar, I. (2008). Problems of feminist leadership among educated women in Ethiopia taking stock in the third millennium. *Journal of Developing Societies*, 24(2), 125–158.

Brush, C.G. and Cooper, S.Y. (2012). Female entrepreneurship and economic development: an international perspective. *Entrepreneurship and Regional Development*, 24(1–2), 1–6.

Buttner, E.H. and Moore, D.P. (1997). Women's organizational exodus to entrepreneurship: self-reported motivations and correlates with success. *Journal of Small Business Management*, 35(1), 34–46.

Carter, N.M., Gartner, W.B., Shaver, K.G., and Gatewood, E.J. (2003). The career reasons of nascent entrepreneurs. *Journal of Business Venturing*, 18(1), 13–39.

Deci, E.L. and Ryan, R.M. (2000). The 'what' and 'why' of goal pursuits: human needs and the self-determination of behavior. *Psychological Inquiry*, 11(4), 227–268.

Deci, E.L. and Ryan, R.M. (2008). Facilitating optimal motivation and psychological well-being across life's domains. *Canadian Psychology/Psychologie canadienne*, 49(1), 14–23.

Deci, E.L. and Ryan, R.M. (2012). Motivation, personality, and development within embedded social contexts: an overview of self-determination theory. In R.M. Ryan (ed.), *The Oxford Handbook of Human Motivation*. New York: Oxford University Press, pp. 85–107.

Eagly, A.H. and Wood, W. (1991). Explaining sex differences in social behavior: a meta-analytic perspective. *Personality and Social Psychology Bulletin*, 17(3), 306–315.

Eisenhardt, K.M. and Graebner, M.E. (2007). Theory building from cases: opportunities and challenges. *Academy of Management Journal*, 50(1), 25–32.

Fafchamps, M. and Quisumbing, A. (2005). Assets at marriage in rural Ethiopia. *Journal of Development Economics*, 77(1), 1–25.

Fisher, R., Maritz, A., and Lobo, A. (2014). Evaluating entrepreneurs' perception of success: development of a measurement scale. *International Journal of Entrepreneurial Behavior and Research*, 20(5), 478–492.

Forbes (2012). Africa's most successful women: Bethlehem Tilahun. *Forbes* magazine. Accessed at http://www.forbes.com/sites/mfonobongnsehe/2012/01/05/africas-most-successfulwomen-bethlehem-tilahun-alemu/.

GEM (2013). *Global Entrepreneurship Monitor 2012: Women's Report*. Accessed 8 April 2016 at www.babson.edu/Academics/centers/blank-center/global-research/gem/pages/reports.aspx.

Gorgievski, M.J., Ascalon, M.E., and Stephan, U. (2011). Small business owners' success criteria: a values approach to personal differences. *Journal of Small Business Management*, 49(2), 207–232.

Hailemariam, A.T., Brigitte, K., and Veldhoven, M. v. (2017). Understanding the motivation of women entrepreneurs in Ethiopia. In T.S. Manolova, C.G. Brush, L.F. Edelman, A. Robb and F. Welter (eds), *Entrepreneurial Ecosystems and Growth of Women's Entrepreneurship: A Comparative Analysis*. Cheltenham, UK and Northampton, MA: Edward Elgar Publishing, pp. 148–171.

Henry, C., Foss, L., and Ahl, H. (2016). Gender and entrepreneurship research: a review of methodological approaches. *International Small Business Journal*, 34(3), 217–241.

Hsieh, H.-F. and Shannon, S.E. (2005). Three approaches to qualitative content analysis. *Qualitative Health Research*, 15(9), 1277–1288.

ILO (2003). Ethiopian women entrepreneurs: going for growth. Report, international conference office, Geneva: International Labour Organization.

Jennings, J.E. and Brush, C.G. (2013). Research on women entrepreneurs: challenges to (and from) the broader entrepreneurship literature? *Academy of Management Annals*, 7(1), 663–715.

Kasser, T. and Ahuvia, A. (2002). Materialistic values and well-being in business students. *European Journal of Social Psychology*, 32(1), 137–146.

Kasser, T. and Ryan, R.M. (1993). A dark side of the American dream: correlates of financial success as a central life aspiration. *Journal of Personality and Social Psychology*, 65(2), 410–422.

Kasser, T. and Ryan, R.M. (1996). Further examining the American dream: differential correlates of intrinsic and extrinsic goals. *Personality and Social Psychology Bulletin*, 22(3), 280–287.

Kasser, T. and Ryan, R.M. (2001). Be careful what you wish for: optimal functioning and the relative attainment of intrinsic and extrinsic goals. In P. Schmuck and K.M. Sheldon (eds), *Life Goals and Well-Being: Towards a Positive Psychology of Human Striving*. Seattle: Hogrefe and Huber, pp. 116–131.

Kelly, D.J., Brush, C., Greene, P., Herrington, M., Ali, A., and Kew, P. (2015). *GEM Special Report: Women's Entrepreneurship*. Wellesley, MA: Babson College.

Klapper, L.F. and Parker, S.C. (2011). Gender and the business environment for new firm creation. *The World Bank Research Observer*, 26(2), 237–257.

Kooij, D.T., De Lange, A.H., Jansen, P.G., Kanfer, R., and Dikkers, J.S. (2011). Age and work-related motives: results of a meta-analysis. *Journal of Organizational Behavior*, 32(2), 197–225.

Lang, F.R. and Carstensen, L.L. (2002). Time counts: future time perspective, goals, and social relationships. *Psychology and Aging*, 17(1), 125–139.

Marlow, S. and McAdam, M. (2013). Gender and entrepreneurship: advancing debate and challenging myths; exploring the mystery of the under-performing female entrepreneur. *International Journal of Entrepreneurial Behavior and Research*, 19(1), 114–124.

Marlow, S. and Patton, D. (2005). All credit to men? Entrepreneurship, finance, and gender. *Entrepreneurship Theory and Practice*, 29(6), 717–735.

Molla, T. and Gale, T. (2015). Inequality in Ethiopian higher education: reframing the problem as capability deprivation. *Discourse: Studies in the Cultural Politics of Education*, 36(3), 383–397.

Patton, M.Q. (1987). *How to Use Qualitative Methods in Evaluation*, London and New Delhi: Sage.

Patton, M.Q. (2002). Qualitative interviewing. *Qualitative Research and Evaluation Methods*, 3, 344–347.

Ritchie, J., Lewis, J., Nicholls, C.M., and Ormston, R. (2013). *Qualitative Research Practice: A Guide for Social Science Students and Researchers*, Thousand Oaks, CA: Sage.

Ryan, R.M. and Deci, E.L. (2000). Self-determination theory and the facilitation of intrinsic motivation, social development, and well-being. *American Psychologist*, 55(1), 68–78.

Sarasvathy, S.D., Menon, A.R. and Kuechle, G. (2013). Failing firms and successful entrepreneurs: serial entrepreneurship as a temporal portfolio. *Small Business Economics*, 40(2), 417–434.

Simpson, M., Tuck, N., and Bellamy, S. (2004). Small business success factors: the role of education and training. *Education + Training*, 46(8/9), 481–491.

Singh, G. and Belwal, R. (2008). Entrepreneurship and SMEs in Ethiopia: evaluating the role, prospects and problems faced by women in this emergent sector. *Gender in Management: An International Journal*, 23(2), 120–136.

Stewart Jr, W.H., Carland, J.C., Carland, J.W., Watson, W.E., and Sweo, R. (2003). Entrepreneurial dispositions and goal orientations: a comparative exploration of United States and Russian entrepreneurs. *Journal of Small Business Management*, 41(1), 27–46.

Toledo-López, A., Díaz-Pichardo, R., Jiménez-Castañeda, J.C., and Sánchez-Medina, P.S. (2012). Defining success in subsistence businesses. *Journal of Business Research*, 65(12), 1658–1664.

Vansteenkiste, M., Duriez, B., Simons, J., and Soenens, B. (2006). Materialistic values and well-being among business students: further evidence of their detrimental effect. *Journal of Applied Social Psychology*, 36(12), 2892–2908.

Wach, D., Stephan, U., and Gorgievski, M. (2016a). More than money: developing an integrative multi-factorial measure of entrepreneurial success. *International Small Business Journal*, 34(8), 1098–1121.

Wach, D., Stephan, U., and Gorgievski, M. (2016b). More than money: developing an integrative multi-factorial measure of entrepreneurial success. *International Small Business Journal*, 34(8), 1098–1121.

Warr, P. (2008). Work values: some demographic and cultural correlates. *Journal of Occupational and Organizational Psychology*, 81(4), 751–775.

Watson, J. (2002). Comparing the performance of male- and female-controlled businesses: relating outputs to inputs. *Entrepreneurship: Theory and Practice*, 26(3), 91–101.

Worku, N. (2000). Fanonet: ethnohistorical notes on the Gurage Urban Migration in Ethiopia. *Ufahamu: A Journal of African Studies*, 28(2–3), 43–73.

World Economic Forum (2015). Global gender gap report 2015. Accessed 2 January 2016 at http://reports.weforum.org/global-gender-gap-report-2015/rankings/.

2. Value creation through women's entrepreneurship

Shandana Sheikh, Shumaila Yousafzai, Federica Sist, Aybeniz Akdeniz AR and Saadat Saeed

Entrepreneurial outcomes have been studied in terms of financial performance, wealth creation, firm survival, improvement in the quality of life (Baumol et al., 2007; McMullen and Warnick, 2015), and promotion of economic growth in developed and developing economies and across industries (Audretsch et al., 2006; Baumol, 1986). Although evaluation of entrepreneurial activity in these terms is important, it often results in a one-sided analysis in which entrepreneurship is evaluated and appraised solely in monetary terms, without reference to its social impact (Zahra et al., 2009) – that is, without mention of other kinds of value that come from it. The focus on financial outcomes excludes social entrepreneurship, which is based primarily on fulfilling a community's unmet needs and creating social value. However, restricting the discussion of non-monetary value creation in entrepreneurship to social entrepreneurs limits the full scope of value created by all entrepreneurs, not just social entrepreneurs. It also limits the contribution of entrepreneurial activity that is initiated by disadvantaged and marginalized groups such as women, ethnic minorities, the disabled, and youth (Welter, 2011), even though these groups often create significant value beyond financial value. Such value takes multiple forms and occurs at various levels, so it must be documented if the full contribution that entrepreneurs make to the economy and society is to be recognized.

In response to the limitation in the current entrepreneurial literature regarding the full impact of and value creation by entrepreneurial activity, we seek to fill part of the resulting gap by studying the entrepreneurial outcomes of rural women entrepreneurs in the context of Pakistan, an economically developing country. Although women entrepreneurs are often seen as the rising stars of the economy (Vossenberg, 2013) and the way forward (World Economic Forum, 2012), the disconnect between the performance of women-owned enterprises compared to those of their male counterparts still holds (Ahl, 2006; Marlow et al., 2008; Eddleston and Powell, 2008), largely because of a one-sided performance evaluation that disregards value-related outcomes beyond financial that accrue at multiple levels and have long-term impact on the *creators* (women entrepreneurs) of this value, as well as on the *recipients* who are affected by it.

It is difficult to define the multiple realms of value that result from women's entrepreneurial activity (WEA), as entrepreneurs and their contexts differ widely. Scholars have suggested that the extent to which the social value from an entrepreneurial venture is created depends on the concept (that is, the business idea), the resources available, and the *ability and the skills* of the entrepreneur to execute and implement the idea (Zahra et al., 2009). Therefore, we argue that not all entrepreneurs are cut out for or aspire to high growth and performance. While women entrepreneurs are often labelled underperformers in business for low growth and low success rates, and are, therefore, under-recognized in the sphere of social value creation, these criteria are what society expects women to achieve, not necessarily what women expect or want to achieve. We argue that performance and success are what women perceive them to be. Women entrepreneurs may not have high profit margins but may be satisfied with the balance between their businesses and personal lives; they may not have high-tech firms or a physical presence on the high street but may contribute to their families' and households' needs and wants. Hence, one must look beyond standard measures of performance and success and focus on what success and performance means to the woman entrepreneur. Each woman has her own story and offers her own unique value to add to her entrepreneurial environment.

In adopting a woman's perspective on value creation in entrepreneurship, we explore the lived experiences of women entrepreneurs to document the value they create across various frontiers (Welter and Xheneti, 2015). Specifically, we explore how women entrepreneurs in Vehari, a district of Southern Punjab in Pakistan, create value through their entrepreneurial activity. As part of a larger project, our sample consisted of 150 women who initiated entrepreneurial activity after taking part in a training programme offered by the United States Agency for International Development (USAID). In this study, we present exemplary cases from the narrative accounts of two women entrepreneurs and highlight the unique ways in which they create value and contribute to the economy and society. Our findings suggest that women create value at multiple levels, which we categorize as value to their lives (*individual value*), to their businesses (*business value*), to their families and households (*household/family value*), and to their society (*society/community value*).

THE IMPORTANCE OF STUDYING VALUE CREATION IN WOMEN'S ENTREPRENEURSHIP

Researching women's entrepreneurship through a value-creation lens and in a rural and/or developing economy context helped us to clarify the diverse ways in which women entrepreneurs add value beyond economic gain and wealth creation. This approach helps to highlight the importance of women as agents of change for society and the economy. Our study has important implications for policy-making in that it directs attention to the role of women entrepreneurs in the economy, regardless of their businesses' size and formal status, and provides evidence for the value of policy-makers facilitating women entrepreneurs' efforts and support-ing their value-creation activities. Through our study, we challenge the underperformance hypothesis associated with women entrepreneurs and argue that women do not underperform in their businesses but that they add value, even in constrained environments. Our work may direct future researchers to shift the focus of research from questions such as 'what do entrepreneurs do?' to 'how do they do it?' (in order to focus on the unique ways in which each woman entrepreneur creates value), and 'for whom do they do it?' (in order to focus on the multiple value outcomes women entrepreneurs create and the beneficiaries of that value) (Zahra et al., 2009). This refocusing will help to cultivate a debate that emphasizes *social capital* as an *enabling resource*, *the social environment* as a *context*, and *social benefit* as an *outcome* of any type of entrepreneurial activity. Evaluating the outcome dimension with a social lens across various forms of entrepreneurship facilitates a multi-dimensional analysis of the growth and performance of women entrepreneurs' enterprises (Korsgaard and Anderson, 2011). This line of research has the potential to initiate a break from dominant methods of positivistic research to more exploratory ones that involve qualitative techniques that help to capture the real impact of entrepreneurship at multiple levels.

REALMS OF VALUE IN WOMEN'S ENTREPRENEURSHIP

Regardless of the country in which they operate, female entrepreneurs face constraints that often prevent them from realizing their full poten-tial in business or achieving the same level of growth and performance as their male counterparts. Such differences between males and females are attributed to a variety of factors, including lack of financing, inad-equate educational background, lack of role models, weak social status, and demands on time with respect to family responsibilities (OECD, 2004). Developing countries like Pakistan, which are characterized by political instability, weak legal and institutional structures, low economic growth, and strong socio-cultural, religious and gender norms present unique challenges to rural female entrepreneurs. Notions of entrepreneurship portray business ownership and entrepreneurship as mostly masculine (Ahl, 2006; Marlow et al., 2008), suggesting that women are not fit to take on the role of entrepreneur (Achtenhagen and Welter, 2005).

Acknowledging the constrained environment in which women entrepreneurs operate in Pakistan, we argue that women entrepreneurs are creators of value who contribute significantly to the country's economic and social well-being (Morris and Lewis, 1991). We focus on value creation beyond economic outcomes, which we refer to as social value creation, that is, the social change and value that women entrepreneurs create through their business activities. Evaluating entrepreneurial activity through this lens changes how women entrepreneurs are studied and judged in terms of their performance and success. Going beyond the standard measures of growth and performance in business, we highlight significant other measures, value outcomes that make women successful in business and in their personal lives. This approach challenges the 'otherness' of women entrepreneurs as inferior, not fit for business, and underperforming.

Our findings highlight several forms of value that women create through their entrepreneurial activity. Although women entrepreneurs in Pakistan tend to be micro-entrepreneurs and operate in the informal economy and in a constrained entrepreneurial environment, they contribute to a plethora of other value outcomes that result from their entrepreneurial activity. These value outcomes, as reflected in our participants' narratives, accrue at four levels: (i) the *individual level* (value that accrues to the female entrepreneur herself); (ii) the *business level* (value that accrues to the entrepreneurial activity itself); (iii) the *household level* (value that accrues to the entrepreneur's family, household, and its members); and (iv) the *community or society level* (value that accrues to society). We present these four levels in our proposed framework of value creation (Figure 2.1). We deconstruct women's narratives to explore these multiple value outcomes in the next section.

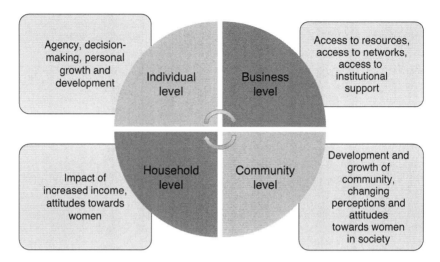

Figure 2.1　Realms of value creation in women's entrepreneurship

EXAMINING VALUE CREATION THROUGH THE NARRATIVES OF TWO WOMEN ENTREPRENEURS

BOX 2.1　NARRATIVE 1: RAMEEN, THE COURAGEOUS MOTHER, WIFE AND ENTREPRENEUR

Before Rameen started her business, there were times when there was nothing to eat in the house and sometimes her six daughters went to school hungry. Now a 38-year-old livestock extension worker, Rameen started her business five years ago. She specializes in livestock health and offers services that include vaccination, ear tagging, treatment of diseases and injuries in animals, and the sale of medicines for animal health. A widow, Rameen has six daughters, two of whom were married recently, and a newborn daughter from her second husband.

Rameen explained how her perseverance and hard work kept her focused in her business. Reflecting on the negative attitudes of the people in her village ('it seems like the people in this house are dying of hunger if a woman needs to go outside and work'), Rameen kept herself motivated and continued her efforts in business until people finally realized that she was doing some valuable work. Rameen appreciated that her education gave her the ability to take part in the livestock extension training given by USAID, which convinced people of her business skills. She believes that education is an asset that a woman can cash in on at any time in her life, just as she had done.

The business challenged the stereotypical notion that a woman can only do housework. As she gained experience in business, Rameen's confidence also improved and she began to overlook negative comments like 'you are a woman, and you will not be able to control the animal' and convinced her clients that she could do so. Previously, she would be scared to leave the house, fearing people's comments, but she gradually overcame this fear and started believing in her ability to do business. A year after she started her business, Rameen started receiving recognition for her work from the people in her village and others who heard about her skill in treating animals.

Rameen's story reflects an underlying belief in herself and the confidence to fight against all odds to achieve. She did not succeed from the first day she started her business, as she faced barriers from the local community. The local community did not initially trust her because she was a woman and they did not see animal care as a woman's job. To change this perception, Rameen went to every house in her village: 'I told them that I would be available any time they needed my services, whereas if they relied on the doctor, their animal could die if the doctor didn't come in time. Slowly, they started calling me, and I would go any time they needed my help'.

The work isn't easy. Once, a cow to which she was giving an injection objected, and she was hurt badly, but she did not show any discomfort or pain in front of her client for fear of confirming their perception that a woman could not control animals.

As time passed, Rameen built her reputation and her clientele. She started off with 20 clients but was eventually making 200 visits a day, working from morning until evening. At first, her clients were in her village, but when she acquired clients outside her village, she rented a bike and hired a boy who drove her from one house to the next. Within a year, Rameen had rented a shop from which she sells the medicines, increasing her visibility and her clientele. Her experience in business taught her marketing and communication skills that help her to attract and retain customers. She made a board with pictures of animals on it and information about the kinds of services and medicines she offered. She also made business cards that she gives to her clients so they can call her any time they need her services and can refer other potential customers to her.

A major part of Rameen's income is used to buy medicines for the business and to pay rent for the shop. The income from her business also pays for her daughters' education, clothing, weddings and day-to-day needs. She has also improved her living conditions in the house, adding a water pump and a gas meter. She bought a cow as a wedding gift for her daughter and some land next to her house. She has a feeling of satisfaction and achievement in being an entrepreneur, not only because she runs a successful business but also because the business has earned her respect both inside and outside her home. There is a difference between how her husband and her in-laws treated her before and after she became a businesswoman. Although she did not talk about any violence or maltreatment from her family, she noticed that she was valued more after becoming an entrepreneur. Her husband appreciated her in that she provided a benefit to his animals by treating them at any time they were sick and in that he did not have to spend money calling a doctor.

During her journey to becoming a successful entrepreneur, Rameen also made significant contributions to society, particularly by convincing people of her abilities, even though she is a woman. Through her hard work she changed people's minds about the kind of work that women can do. Seeing Rameen's success, other women in the village also began aspiring to start businesses, and Rameen started taking women from her neighbourhood on client visits, particularly those who were sitting idle at home and faced difficulties managing their expenses. She teaches women the skills she learned from her business and encourages them to start their own businesses. She says to these women, 'If you keep sitting at home, who will know what you can do? Come with me and learn how to practise the skills on the animals. Only when you go out will you develop the confidence to have people get work done by you'. Two of the five women she has trained have started their own businesses, which gives Rameen a feeling of accomplishment and satisfaction. As a role model to the women in the village, Rameen provides advice and support to those who ask her for help in any matter, personal or professional. She is known as the leader of the women in her village.

BOX 2.2   NARRATIVE 2: AMEERA, THE DOING-GOOD ENTREPRENEUR

Ameera, age 25 and the mother of a seven-month-old daughter, started her business four years ago. While studying for her bachelor's degree, Ameera participated in the training offered by the USAID programme and became a livestock extension worker. Ameera offers services that include animal vaccination, deworming, and treatment against disease. She started her business with a stock of medicines that she received as part of the USAID training's initial tool kit.

Ameera reinvests most of her income in medicines for further sales, with the rest going to household expenses. She feels independent in being able to spend her own money, knowing that she does not have to answer to anyone about how much and where she spends the money, so she enjoys getting sweets from the bakery for her family or something for her daughter. She likes making identical clothes for her daughter and herself. Ameera's business also financed her bachelor's degree, even after marriage, and she is pleased that she did not have to ask for money from her husband or her father-in-law.

Before she started her business, she did not have an inkling that she could run a business or do anything other than housework. Over time, her knowledge about the business and her confidence in dealing with people grew. She hardly communicated with anyone before starting the business and did not know how to talk to clients, especially men. Over time, the business gave her the skills to carry out conversations with her customers and inform them about the benefits of certain medicines and treatments that were available for their animals. It was difficult to convince clients, especially men, of her capabilities since they perceived a woman as inferior, but experience taught her the skills to convince her clients about her ability to provide services for their livestock and the benefits of those services.

While Ameera's family supported her participation in the training programme, she faced challenges when she first started her business. For example, people would say bad things about her because she was working outside her home, and she wasn't initially confident about her abilities as a business owner. People told her husband that a woman should stay within the boundaries of her home and take care of the family and the house, and since people perceived livestock workers as male, they cast doubt on her ability as a livestock extension worker. However, Ameera believed that, if women could feed the animals and clean up after them, they could also treat them. Over time, she changed the negative perceptions about her and working women in general by proving her skills and abilities as a businessperson.

Ameera worked hard through the years and availed herself of every opportunity that could benefit her business. She took a 15-day training course in her village that taught her about new medicines and treatments for animals' diseases. The training gave Ameera an edge in her business, as she could bring in new treatments for the animals. She bought and recommended a new vaccine for cows, and very few cows died thereafter. As she explains, 'This has immensely helped me to expand my business since previously animals became weak and eventually died from this disease. With this new vaccine, the animals are protected against it'.

Since Ameera's business has become successful, her father-in-law, who is the head of the household, asks her opinion on matters concerning the house. As the only woman in the house, she has to manage her time between the housework and her business, and her husband helps her, preparing vegetables and meat for her to cook later and bringing food from outside if he notices that Ameera is particularly busy.

For Ameera, it is not important just to earn money from her business but to help people look after their animals in such a way that they can increase the benefits from their livestock. One of the first few animals that she treated in the village belonged to a person who lived near her. The goat was in a serious condition and was extremely weak. The private doctor who had checked it could not find a cure for the goat's disease and told its owner to slaughter it because there was no chance of its survival. Ameera gave the goat an instant energy-inducing injection and some high-quality medicine, and the goat was healthy by the fourth day of treatment. This was one of the first incidents where Ameera felt that she had done some good to the people in her community. Thereafter, the people of the village encouraged Ameera to take part in new training and to learn new ways of increasing animal productivity and treating diseases.

In another incident, Ameera noticed that one of the families in her neighbourhood was giving hormone injections to their cows to increase milk production. Ameera stopped at their house and told them how harmful the injection was to the cow and to the people who consumed its produce. She educated them about other natural ways they could increase milk production without harming the animal or themselves. The neighbour stopped giving injections to their animals and shifted on to more natural ways of increasing their animals' produce.

Now Ameera is known as Doctoraani ('the lady doctor') and is a source of pride for her community. She has more than 200 customers, some of whom she visits on a regular basis, while others she visits every quarter to vaccinate their animals. Word of mouth and referrals help her to expand her business, and hard work helps her earn a good reputation.

Once Ameera was confined to her home and did not meet many people, but now she goes out to meet clients, family and friends. Her life has expanded, and she has benefited her community in the process.

MULTIPLICITY OF VALUE IN WOMEN'S ENTREPRENEURSHIP: THE CREATOR'S AND THE RECIPIENT'S PERSPECTIVES

The two narratives show that Rameen and Ameera can break through gender bias and strict socio-cultural norms and prove their ability by initiating entrepreneurial activity and creating value at multiple levels.

Entrepreneurship provides women with opportunities that can help them to improve their bargaining power in their personal lives (for example, enhanced agency and decision-making), promote their personal growth and development, and improve their overall well-being and quality of life (Beath et al., 2013; Haneef et al., 2014; Haugh and Talwar, 2016; Kantor, 2003). The narratives of Rameen and Ameera confirm this view, showing that women entrepreneurs can create value for themselves (*value at the individual level*) through enhanced agency, greater involvement in decision-making, and enriched personal growth and development. Agency includes factors like engagement in paid work outside the home, management and control over family assets, mobility outside the home, and involvement in household and family decisions as well as investment and property-related decisions (Schuler et al., 2010). As is evident from Rameen's and Ameera's accounts, their business start-ups enable both women to exert agency over their life choices and to improve their involvement in decision-making regarding their lives and family/household matters, and running their businesses significantly contributes to their personal development. Women in conservative societies like that in Pakistan often need permission from their families or must be accompanied by a male member of the household to leave their homes, even to visit a doctor or a family member, or to attend social events (Kantor, 2003). However, starting a business enables women to step outside the boundaries of their homes and engage in productive activities outside, thus breaking through the gender-biased norms of society. Business start-ups also increase women's self-confidence, self-esteem, and overall happiness and satisfaction in life. They enable women to learn about business dealings, develop communication skills, and market their businesses. Improvement in all of these aspects of life tends to elevate their status, leading to overall development and growth for women in general (Sahab et al., 2013). Moreover, through their entrepreneurial activity, women's perceptions are transformed regarding gender roles in the society, attitudes toward and tolerance of discrimination against women, and decisions regarding their personal lives and families. Research suggests that entrepreneurial activity increases women's control over their investments and assets, to which women usually do not have access prior to starting businesses (Beath et al., 2013). Our findings suggest that savings from their businesses give women the opportunity to make independent choices regarding asset purchases and day-to-day expenses.

Beyond individual value, women entrepreneurs also create value for their businesses (*value at the business level*) through *increased access to resources* (primarily social networks and information flows) and *experience in running the business*, both of which help them to create opportunities in their businesses and generate value for them. Our findings suggest that running a business gives women entrepreneurs access to new clients and customers, as well as links to the market so they can sustain their businesses and succeed. For example, through existing clients, women get word-of-mouth referrals to new customers, which helps them to build their reputations. Beyond social networks, *human capital* – a combination of education, experience, and learning – significantly helps women entrepreneurs generate value in their businesses. Learning by doing plays a significant role in enhancing entrepreneurs' intellectual development, adds to their human capital throughout the entrepreneurial process, and helps the entrepreneur to make good decisions and take sound action in times of uncertainty (Malerba, 2007; Shane and Venkataraman, 2000). The two narratives presented above reflect this view by showing that the two women's experiences in doing business and dealing with clients increase their knowledge about medicines, certain animal diseases, and treatments.

Entrepreneurship can also lead to significant changes in the household and family unit (*value at the household level*), including increased income and changes in attitudes toward women to perceiving women as independent and entrepreneurial. The positive impact on household members can be seen in improved standards of living and increased family happiness and well-being (Dsizi and Obeng, 2013; Haugh and Talwar, 2016; Kabeer, 2001). This positive impact is reflected in the two narratives, which describe how higher income supported household expenses, improved the households' living conditions through better sanitation and water facilities, and improved the family's well-being and satisfaction. The narratives also reveal a change in others' attitudes after the women embarked on their entrepreneurial journeys. In this regard, scholars have discussed the spillover effects of work on family (Greenhaus and Powell, 2006), including increased love and respect from the family (Hammer et al., 2002), improvement in women's status, increased recognition and respect for work, sharing of domestic responsibilities, and fewer instances of genital mutilation, domestic violence and abuse, polygamy, and early marriages. The narratives herein reflect these benefits, showing that the women are valued for their knowledge and business acumen and are respected more by their family members and spouses. It also resulted in changes in attitudes about gender roles, as domestic responsibilities are shared so the women have time for their businesses.

Women also impact the lives of other members of society through their business activity, thereby contributing to value creation at the community level. Women's entrepreneurship provides value by contributing to their communities' development and growth and changing perceptions of and attitudes about women in society, increasing support for female entrepreneurs. In terms of development and growth, women create value by offering a service that meets the needs of the community and its members. With most of the community relying on livestock for their income, the women in the two narratives provide convenient and low-cost services to the people in their communities. For example, in societies with strict norms that restrict a woman's mobility outside the home, a female-based enterprise like a health-related service may be a significant source of services to other women in the community. Female entrepreneurs also add value by influencing the personal lives of the members of the community. By becoming entrepreneurs and achieving success in their businesses, women become role models and set an example for other women, encouraging them to become entrepreneurial and contribute to the community in a similar way (Haugh and Talwar, 2016). Research has suggested that entrepreneurship may enable women to play an active role in resolving conflicts between members of the society because of the respect they enjoy and their status in the society. Such role models can assist other women to set up their own businesses by increasing their confidence and improving their skill sets (Haneef et al., 2014; Korsgaard and Anderson, 2011). This notion is also confirmed in our finding that entrepreneurial women teach other women in the village skills related to doing business and encourage them to initiate their own entrepreneurial activities.

In the context of changing perceptions toward women, our findings suggest that, through their persistent efforts, women demonstrate their ability to do business, thereby breaking with the gender-based stereotypical norms associated with entrepreneurship. Despite the negative remarks the women heard in the initial phases of their business start-ups, they built their names as competent, reliable and knowledgeable entrepreneurs. Hence, through their entrepreneurial efforts, women can prove that they can be agents and value-creators for society. They can exercise agency over their life decisions, overcome society's resistance to pursue their goals in their personal and professional lives, and gain increased respect and recognition in society (Haugh and Talwar, 2016).

MOVING FORWARD: RECOGNIZING AND LEGITIMIZING WOMEN'S ENTREPRENEURSHIP AS AN AVENUE FOR VALUE CREATION

Entrepreneurship is a multi-faceted concept in which several factors, including the entrepreneurial context, the individual entrepreneur, the entrepreneurial environment, and the entrepreneurial product or service, combine to create the outcomes of the entrepreneurial process. Most research has documented the entrepreneurial outcomes of WEA through an economic lens, such as in terms of employment generation and poverty alleviation, while less attention has been paid to the multi-level value creation and change that female entrepreneurs bring to a society. Our study sought to address this gap by highlighting some of the aspects of value creation from WEA in rural areas of a developing country – in this case, Pakistan. In doing so, we challenge the stereotypical underperforming image associated with women entrepreneurs and highlight that women entrepreneurs, despite their constrained environments and the size, type and scope of their businesses, create value in multiple forms, including value for themselves (individual value), value for their families and households (household value), value for their businesses (business value), and value for society (society value). Our study suggests that the contribution of marginalized and invisible women in the economy be recognized and that they be included among society's change agents who create value through entrepreneurship. Scholars should move beyond the value generation of high-growth-oriented and financially successful firms to focus on entrepreneurs who create value in their own ways and in the presence of significant challenges in their entrepreneurial environments (Aslund and Backstrom, 2015).

Our work opens a debate on women as creators of value in entrepreneurship and encourages researchers to advance this debate by exploring unconventional value outcomes in multiple contexts, business sectors, industries and countries. Our research also opens debates around the interplay of gender and entrepreneurship. Previous research that compares men and women in entrepreneurship has been based primarily on the economic contributions of entrepreneurship, focusing on wealth creation, performance, growth orientation and profit-making, largely ignoring the contribution of entrepreneurs who create social value. Comparisons based on value creation by men and women in entrepreneurship will help to highlight the value of female entrepreneurs from a variety of perspectives and ensure that the impact of entrepreneurial activities initiated by men and women is evaluated in a more meaningful way.

REFERENCES

Achtenhagen, L. and Welter, F. (2005). (Re-)constructing the entrepreneurial spirit. Paper presented at the Babson College Entrepreneurship Research Conference (BCERC).

Ahl, H. (2006). Why research on women entrepreneurs needs new directions. *Entrepreneurship Theory and Practice*, 30(5), 595–621.

Aslund, A. and Backstrom, I. (2015). Creation of value to society: a process map of the societal entrepreneurship area. *Total Quality Management and Business Excellence*, 26(3–4), 385–399.

Audretsch, D.B., Keilbach, M.C. and Lehmann, E.E. (2006). *Entrepreneurship and Economic Growth*. New York: Oxford University Press.

Baumol, W.J. (1986). Entrepreneurship: productive, unproductive, and destructive. *Journal of Business Venturing*, 11(1), 3–22.

Baumol, W.J., Litan, R.E. and Schramm, C.J. (2007). *Good Capitalism, Bad Capitalism, and the Economics of Growth and Prosperity*. New Haven, CT: Yale University Press.

Beath, A., Christia, F. and Enikolopov, R. (2013). Empowering women through development aid: evidence from a field experiment in Afghanistan. *American Political Science Review*, 107(3), 540–557.

Dsizi, S. and Obeng, F. (2013). Microfinance and the socio-economic wellbeing of women entrepreneurs in Ghana. *International Journal of Business and Social Research*, 3(11), 45–62.

Eddleston, K.A. and Powell, G.N. (2008). The role of gender identity in explaining sex differences in business owners' career satisfier preferences. *Journal of Business Venturing*, 23(2), 244–256.

Greenhaus, J.H. and Powell, G.N. (2006). When work and family are allies: a theory of work–family enrichment. *Academy of Management Review*, 31(1), 72–92.

Hammer, L.B., Cullen, J.C., Caubet, S., Johnson, J., Neal, M.B. and Sinclair, R.R. (2002). The effects of work-family fit on depression: A longitudinal study. Paper presented at the 17th Annual Meeting of SIOP, Toronto.

Haneef, C., Pritchard, M., Hannan, M., Kenward, S., Rahman, M. and Alam, Z. (2014). Women as entrepreneurs: the impact of having an independent income on women's empowerment. Online. Available at http://www.enterprise-development.org/wp-content/uploads/Women-as-Entrepreneurs_The-impact-of-having-an-independent-income-on-womens-empowerment_August-2014.pdf. Accessed on 20 April 2016.

Haugh, H.M. and Talwar, A. (2016). Linking social entrepreneurship and social change: the mediating role of empowerment. *Journal of Business Ethics*, 133(4), 643–658. Available at https://doi.org/10.1007/s10551-014-2449-4.

Kabeer, N. (2001). Resources, agency and achievements: reflections on the measurement of women's empowerment. *Development and Change*, 30(3), 435–464.

Kantor, P. (2003). Women's empowerment through home-based work: evidence from India. *Development and Change*, 34(3), 425–445.

Korsgaard, S. and Anderson, A.R. (2011). Enacting entrepreneurship as social value creation. *International Small Business Journal*, 20(10), 1–17.

Malerba, F. (2007). Innovation and the dynamics and evolution of industries: progress and challenges. *International Journal of Industrial Organization*, 25, 675–699.

Marlow, S., Shaw, E. and Carter, S. (2008). Constructing female entrepreneurship policy in the UK: is the USA a relevant role model? *Environmental Planning C,* 26(1), 335 351.

McMullen, J.S. and Warnick, B. (2015). The downside of blended value and hybrid organizing. *Academy of Management Proceedings,* January. Available at doi: 10.5465/AMBPP.2015.10130abstract *ACAD MANAGE PROC January 2015.*

Morris, M.H. and Lewis, P.S. (1991). Entrepreneurship as a significant factor in societal quality of life. *Journal of Business Research,* 23(1), 21–36.

OECD (2004). Promoting entrepreneurship and innovative SMEs in a global economy: towards a more responsible and inclusive globalization. Online. Available at http://www.oecd.org/cfe/smes/31919215.pdf. Accessed on 12 June 2016.

Sahab, S., Thakur, G. and Gupta, P.C. (2013). A case study on empowerment of rural women through micro entrepreneurship development. *Journal of Business Management,* 9(6), 123–126.

Schuler, S.R., Islam, F. and Rottach, E. (2010). Women's empowerment revisited: a case study from Bangladesh. *Development in Practice,* 20(7), 840–854.

Shane, S., and Venkataraman, S. (2000). The promise of entrepreneurship as a field of research. *Academy of Management Review,* 25, 217–226.

Vossenberg, S. (2013). Women entrepreneurship promotion in developing countries: what explains the gender gap in entrepreneurship and how to close it? Online. Available at ftp://ftp.repec.org/opt/ReDIF/RePEc/msm/wpaper/MSM- WP2013-08.pdf. Accessed on 6 July 2015.

Welter, F. (2011). Contextualizing entrepreneurship: conceptual challenges and ways forward. *Entrepreneurship Theory and Practice,* 35(1), 165–184.

Welter, F. and Xheneti, M. (2015). Value for whom? Exploring the value of informal entrepreneurial activities in post-socialist contexts. *Exploring Criminal and Illegal Enterprise: New Perspectives on Research, Policy and Practice,* 5, 253–275.

World Economic Forum (2012). Women as the way forward. Annual meeting. Online. Available at http://www.weforum.org/videos/women-way-forward-annual-meeting-2012. Accessed on 10 May 2015.

Zahra, S.A., Gedajlovic, E., Neubaum, D.O. and Shulman, J.M. (2009). A typology of social entrepreneurs: motives, search processes and ethical challenges. *Journal of Business Venturing,* 24(5), 219–532.

3. Stepping into power: women leaders and their journey of self-redefinition

Milka Milliance

In the collective imagination, and even across cultures, power has been relegated to the realm of the masculine and is perceived as belonging primarily to men (Clark Muntean and Özkazanç-Pan, 2015). More importantly, until recently the vast majority of women globally occupied little, if any, space in the public domain. However, with more women receiving university degrees and pursuing white-collar occupations, the opportunity for women to lead organizations should be substantial. While the world does not lack competent women to lead or start new organizations, few reach such senior leadership positions in their companies, and now, more than ever, women around the world are launching companies that service their needs in the marketplace.

Women's lack of motivation, inability to marshal resources, or descent into traditional gender roles are seen as the drivers for their failure in entrepreneurship (Brush et al., 2004). Little ethnographic work has been undertaken to explore the narratives, voices, and psychologies of women who leave their corporate careers to start their own companies. Perhaps the reasons and motivations for such actions vary widely, but it is with the explorative power to uncover women's motivations that women can also allow themselves the opportunity to learn who they truly are and what matters to them. Moreover, who decides what a leader or an entrepreneur looks like is firmly integrated into the hetero-normative social structure of a society's dominant power base.

Like men, as women move into positions of leadership they are confronted with the interplay of power in the public domain as well as in the intimately personal realm of the self. Today, more than ever, it is important to question how the ideas of power and exercising power impact women's experiences, as it is their perceptions of themselves – particularly whether they believe that they are empowered and can make powerful choices – that may destabilize the status quo.

In addition, the selective narratives chosen by the media, academics, and 'culture-makers' that convey men's and women's successes and failures in entrepreneurial leadership shape the conventional understanding of who can claim the identity of a leader or an entrepreneur (Ahl and Marlow, 2012). Since women have been written out of most of the historical narrative of those who wield power and have often been placed in the periphery of power, it is not surprising that, for women in leadership roles, there is nary a historical context in which to place themselves where societies can locate them and see them as leaders.

How many of us know the stories of very powerful women leaders in history across cultures who were not just figureheads but stateswomen, writers, poets, or artists? All of the known 'greats' in every aspect of life are constructed in the vision of the hyper-masculine. Few people know of Hatshetsup, the first and longest-reigning woman pharaoh in Egyptian history; Empress Wu of China; Empress Theodora of Byzantium, who with Emperor Justinian rebuilt Constantinople; or Christine de Pizan, a French noblewoman during the Renaissance who was one of the first feminist writers and author of *City of Ladies*. There are many more stories of powerful women whose leadership narratives do not exist in the collective imagination (Foreman, 2016). These women wielded power for long periods of time, however their stories were kept outside of the historical narrative by male leaders and male historians.

Fast-forward to the twenty-first century and celebrated women business leaders like Oprah, Martha Stewart, and Dame Anita Roddick created companies that served the needs of women. They were interested in making money while also raising human consciousness, promoting healthier lifestyles and a more sustainable planet. Their value proposition was also a call to arms to bring change that positively impacted the lives of many. Their perceptions and use of power are located in personal experiences with which other women could identify, thereby uplifting them and shifting their perceptions of themselves (Ahl and Marlow, 2012).

In building women-centered business models, the most successful twenty-first-century women entrepreneurs did not follow the traditional male entrepreneurial paradigm of subordinating their own goals to growing a company (Brush et al., 2004). Oprah's and Martha Stewart's authenticity embodied the very ideas of empowerment and so was the hallmark of their success. Perhaps if we paid attention to how they used the power of gender to build corporate empires that served the unmet needs of half of the world's population, we – women – would realize that we have been asking the wrong questions about women and entrepreneurship.

These women reshaped an entire generation's view of a female leader's relationship to power. They inspired women to renegotiate their relationships with what it means to have power and to be leaders on their own terms. Because of Oprah and Martha Stewart, we also got Jessica Alba, an actress-turned-entrepreneur, who created the Honest Company, now valued at $1.7 billion, and Sophia Amoruso, creator of Nasty Gals and #GirlBoss, whose net worth *Forbes* estimated at $280 million in 2015. These are all women who built massively successful companies with primarily female consumer bases because they each found a need in the marketplace that was based on their own need.

Only when women begin to ask themselves, 'What do I need?' and when we overcome all the internal and external obstacles that keep us from building businesses and investing our dollars will there be a paradigm shift that leads to many more successful female entrepreneurs and leaders. We explore this theme through a multi-disciplinary review of the literature across the fields of entrepreneurship, leadership, gender studies, and archetypal psychology that takes a radical feminist point of view to disavow the notion of gender neutrality in entrepreneurial leadership.

I locate myself at the intersection of actor and observer in this analysis because my story is part of the greater narrative of women, especially women of color, who regularly encounter the perception that they are deficient because they do not fit the hetero-normative views of masculine leadership or entrepreneurial motivation, even though black women have always taken strong leadership roles in their communities.

I draw on these case studies to give voice and meaning to and to empower the women who have started businesses that the entrepreneurship literature considers 'low-growth and lifestyle' businesses. Although some of the greatest women entrepreneurs have built 'lifestyle' businesses, the hetero-normative definition in which entrepreneurship is defined suggests that they should never have succeeded because their expressed goals and aspirations were multi-dimensional. In *Clearing the Hurdles: Women Building High Growth Businesses*, Brush et al. (2004) devote an entire chapter to how a woman's expressed aspiration, when it is not as singular as a man's, is seen as suspect, so she appears less credible.

More women are paving their leadership paths by challenging their own attitudes regarding power. I am curious about how they distill their experiences to take control of their lives, not waiting for power to be conferred by others but claiming their power. Srilatha Batliwala is a scholar practitioner whose work on the practical use of power provides a useful theoretical framework with which to examine the notion of power vis-à-vis its application (empowerment) among women who are renegotiating their relationship with power. While there are many competing definitions of power, the one that prevails in this analysis is a radical feminist view of entrepreneurship that suggests not only that men and women are different but that the dominant masculine values of entrepreneurial success should be rejected wholesale so women can find their own definition of success and their own path toward what they perceive as worthwhile entrepreneurial endeavor (Clark Muntean and Özkazanç-Pan, 2015).

In her research work, *Feminist Leadership for Social Transformation: Clearing the Conceptual Cloud*, Batliwala (2010) describes *intrinsic power* as a set of an individual's personality traits, talents, capabilities, knowledge, and experience that is unique to her life circumstances. This definition of power supports the foundation of leadership development, which is grounded in talent, capabilities, prescribed preferences, and certain personality traits. Therefore, people either are inclined to or are selected for leadership roles. By locating the notion of intrinsic power in the discourse of women and leadership, we dismantle the traditional notion of power as something that exists primarily in the masculine realm and that women possess only in smaller quantities, if at all. This definition permits women, a group perceived as subordinate and as having no power, to reframe their conceptions of and relationships with the notion of power.

The path that a few leaders take to develop organizations or lead movements that support the advancement of women and their leadership potential often begins with their intrinsic power. It was my experience working at global consultancies and advising leaders that challenged me to rethink my own idea of what it means to be women in global organizations and entrepreneurial environments, how women choose to collaborate or not to collaborate with each other, and how they lead their teams.

Given the masculine normative values in the existing leadership discourse, women are rarely cast as heroines in their own narratives and have instead become second-rate heroes encased in female bodies (Murdoch, 1990). So how effective has traditional leadership development been in meeting the needs of women leaders? Research shows that little effort has been made to ensure that the leadership needs of women are reflected back to them. In 'Taking gender into account: theory and design for women's leadership development programs', Ely et al. (2011) expose how second-generation gender bias in the workplace has affected the *identity work* that is crucial to the development of women who are potential leaders. The authors propose taking a gendered approach to the development of women using frameworks that take into account how gender shapes their leadership journey. Their research and analyses provide evidence of what women achieve by doing identity work, a set of relational and social processes that leaders internalize in order to see themselves and to be seen by others as leader-like.

It is through an increased sense of self and an evolutionary journey that one becomes a 'perceived' leader. To borrow from Ralph Waldo Emerson's essay 'Self-reliance,' the notion of 'trust thyself' is founded on the belief that one's self-identity is based on an individuation process by which one believes that 'what is true in your heart is often true in the heart of others.' Therefore, the personal becomes the public and collective experience to which we can relate (Batliwala, 2010). This is precisely the journey that women leaders like Oprah and Jessica Alba have undertaken to achieve success. The intersectional experiences of women across race, class, and ethnicity, while different, are also familiar to each other. Gender and racial bias has always played a role in what narratives are selected, what stories are valued, and whose experiences matter. It is an invisible power that permeates the media, our political and economic institutions (Ahl and Marlow, 2012), and our collective private lives and that can either empower or disempower women to trust ourselves, our intuitions, and our lived experiences and personal truths (Ely et al., 2011). It is in the individual and the collective heroine's leadership journey that women will find the self-confidence and pride necessary to attain the self-efficacy to manifest their dreams into the world.

THE HEROINE'S DEPARTURE: THE EMERGENCE OF THE FEMININE

While many feminist theorists have written about women's psychological development, the search for personal significance requires that we differentiate women's individuation journey from men's (Harding, 1971). Some women do not choose leadership roles in larger companies but turn instead to entrepreneurship. Why? What are the motivations and drivers for those who embark on that journey? Some, not all, of these questions are explored in the ethnographic narratives of the women profiled in this analysis.

My construction of a woman-centered leadership framework is defined by the actor's (women's) active choice to lead with feminine principles, which I define as authentic and creative behaviors that lead to relatedness as a leader. The notion of feminine and feminist leadership has been depicted as a polarity, especially during the second-wave feminist movement that perceived the word 'feminine' with suspicion, as women sought equal treatment with men (Murdoch, 1990; Bolen, 1985) However the post-feminist generation embraces and imbues the word 'feminine' with power, pride, wholeness, and strength.

My working definition of feminine leadership is informed by the pro-women branding platforms that millennials are launching to empower themselves. There are thousands of self-made millionaires who market their services on social media and have millions of followers as part of their tribes. Marketers pay many of them top dollar because they are powerful influencers. For many of these women social-media influencers, the traditional professional path of working at a large corporation became less of an option when it became clear that there was no 'place' for them at large organizations that hired 'diverse' candidates who were expected to conform and behave like white men. As such, they sharpened their skill set before leaving to build their brands. Unlike most of their peers, these women did not take the traditional path and conform to the dominant masculine values that prevail in corporate cultures. Some stick it out in industries that are not considered desirable and find themselves increasingly isolated, unhappy, and burned out. Often they do not realize that the personal challenges they face are symptomatic of living in such a way that cuts them off from their feminine sides while identifying with the masculine (Murdoch, 1990).

It has become increasingly clear that the corporate paradigms in which most women work and the leadership approaches that they have learned to adopt are not working for many of them (Ely et al., 2011). If these paradigms and approaches were truly inclusive and gender-neutral, more women would be in senior leadership roles at leading companies, but they are not. Instead, many find themselves stuck in middle-management roles with little hope that they will be afforded the same opportunities as their male counterparts. This assessment of the state of women in leadership does not preclude all the cultural biases and structural impediments that prop up the hetero-normative values that prevail, nor does it find any deficiency in women. However, it is an assessment that must be constantly questioned and examined through new lenses. As Einstein (1946) said, 'No problem can be solved by the same level of consciousness that created it.' The research by gender and post-feminist scholars rightly points us to the need for women to remove their masks and confront their shadows so they can succeed in a male-dominated environment (Stover, 2015).

Turning inward is required for anyone who wants to step into leadership in order to gain the self-confidence and influence needed to rally others. This imperative is completely unknown to many women. Men have heroes and models that embody and exude leadership that they have known since they were children through story, history, and myth that exalt the masculine. However, effective leadership requires reframing situations and making one's ideas into lived experiences and reality. The feminine leadership journey to creativity and innovation is related directly to a woman's path toward personal development and greater self-efficacy. Many never take this journey, but for those who do, it is often initiated by a life-changing event that demands becoming one's own heroine, rather than waiting for a hero.

THE HEROINE'S JOURNEY: THE FORMATION OF SELF-IDENTITY

Regardless of women's endeavors, if they have not conformed to the masculine achievement paradigm, their value in the eyes of society is questionable. The accepted narrative favors the male hero on an outwardly focused journey of self-expression (Campbell, 1988). The masculine rebirth becomes the quest for individuation – the hero myth – which is replayed in literature and film and embedded in our collective unconscious. The hero archetype is universally recognized and is our ideal entrepreneur (Brush et al., 2004).

Approaches to leadership development have favored personal transformation through the lens of the hero myth and a hyper-masculine journey that favors 'power over' others. Moreover, the question concerning how the hero myth, with its highly masculine logic, plays into our conception of the feminine self, the female identity, and its individuation process is left unanswered. How has our conception of our journeys to personal transformation influenced the leadership development models that should help us deploy power and lead more authentically? How can women leaders be developed when their experiences stand outside of the narratives of leadership, change, and transformation (Murdoch, 1990; Bolen, 1985)?

C.G. Jung's archetypal corpus in the field of psychology illuminates our understanding of *individuation*, *subjective experiences*, *mutuality*, and *inter-dependency*, all of which have informed the field of leadership development (albeit in a more simplified way). Jung's corpus is even more central to developing leadership models that value the experiences of women. A comparison between the two models – the hero's journey vs the heroine's journey – makes clear that the paths toward personal development for men differ from those for women. The biological and socio-cultural constructs of sex and gender play roles in our subjective and objective experiences, so how we experience our inner and outer worlds and our collective experiences affect our sense of who we are (Bolen, 1985). These steps in the heroine's leadership journey are predicated on a subjective *inner* experience of self-identity and a collective *outer* experience that supports self-efficacy.

The heroine's leadership approach (Figure 3.1) uses Jungian theories of the exploration of the inner and outer worlds of subjective and objective experiences to foster an individuation process that is feminine at its core. It explores the worlds of one's feelings and emotions to reconnect the self to one's intuitive intelligence. Given the predominance of the intellect, the mind, and rational thought, we take a holistic approach by creating a strong mind–body connection during the coaching process. Locating the Jungian-inspired individuation process in this chapter demonstrates how what we might constitute as a crisis can often be an opportunity for a

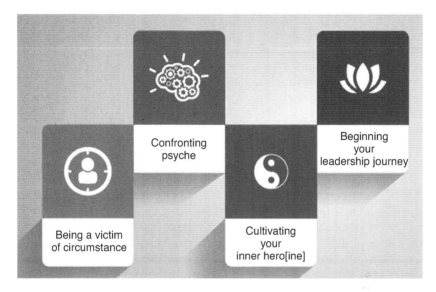

Figure 3.1   The Heroine's Leadership Journey transition model

woman who is ready to become her own heroine to dig deeper to unearth an unpolished diamond. Figure 3.1 depicts the four steps in our Heroine's Leadership Journey.

THE HEROINE'S LEADERSHIP JOURNEY

Step 1   The Victim of Circumstance: A woman's personal narrative, filled with negative thoughts and limiting beliefs, traps her in a behavioral loop.

Step 2   Confronting the Psyche: The woman raises a mirror to reflect her shadow side of unmet needs and desires. Poor physical, psychological, and spiritual health has created imbalance, high levels of stress, depression, or sickness. The inability to make sense of one's life choices has created disassociation and general unhappiness about a life not lived.

Step 3   Cultivating the Inner Heroine: This step occurs only when a woman chooses to explore her inner world of feelings, thoughts, emotions, and desires to take a step toward personal transformation. Ignoring the call to begin the inner quest toward self-knowledge can create physical, mental, and emotional havoc.

Step 4 Beginning the Leadership Journey: The woman embraces the heroine's journey toward forming a self-identity, which gives her the courage to have more self-efficacy and integration with the masculine. This embrace is a step toward forming a more balanced leadership style that embraces the feminine and masculine.

Let's examine a feminine leadership model that presupposes a world in which certain attributes and personality traits are believed to be effective leadership competencies. The women we showcase are living their heroine's journey and conceiving their companies from a creative source – essentially from within – as their way of reconnecting to their whole selves. They carved paths that laid out the narrative of their stories – their journeys toward manifesting something new in the world.

Some women's leadership journeys led them down the path to entrepreneurship. It began with the recognition that, to be successful on their own terms, they had to transform themselves from the inside out. Doing so required an inward journey that allowed them to tap into their intrinsic power. In addition, the manifestation of their self-transformations led them to reconnect with their most feminine leadership attributes, a set of innate characteristics that the world increasingly values as crucial to leadership.

Gerzema and D'Antonio's (2013) *The Athena Doctrine* claims that the world is shifting to a paradigm that embraces traditionally more feminine leadership attributes rather than the traditional masculine ones. In a study conducted with 64 000 people across 13 countries, two-thirds of the participants agreed 'the world would be a better place if men thought more like women.' The study suggests that the future will require that both men and women embody these traits.

Within a feminine leadership paradigm, women must use all of their resources without succumbing to the concepts of domination or separation of the self to achieve their objectives. Feminine leadership does not embrace separation from community and others in order to go on a heroic quest in order to be transformed; instead, the call for change occurs within, when women conquer their fears, gain the courage to acknowledge and serve their own needs, and create a vision of the world they would like to see – the first step toward self-efficacy. While men slay their dragons in the outside world, as often depicted in hero myths, women must grapple with the cut-off parts of themselves, which are predicated on the subordination of the feminine. Actively engaging social constructs like gender and race, especially when they remain unexplored and effectively unchallenged, is an important step to deconstructing misguided notions of gender neutrality. When we follow this logic, we embrace a social dynamic that embraces difference, rather than elevating oppressive ideologies of 'equality.' In essence, we minimize the possibility of a binary and atavistic relationship that perpetuates dysfunction of thought and action within the self.

The following case studies present the narratives of women who transitioned into entrepreneurship rather than staying on the corporate path, even when they were considered high potentials.

Stepping into Power: Heroine's Journey Case Studies

Women entrepreneurs are creating businesses that reflect their values, identity, and aspirations. Some women are reimagining the definition of success from that of limited individual achievement to one that is based on collective achievement. Exploring how women organize, create networks, and build ecosystems to maximize their opportunities as female entrepreneurs is significant because it gives us a view into why gender still matters in entrepreneurial leadership. Are women building relationships that are mutually beneficial? How does inter-gender competition vs collaboration influence their perception of individual vs collective success? These questions illustrate a useful way to reimagine how women can actually empower themselves and each other by encouraging other women to show their uniqueness, rather than conforming to a hetero-normative masculine framework.

Transformational leadership provides multiple lenses through which to reframe how we, as women, can harness our leadership skills to reimagine a holistic ecosystem. This approach supports a culture that shares and redistributes power by empowering women as a group to develop their whole selves radically. In many instances women leaders already use feminine leadership to foster collaborations that support one another's businesses. Instead of favoring the more masculine leadership principles premised on *power over*, they are using *power within* to collaborate and achieve results (Batliwala, 2010). Through the work of these women, we can see the heroines of tomorrow, who are writing their own narratives of leadership.

Being aware of the traditional hero-worship cult of leadership, the women of our case studies have knowingly or unknowingly flipped the paradigm on its head and become their own heroines on their paths to success. By introducing soulfulness into leadership these women have created space for collaboration, empowerment, and imagination. They have also fully integrated their feminine identities into their leadership brands. Within a week of moving to Miami, I was pulled into a world of entrepreneurship in professional services. I have different relationships with these three different women. I coached the first and collaborated with the second to deliver women-centered workshops. They represent a uniquely different facet of women who have transitioned into entrepreneurship from corporate jobs.

The Masculine Whelm, Leading an All-male Team

Marisol (not her real name) had a long list of professional accolades that demonstrated her achievements. She launched her career as a digital designer at a major European media company, founded a non-profit organization to empower women professionals, and obtained many fellowships at prestigious institutions, in addition to working as a director at a large media company in the US. She was at the top of her field, was very well networked, and was in high demand.

After years of success, Marisol was depressed, confused, and physically, emotionally, and mentally exhausted. She was leading multiple projects, living a bi-coastal life, and traveling internationally as the leader of a mostly male team. Like many young, overworked professionals, because of her success and increasing workload, when I met her she was anxious, approval-seeking, and required validation for her choices. Shattering glass ceilings in a male-dominated industry was taking its toll on her, but she had been doing everything that everyone had always told her to do. As a smart and ambitious woman, she had nowhere to go but up, until she came crashing down – gradually at first and then more quickly.

After working at an intense pace for several years, she felt it all starting to unravel. The personality traits that had ensured her success – her assertive, charismatic, and optimistic attitude – brought her so many opportunities that it became impossible to manage them all. While power was conferred to her institutionally, her intrinsic power – her power within – remained hidden, even to her. The more opportunities she took on, the less time she had to develop her personal sense of self and the leadership skills she needed in order to be effective in her numerous roles. She found herself living a life based on other people's vision of success, not her own. It was a harsh awakening, and it had a deleterious effect on her self-confidence.

With her can-do attitude, she could never say no to an opportunity. She made choices based not on her needs but to fulfill the expectations of her managers and mentors and the male leaders in her life. If Marisol had been more self-aware she would have realized that she did not have to pursue every new opportunity. Her sense of power did not come from within; it came from that which was given to her – the power that was conferred through her role, her boss, and her company (Batliwala, 2010).

Marisol is a classic Gladwellian 'Connector.' Even though she was spread thin, everything was possible in her mind. With every opportunity she accepted, her power over her own life diminished (Gladwell, 2000). She tried to manage her team from afar, keep her bosses happy, and maintain her commitment to all the initiatives of which she was part – all at the expense of her inner health. Her team no longer trusted her because she was often traveling and building strategic relationships and not present to effectively direct and guide them. She felt hopeless.

We agreed that a leadership transition program was what she needed to help free her from being stuck. I helped Marisol take a step back to explore her situation, to understand her decisions, choices, and desire to over-achieve. The more we explored her notion of success, the more it became clear that it was not self-defined but was envisioned and directed by others. With holistic and mindfully adapted coaching, Marisol stepped into her intrinsic power and went from feelings of despondency and hopelessness to greater clarity and the courage to transform herself and her situation. Marisol turned her situation around by first going inward to find her inner heroine and then laying the groundwork for her new company.

Women-centered Business Collaboration and Sacred Space

The Creative Girls is an organizational collaboration among three Hispanic women who pooled their resources to host workshops and events in a corner storefront in Miami's Little Havana that center on branding, digital strategy, and social media services for entrepreneurs – with a feminine twist.

Gabriela is a single mother and the founder of a boutique social media consulting company that serves women entrepreneurs, Nadia is a branding expert who consults with both small and large companies, and Jennifer had previously founded and closed a creative strategies consulting company.

Collaborating with these women professionally was a departure from the 'norm' I had seen in the hyper-competitive, masculine world of management consulting. In many ways, they had all gone through their own heroine's journey of personal transformation that gave them the courage to step out of their corporate careers to fill their need to work independently and, more importantly, to live more balanced and healthy lives.

Gabriela and Nadia's joint business venture, The Branding Goldmine, is a bi-annual workshop that they lead for women creative entrepreneurs who want to develop an integrated brand and social media strategy that can be implemented quickly. This feminine-centered interactive workshop is a soulfully effective way to learn-by-doing that can be much more inspiring than more conventional types of professional training. Women business owners in the arts, product development, and professional services come together to tap into a creative inner place and develop creative business strategies.

The female-centered workshop environment is collaborative and nurturing. Unlike mix-gendered environments that men often dominate by speaking over each other and talking down to female colleagues, no one is afraid to speak up and share her perspective. The Creative Girls' office feels like a feminine space that supports its female participants' right to be vulnerable and to share their most heartfelt desires for their creative businesses.

From a business perspective, this model of collaboration is one that would work well for women who are interested in working as independent contractors or starting new businesses. First, it is cost-effective and keeps overheads low since office space is shared with others. Second, it provides structure and a readily available support system that limits isolation and expands one's networks. Third, joint collaboration on new opportunities limits certain business risks.

The examples provided by Marisol and The Creative Girls reveal different approaches to beginning a journey down an entrepreneurial path. Marisol's initial break into entrepreneurship was abrupt and professionally painful, and she needed a leadership coach for guidance and support and the validation that she could live with her choices and their consequences. Given the opportunity to move quickly into entrepreneurship, she also had to get her emotional house in order to rebuild her self-confidence and sense of self-efficacy.

Gabriela's journey was more gradual. As opportunities revealed themselves, she continually rebalanced her personal needs with her professional aspirations. For her, like most single mothers, she needed time to spend with her young son, and starting her business gave her the flexible schedule that she needed. Finding other women with similar business goals and life perspectives reassured her that she was not going at it alone.

CONCLUSIONS

Relationships are at the center of entrepreneurship, especially for women who seldom have access to new technologies or capital when they launch a business. The old-boys' network, even though mediated by an impersonal market, is well aware of the importance of social networks, trust, and influence in deal-making. Leveraging social networks effectively remains a challenge for women who seek to climb the corporate ladder, especially when they believe that there is room for only one woman at the top (Barsh et al., 2008). However, the importance of building strong social networks and relationships is clear to women entrepreneurs. They, more than their corporate counterparts, value their relationships with other women differently and realize that these relationships are often their most valuable currency.

In the zero-sum game that is often played in becoming an executive in a large corporation, women continue to be at a disadvantage. They try to mold themselves into the hetero white male model of leadership that keeps them from using the very skills, competencies, and talents that would make them exceptional leaders. In the US, many women, especially black women, are starting to take the entrepreneurial path and are changing the entrepreneurial landscape by building new professional-service models that are a reflection of how people want to live their lives and work. These women are able to launch their companies after a journey of personal transformation, their heroine's journey that gave them the confidence to approach entrepreneurship in a new way.

Each step taken inward for these women was a step toward an outward manifestation that culminated in greater creativity and a subsequent business opportunity. A greater sense of self that increased awareness, confidence, and efficacy enabled our heroines to create something new, even under difficult circumstances. In addition, their heroine's journey was the first stage in achieving greater *authenticity* in the *Artemis Leadership Compass* (see Figure 3.2); without it, there is little space to move into *creativity* and *relatedness*, the second and third phases of the model.

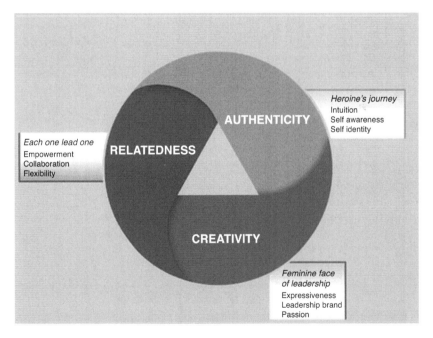

Figure 3.2 The Artemis Woman-Centered Leadership Compass

I hope that raising questions related to women's empowerment will help reframe how we think of women entrepreneurs. Perhaps others will explore some of these questions in their work, which can only support the development of scholarship on women in entrepreneurship and encourage more informed policy decisions. How resources are allocated from the policy level to ensure an equal playing field and equal market access is one of these important questions.

What is the overall perception of both women and men of the value of the services women provide in the market? How can leadership and entrepreneurial programs for women do more to support their success and move the dial on change so we have women leaders who represent the social and economic needs of people worldwide? Are leadership programs and accelerators doing enough to change the external and internal factors that play a role in women's confidence and self-efficacy?

Currently, women who lead these types of efforts for women leaders and entrepreneurs are either unaware of or dismissive of approaches that challenge the hetero-male model to entrepreneurial success. As such, they perpetuate the low rate of success for women entrepreneurs by not seeking a way to support the personal development needs of the women in their programs. A young woman at the Miami WIN accelerator program mentioned that one of her big challenges was the lack of support the women were given for their self-development needs. While hard skills and mentoring was available, the deeper support they needed on the lonely journey that is entrepreneurship was just not available to them. More can be done to help women build resiliency by coaching and designing learning programs that honor their woman-ness and the inner journey that is as crucial as learning how to create a balance sheet.

I ask these questions because they are as relevant today as they were 50 years ago, given the slow pace of change in women's representation in institutions and as entrepreneurs. Given that we cannot afford to continue to ignore 'our self,' half the population and half the brainpower needed to solve the world's problems, it means that we cannot continue doing things the same way. We must ask better questions so we find better solutions, rather than assuming that what works for men can always be adapted for women.

As women take their first steps toward becoming their own heroines, they must remember that they already have all the inner strength and power to be effective leaders and entrepreneurs – in their own way, a way that is often better and more powerful than the models on which the world is currently built.

REFERENCES

Ahl, H. and Marlow, S. (2012). Exploring the dynamics of gender, feminism and entrepreneurship: advancing debate to escape a dead end? *Organization*, 19(5), 543–562.

Barsh, J., Cranston, S., and Craske, R.A. (2008). Centered leadership: how talented women thrive. *The McKinsey Quarterly*, 4, 35–48.

Batliwala, S. (2010). *Feminist Leadership for Social Transformation: Clearing the Conceptual Cloud*. Bangalore: AWID (Association for Women's Rights in Development).

Bolen, J.S. (1985). *Goddesses in Everywoman: Powerful Archetypes in Women's Lives*. San Francisco: Harper.

Brush, C., Carter, N.M., Gatewood, E., Greene, P.G., and Hart, M.M. (2004). *Clearing the Hurdles: Women Building High Growth Businesses*. Upper Saddle River, NJ: Prentice Hall.

Campbell, J. (1988). *The Power of Myth with Bill Moyers*. New York: Random House.

Clark Muntean, S. and Özkazanç-Pan, B. (2015). A gender integrative conceptualization of entrepreneurship. *New England Journal of Entrepreneurship*, 18(1), 27–40.

Einstein, A. (1946). Atomic education urged by Einstein. *The New York Times*, 25 May, p. 13.

Ely, R.J., Ibarra, H., and Kolb, D. (2011). Taking gender into account: theory and design for women's leadership development programs. *Academy of Management Learning & Education*, Special Issue, 10(3), 1–53.

Foreman, A. (2016). *The Ascent of Women*. Documentary, BBC2 and Netflix.

Gerzema, J. and D'Antonio, M. (2013). *The Athena Doctrine: How Women (and the Men Who Think Like Them) Will Rule the Future*. New York: Young & Rubicam Brands.

Gladwell, M. (2000). *The Tipping Point*. New York: Little, Brown.

Harding, E.M. (1971). *The Way of All Women: A Classic Study of the Many Roles of Modern Women*. London: Rider.

Murdoch, M. (1990). *The Heroine's Journey*. Boston: Shambahla Publications.

Stover, S.A. (2015). *The Book of She: Your Heroine's Journey into the Heart of Feminine Power*. Novato, CA: The New World Library.

FURTHER READING

Campbell, J. (2008). *The Hero with a Thousand Faces*. Novato, CA: The New World Library and Joseph Campbell Foundation.

Jung, C.J. (1970). *Four Archetypes*. Princeton, NJ: Princeton University Press.

Jung, C.J. (1990). *The Undiscovered Self*. Princeton, NJ: Princeton University Press.

Kelley, D., Brush, C., Greene, P., Herrington, M., Ali, A., and Kew, P. (2015). GEM women's special report: women's entrepreneurship. Wellesley, MA: Babson College.

Lesser, E. (2000). *The Seekers Guide: Gender and Self – Gods and Goddesses Within*. New York: Villard.

Moore, T. (1992). *Care of the Soul: A Guide for Cultivating Depth and Sacredness in Everyday Life*. New York: HarperCollins.

Smyer, I.F. (2013). *Relationship Within*. Bloomington, IN: Balboa Press.

PART 2

Challenging the underperformance hypothesis
and acknowledging the constrained
performance of women entrepreneurs

4. Hitting the top: is there a glass ceiling for high-growth women entrepreneurs?

Ruta Aidis

Entrepreneurship is often portrayed as an alternative to traditional 'work' that offers women freedom from bosses, independence, and success. There is a popularized notion[1] that by dreaming big, women can apply their skills and talents to pursue their entrepreneurial endeavors and the rest will fall into place. Though this may be true in some cases, removing entrepreneurship from the realm of 'work' minimizes the gendered institutional embeddedness that affects women's entrepreneurship development.

For this reason authors such Jennings and McDougald (2007) and Eikhof et al. (2013) have suggested that it may be more relevant to view entrepreneurship for women as another form of work. In this regard, it is also useful to differentiate between types and levels of entrepreneurs in a similar way to workers in terms of different levels of authority and responsibility. When women's businesses are small-scale with few if any employees they are generally less dependent on outside resources for success. However, as entrepreneurs, male or female, grow their businesses, their dependence increases on the availability of external resources such as knowledge, networks, and funding. It is at this point of entrepreneurship that gender leadership bias as related to leadership may create an additional barrier for women.

Institutional theory has been used to understand the gendered impediments throughout the entrepreneurial process (Welter and Smallbone, 2011; Aidis et al., 2015). Gender role congruity theory provides additional insights as to the effects of gendered expectations for leadership. Women who grow their businesses occupy leadership roles (often by default) that have traditionally been associated with male characteristics and stereotypes and as a result encounter additional gender-specific barriers.

Gender leadership bias is well documented in context of the corporate sector. First constelled in the 1990s, the 'glass ceiling' phenomenon continues to be a visible feature of the corporate environment worldwide. Even though women are increasing their participation in management positions, far fewer women occupy senior executive roles or are members on boards of directors. This contributes to the tokenism of senior-level women which limits women's leadership opportunities and power in organizations. For example, on US boards, new women board members are usually appointed to replace leaving women board members but rarely to replace leaving male board members (Tinsley et al., 2014). Since there are so few women on boards, this process invariably maintains a small 'token' presence of women.

Could this dynamic be occurring for growth-oriented women entrepreneurs? A recent survey of small business owners in the US found that 77 percent of female business owners believe that women and minorities are affected by the glass ceiling while 46 percent of the female business owners felt limited by the glass ceiling (Bank of America, 2016). These results indicate that it may not be possible for women entrepreneurs to circumvent the glass ceiling by leaving the corporate sector and becoming their own boss as entrepreneurs. Moreover, the institutional nature of gendered leadership bias indicates that it is a systemic, cultural phenomenon that may affect growth-oriented entrepreneurs in a similar way to executives.

COMPARATIVE DATA ON THE GLASS CEILING IN THE PRIVATE SECTOR

The glass ceiling has been defined as the 'unseen, yet unbreachable barrier that keeps minorities and women from rising to the upper rungs of the corporate ladder, regardless of their qualifications or achievements' (US Federal Glass Ceiling Commission, 1995, p. 6). In this section, we present some of the existing comparative data on how women are perceived as executives as well as data on the percentages of women in senior decision-making positions that illustrate the existence of the glass ceiling in the corporate sector. We utilize data from a 31-country sample that includes a range of different regions and countries at various levels of economic development to provide a 'global' perspective. We begin with insights into the perception of women as leaders based on survey data collected by the World Values Survey. In each country, the respondents were asked the following statement: 'On the whole, men make better business executives than women do.' The percentages of men and women respondents that disagreed with this statement are shown in Figure 4.1. Three trends are worth highlighting: First, perception bias exists for women executives in all countries sampled. Second, in general, male respondents exhibit a higher degree of perception bias than female respondents. Third, the R-squared

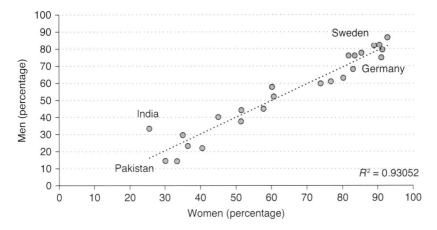

Source: World Values Survey (2015) data shown from most recent year. Percentage of respondents that disagree with the question, 'On the whole, men make better business executives than women do' (V53).

Figure 4.1   Perception bias for women executives

statistic of 0.93 indicates that the relationship between male and female perceptions are highly significant and follow a similar high or low bias trend. As gender congruity theory predicts, it is not surprising that in general, male and female leadership perceptions follow a similar trend. However, outliers exist for several countries: In Germany the difference between female and male perception bias is high at over 17 percent while in India gendered perception bias is high for both men and women, however male perception bias is somewhat lower than female leadership perception bias.

The next three figures present the percentages of women in three types of senior corporate positions: Figure 4.2 presents the percentages of women CEOs in a country's largest publicly traded companies;[2] Figure 4.3 shows the percentages of women senior managers; and Figure 4.4 presents the percentage of women on corporate boards. If these three senior corporate positions were characterized by gender parity, we would expect to see a 40–60 percent ratio of women. The overall percentages for women CEOs shown in Figure 4.2 are well below gender parity and do not even reach 10 percent for any single country. Out of the sampled countries, Nigeria shows the highest percentage of female CEOs at 8 percent while six countries including Germany and Japan have no female CEOs. In most cases, the lack of women CEOs is not even reflective of the relatively high percentage of women active in the labor force. For example, in the US,

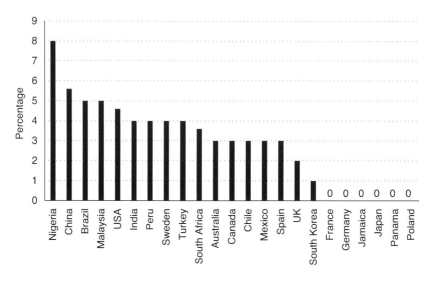

Source: 2015 Global Women Entrepreneur Leaders Scorecard (Aidis et al., 2015).

Figure 4.2   Percentage of women CEOs

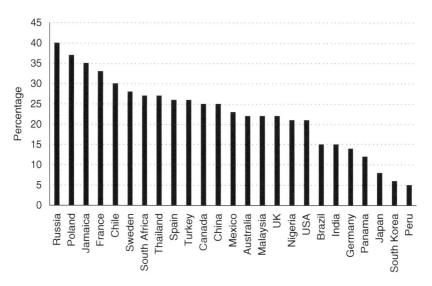

Source: Figure adapted from Aidis et al. (2015). Original data sourced from Grant Thornton International Business Report (IBR) (2014; 2015) and Catalyst (2014).

Figure 4.3   Percentage of women senior managers

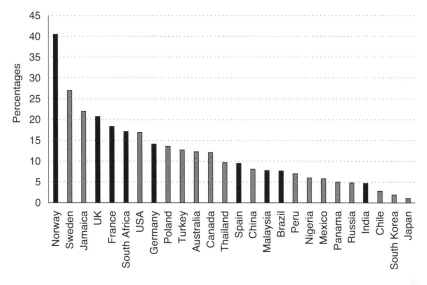

Note: Darker columns indicate countries which have introduced a quota for women on boards.

Source: Figure adapted from Aidis et al. (2015). Original sourced from Catalyst (2014).

Figure 4.4   Percentage of women on boards

where currently 4.6 percent of CEOs are women, women would make up 47 percent of CEOs if the rate were representative of the female working population.

Compared to the percentages for women CEOs, the percentages of women in senior management positions are generally higher but in most cases still do not reach gender parity. As shown in Figure 4.3, the one exception is Russia with 40 percent female senior managers followed by Poland (37 percent) and Jamaica (35 percent) which are only slightly below gender parity levels. Surprisingly, many advanced market economies are characterized by relatively low percentages of female senior managers: The percentage of female senior managers is only 21 percent in the US and even lower in Germany (14 percent), Japan (8 percent), and South Korea (6 percent).

Figure 4.4 presents the percentages of women on boards. A comparison of Figure 4.3 with Figure 4.4 shows that high percentages of women senior managers do not necessarily correspond with higher percentages of women on boards. For example, in Russia, while 40 percent of senior managers are women, less than 5 percent of board members are women.

In order to increase the percentages of women on boards, nine countries shown in Figure 4.3 (the UK, France, Germany, Norway, Poland, Spain, South Africa, Malaysia, and India) have introduced quotas. The quotas range from at least one woman on every board for listed companies in India to 50 percent of women on boards in South Africa. Norway shows the highest percentage of women on boards which reflects the success of a mandatory quota of 40 percent women on boards introduced in 2003. A longitudinal study on women on boards in the US (2002–2011) indicates that tokenism continues to characterize women's participation on boards: A significant predictor of a woman being appointed is whether a woman has just left that board (Tinsley et al., 2014). However, gender-balanced quotas, such as those implemented in Norway, have been successful in increasing and sustaining higher participation of women on boards.

The data available on women CEOs, senior managers, and women board members provides a fairly consistent portrayal of the glass ceiling's existence regardless of a country's regional location or level of economic development, women's participation in the labor force or women's educational attainments. However, equally insightful are the large data gaps that exist even for this relatively small sample of countries: Out of 31 countries sampled, data on the percentages of women CEOs in the largest publicly traded companies, senior managers and board members were not available for six countries including Uganda, Ghana, Tunisia, Egypt, Pakistan, and Bangladesh. In Russia and Thailand, there were no data available on the percentages of CEOs in the largest publicly traded companies and in South Africa there were no data available for the percentages of women on boards. In this regard, lack of data is a serious issue as it perpetuates the invisibility of women's participation in senior corporate positions and interferes with benchmarking and comparative research.

INSTITUTIONAL THEORY AND GENDER ROLE CONGRUITY THEORY

Institutional theory combined with gender role congruity theory provides a useful theoretical foundation for understanding how gender bias for women in leadership positions can permeate all sectors of society including entrepreneurial activity.

In theory, institutions have been created to facilitate economic transactions, and to increase efficiencies in economic systems (North, 1990). However, there is increasing evidence that the persistence of gender bias in formal and informal institutions can lead to market failures and create economic inefficiencies. A growing body of research indicates that women entrepreneurs function in a gendered context where different cultural customs, laws, traditions, and beliefs grant different levels of gendered privilege. As a result, studies in the field of women's entrepreneurship have adopted an institutional lens to better understand gendered barriers in entrepreneurship (de Bruin et al., 2007). Some of these studies have identified that existing gendered restrictions affect women's abilities to not only start but also scale their businesses (Aidis et al., 2015).

An example of formal institutional impediments that affect women entrepreneurs globally are gendered legal restrictions. A recent study by Women Business and the Law[3] indicates that increased levels of gendered legal restrictions result in fewer female-owned businesses (World Bank, 2014). Unequal inheritance rights and property ownership[4] as well as work restrictions limit women's abilities to accumulate wealth and access to resources that could be used as start-up capital or as collateral. Moreover, in 28 economies, the husband is legally considered the final decision-maker for the household, which in practice mandates married women entrepreneurs to defer to their husbands regarding decisions that affect their businesses (ibid.).

Though often less visible than formal institutions, informal institutions such as expectations and beliefs exert a subtle yet powerful impediment for women entrepreneurs. Even in countries where legal rights are insured, the gender wage gap (78 percent in the US[5]) results in working women being financially disadvantaged compared to working men. Since most business start-ups are self-financed, this puts women entrepreneurs in an unfavorable position. Moreover lower levels of wealth accumulation amongst working women may also impact the development of women who can act as investors for growth-oriented businesses. Importantly, and contrary to popular opinion, research on the gender pay gap in the US was not found to be specifically related to women working in different industries or because mothers choose to work fewer hours than other workers (Labaton, 2014). The combination of less personal wealth (influenced by the gender pay gap) and more limited access to external financing influences the pervasive undercapitalization of women's entrepreneurial pursuits so that they tend to stay small and not grow to their fullest potential.

Moreover, pervasive gendered beliefs and expectations that women are less capable as entrepreneurs hampers growth-oriented women entrepreneurs' access to finance. Researchers found that male investors preferred pitches presented by male entrepreneurs compared with pitches made by female entrepreneurs even when the content of the pitch was exactly the same (Brooks et al., 2014). The male-narrated pitches were rated as more persuasive, logical, and fact-based than were the same pitches narrated by a female voice (ibid.). Beliefs that men are more suited for entrepreneurship as well as data that show men as more likely to own larger, more profitable businesses than women contribute to the stereotype 'think successful entrepreneur – think male' (Eddleston et al., 2016, p. 497). Moreover, these results illustrate how gender bias can trigger behavior that runs contrary to economic rationale since research also indicates that businesses led by women entrepreneurs perform as well as or better than those led by men[6] (Brush et al., 2014). In addition, since venture capitalists (VCs) remain overwhelmingly male the notion 'think venture capitalist – think male' prevails. In 2016, of the top 100 VC firms in the US, only 7 percent of the VC partners were women (Teare and Desmond, 2016). This may be strongly influenced by the generally small size of a typical VC firm (median 3 partners) (Gompers and Wang, 2017). In effect, a VC firm making a new hire may have a slight gender preference for hiring a man over a woman. However, in this setting, even a very small bias towards hiring someone of the same gender can lead to persistent low representation from women and other groups not already in the VC industry (ibid., p. 37). Moreover, male VCs overwhelmingly invest in male growth-oriented entrepreneurs. The report by Brush et al. (2014) found that only 2.7 percent of companies who received VC funding had a woman CEO. Data from Crunchbase indicate that only 4.1 percent of women-led companies received VC funding (Crunchbase, 2016) while data from Pitchbook show that only 18 percent of funded companies were founded by women (Nolasco, 2016).

Gender role congruity theory introduced by Eagly and Karau (2002) elaborates on the ways in which gender bias and stereotypes interfere with the acceptance of women as successful leaders. Gender role congruity theory distinguishes between two types of informal institutional norms (descriptive and injunctive norms) as well as between two types of attributes (communal and agentic attributes). Descriptive norms or stereotypes are based on observations of what different types of people do. Common gendered stereotypes portray sex-typical roles such as men occupying higher-status leadership roles as breadwinners while women are portrayed as homemakers and lower-status roles as assistants or secretaries. Injunctive norms are related to ideal gendered qualities that are ascribed to men and women as well as the ideal gendered qualities men and women ascribe to themselves (ibid.). Injunctive norms are further divided into communal and agentic attributes (Eagly, 1987). Communal attributes are characterized by a primary concern for the welfare of others and are more strongly associated with women. In contrast, agentic attributes which include self-confidence, self-sufficiency, and independent and assertive behaviors as well as leadership roles are more strongly associated with men[7] (Eagly and Karau, 2002).

Since leadership ability is more readily associated as a male characteristic or stereotype the notion 'think leader – think male' is far more common than associating leadership with female characteristics. As a result, when women occupy leadership positions, there is both a less favorable opinion of their abilities as leaders as well as a less favorable evaluation of their actual leadership behavior (Eagly and Karau, 2002).

The greater the incongruity between the norms that define the female gender role and leadership role, the more likely it is that women are perceived as less qualified for leadership (Eagly and Karau, 2002). For example, leadership roles in the military or corporate sector align more directly with the male stereotype and male ideal than the female stereotype or female ideal. Therefore women are more likely to be perceived as less qualified for leadership in the military or the private sector. Given the pervasiveness of these beliefs, the gender role congruity theory emphasizes that achieving leadership is more difficult for women than men, because of the common perception that women have less leadership ability (ibid.).

In entrepreneurship research, gender role congruity theory has been used to explore the gendered effects of access to bank financing. Eddleston et al. (2016) find that different standards are used to evaluate the performance of men and women entrepreneurs seeking bank financing. Their results indicate that signals of viability and commitment by male and female entrepreneurs appear to be rewarded differently by capital providers, often putting women at a disadvantage. The authors conclude that existing gender biases have a detrimental effect on women entrepreneurs seeking bank financing.

With fewer women leaders as entrepreneurs or executives, the risk is great that when they fail, negative stereotypes can become further entrenched. The recent failure of Elizabeth Holmes, founder and CEO of Theranos as well as Marissa Mayer, CEO of Yahoo in the US have rekindled skepticism regarding women's overall capabilities as leaders in the private sector (Sydell, 2016). However, given the greater number of men in leadership positions, the frequent failure of male entrepreneurs or executives even in spectacular cases such as Kenneth Lay and the Enron scandal does not result in the same questioning of the 'leadership abilities of men.'

DEFINING HIGH-GROWTH FEMALE ENTREPRENEURS

The depiction of women entrepreneurs in a popular women's magazine in the UK offers an important perspective on the dominant stereotypes for women's entrepreneurship (Eikhof et al., 2013). The authors found that women's entrepreneurship was overwhelmingly portrayed as women escaping corporate culture to launch home-based, female-dominated industries which represented a retreat back to the 'female ideal' through entrepreneurship. By starting small-scale, home-based, part-time activities that provide supplemental income and allow for the balancing women's caretaker role, women embrace traditional 'communal norms' and their businesses do not fundamentally challenge the traditional gender dynamic. Unfortunately quantitative studies have not been conducted to validate how widespread this trend is amongst women entrepreneurs. However, as US Census data indicate, women are much more likely to be part-time self-employed than their male counterparts.

This pervasive view of women becoming entrepreneurs to escape the 'glass ceiling' that characterizes corporate culture renders women entrepreneurs who want to grow their businesses largely invisible. Little is known about high-growth women entrepreneurs as gendered data are limited and a lack of uniform definition for high-growth entrepreneurship hinders comparative research. Yet not all women entrepreneurs fit neatly into a single category. In this section we further discuss the main types of high-growth women entrepreneurs in addition to presenting some of the existing definitions and statistics on high-growth entrepreneurship.

A widely accepted definition of high-growth entrepreneurs was introduced by the Organisation for Economic Co-operation and Development (OECD). It defines these enterprises as exhibiting an average annual growth greater than 20 percent over a three-year period (OECD, 2007). According to this definition, growth can be measured by the number of employees or by turnover. Using the OECD definition, a 2008 study by the UK's Department of Business Enterprise and Regulatory Reform found that high-growth firms in both the US and UK are overwhelmingly founded by men. Only 7 percent of the high-growth firms in the US and 6 percent of the high-growth firms in the UK were founded by women or teams that included women (Audretch, 2012).

Gazelles are often considered a sub-set of high-growth enterprises. Gazelles are defined as enterprises which are up to five years old with average annual growth greater than 20 percent per annum, over a three-year period. For both definitions, only enterprises with at least ten employees are considered.[8] The OECD found that high-growth firms constitute between 3 percent and 6 percent of all firms and less than 1 percent of firms, and less than 2 percent in terms of turnover, is accounted by firms classified as gazelles (OECD, 2007). A definition for high-impact companies introduced by Tracy (2011) takes into account a firm's sales and employment growth. A high-impact company shows sales that at least double over a four-year period and an employment growth quantifier (product of its absolute and percentage employment change) was at least two (ibid.). However, these definitions require large amounts of firm-level, longitudinal data and as a result are difficult to operationalize across multiple countries and regions. A 2011 Ernst and Young study[9] of entrepreneurship in 60 countries found that only three out of every 1000 respondents achieved high growth (Morris, 2012). These high-impact entrepreneurs were defined in terms of their growth aspirations: as those entrepreneurs who intend to increase their number of employees fivefold in the next five years. They also exhibited certain identifiable characteristics: They tended to be college-educated and had internationally oriented businesses.

The 2015 Global Women Entrepreneur Leaders Scorecard adapted the parameters introduced by the 2011 Ernst and Young study to identify high-impact women entrepreneurs.[10] The Scorecard defined high-impact women entrepreneurs as those who exhibit characteristics associated with high-growth outcomes but which may currently be aspirational rather than have already achieved (Aidis et al., 2015). The three criteria used included: college-educated women entrepreneurs, women entrepreneurs who have a market-expanding, innovative business and are intending to employ at least ten people and plan to grow more than 50 percent in five years.[11] Market-expanding, innovative businesses are further identified as the percentage of women entrepreneurs with more than 1 percent of customers outside of the home country.[12]

However, not all women entrepreneurs want to grow their businesses nor will all growth-oriented women entrepreneurs be responsive to the same policy interventions. According to the perspective introduced by the 'Melting Middle,' three groups of growth-oriented women entrepreneurs are present in any given environment: privileged, die-hard, and promising entrepreneurs (Aidis, 2014). As the name implies, privileged entrepreneurs[13] are women who experience fewer entrepreneurial impediments due to their elite or celebrity status. Privileged entrepreneurs have access to networks and resources due to their social status and family connections. Entrepreneurs in this category are not less capable than other entrepreneurs; rather, in addition to their personal skill and talent, they enjoy privileges which allow them to 'function' above the normal limitations of the existing gendered institutional environment. In this way, they do not encounter the same regulatory barriers and they have access to key resources such as financing, contacts, connections, and insider information not readily available to the unprivileged.

The second type of high-growth women entrepreneurs are die-hard entrepreneurs. These entrepreneurs start businesses no matter what the conditions. While people around them may bemoan the regulatory burden, the high level of corruption, or lack of financing or gender-specific barriers, die-hard entrepreneurs develop strategies to overcome barriers. An example of a die-hard entrepreneur is Hassina Syed who despite numerous obstacles, including threats by warlords, government officials, and rival male interests who deeply resent a female in their presence, built a successful business in Afghanistan (Girardet, 2009). Stories of die-hard entrepreneurs often take on an unbelievable 'larger than life' quality and it is often hard for the population at large to relate to these exceptional individuals.

In general, public policy has little influence on the emergence of the first and second group of high-growth women entrepreneurs. However, the third category, 'promising entrepreneurs,' which tends to be most directly affected by gendered impediments, could also benefit the most from public policy interventions that target these gender-specific impediments. These types of gendered impediments often take the form of cultural or religious traditions. For example, some emerging research and anecdotal evidence indicates that social status is often a gendered impediment for married women entrepreneurs from the upper or middle class.[14] Social pressures and expectations as women increase their economic status often serve as a disincentive for women to start or grow their businesses since it conflicts with the prevailing expectations of what is considered appropriate behavior at higher levels of income and social status.

BUILDING EVIDENCE

Previous studies have indicated that there are fewer high-growth women entrepreneurs. Yet the statistics available are characterized by large knowledge gaps and much of the available data are either outdated or based on small sample sizes. For example the percentages for high-growth women in OECD countries is based on data from 2007. The frequently used US statistic that only 2 percent of women entrepreneurs in the US grow past the $1 million mark is quoted from Ernst and Young's 2012 report but is actually based on US Census data from 2007.

Data from 2004–2008 was used by Tracy (2011) to compare the rates of high-impact firms started by men and women. Tracy finds that the success rate for women-owned firms that achieve high-impact status is almost the same as the rate for men-owned firms. However, the big difference lies in the fact that women's firm ownership diminishes with increased firm size. Tracy concludes that as firm size increases, the glass ceiling phenomenon takes a stronger hold (ibid., p. 6). Again the data analyzed by Tracy (2011) and collated by the Corporate Research board are a one-off historical study that has not been updated.

These data, collected annually by the Global Entrepreneurship Monitor

(GEM), are also used to get an indication of the likelihood for women entrepreneurs to achieve high-growth firms. However this approach is subject to data limitations given that the typical small sample size of 2000 respondents often only contains a fraction of respondents that are women entrepreneurs.

In 2015, the Global Women Entrepreneur Leaders Scorecard utilized GEM data and explored the significant differences between growth aspirations for men and women entrepreneurs in a sample of 31 countries to get an indication of the gender business growth gap. T-tests were used and identified significant gender differences in 13 countries. However, in most of the remaining cases, the overall numbers of men and women entrepreneurs captured by the respondent sample size were not large enough to test for significant gendered differences. For example in Panama, only one growth-oriented woman entrepreneur was recorded, and only 7 men entrepreneurs, out of a total sample of 3874 respondents.

For the 13 countries where statistically significant differences were found, the 'gendered business growth gap' was estimated, and identified the magnitude of gendered economic effects on entrepreneurship. For example, in the US, if start-up rates of women's and men's growth-oriented businesses were the same, there would be 1.5 million more growth-oriented women's start-ups in the US economy; in Turkey there would be 872000 more growth-oriented women's start-ups; and in China, there would be 7.4 million more growth-oriented women entrepreneurs.[15] However, given the limitations of individual country sample sizes, the gendered business growth gap could only be calculated for less than half of the 31 countries.

The focus on women's entrepreneurship also tends to overlook the substantial loss of human and social capital that can occur, especially for women transitioning from paid employment in a male-dominated field to starting a business based on a female-dominated activity. Some women use entrepreneurship as an escape from male-dominated corporate environments where they have either experienced the glass ceiling or have felt unwelcome. On the surface, the transition from paid labor to a business start-up is celebrated as an increase in entrepreneurial activity, however it can hide the subsequent loss of human and social capital. For example, in Bolivia, Maria Claudia Mendez worked as a financial-economic analyst for an engineering firm. Initially elated about her new job, Maria soon noticed that she was treated differently from her male colleagues: She worked more hours than most of her male colleagues but earned the lowest salary in her division. Maria Claudia stuck it out for three years but the situation did not improve. A year later, at 30 years of age, Maria Claudia used her personal savings to start a business producing and selling upscale textiles based on natural fibres (Aidis, 2016b). Though Maria Claudia

Mendez was able to successfully transition to entrepreneurship, she exited her highly skilled professional career in the labor market to pursue entrepreneurship in a completely unrelated field (Aidis, 2016a).

In sum, there is growing evidence that a glass ceiling exists for women who scale their businesses in two ways: First, a gendered business growth gap is evident in a number of developed and developing countries. Second, the glass ceiling in the corporate sector can lead highly skilled professional women to exit their careers to start businesses in a completely unrelated field resulting in a substantial loss of human and social capital.

CONCLUSIONS AND RECOMMENDATIONS

Entrepreneurial activity has often been viewed as occurring outside of the normal confines of work. Excluding entrepreneurship from 'work' supports the assumption that women entrepreneurs would not experience the same degree of gendered institutional impediments in growing their businesses as they would in 'climbing the career ladder.' However, data presented in this chapter indicate that women are generally less accepted in leadership positions (by both men and women) and of the 31 developed and developing countries sampled, no single country exhibits gender parity for senior positions in the corporate sector. One strategy that seems to hold promise to break this cycle is the use of voluntary or mandatory quotas in the corporate sector. Holding corporations accountable for gender parity targets is also likely to have a positive spillover effect on increasing the legitimacy and acceptance of women in leadership positions in entrepreneurship.

This chapter puts forth the case that similar patterns are occurring in the corporate sector as well as in entrepreneurship. Women entrepreneurs may be their 'own bosses' yet they also must contend with prevailing 'injunctive norms' which ascribe leadership roles to the male domain. Even if women are successful leaders, their capabilities tend to be questioned and they tend to be less favorably evaluated than their male counterparts. The glass ceiling in the corporate sector as well as the internalized ideals of the female role may also influence women to escape their corporate jobs to start small-scale businesses in female-dominated sectors. Though the resulting business increases the rate of women's entrepreneurship, it often constitutes a tremendous social and human capital loss as the skills and networks developed in corporate jobs are abandoned. The media play a key role in perpetuating this image (Eikhof et al., 2013). These examples become realities as women and men form images of the characteristics and trajectory of successful women entrepreneurs.

In addition, this chapter uses the 'Melting Middle' perspective to distinguish between different types of growth-oriented women entrepreneurs indicating that some types (die-hard and privileged entrepreneurs) will be less affected by gendered barriers due to personal characteristics or elite status. However, the vast majority of growth-oriented women entrepreneurs (promising entrepreneurs) are likely to react to prevailing gendered institutional conditions by not growing their businesses. In this regard, public policy can and should play a pivotal role in addressing the impediments for women to start and grow their businesses.

In sum, the glass ceiling affects women who scale their businesses in three important ways: First, gendered attitudes towards 'leadership' make it less socially acceptable for women to scale their businesses. Second, gendered attitudes towards 'leadership' make it more difficult for women to access needed resources for growth such as venture capital. Third, the trend for women to exit corporate careers after hitting the glass ceiling to become entrepreneurs in completely unrelated business sectors constitutes a large loss of human and social capital.

A number of steps need to be taken. The screening of governmental entrepreneurship promotion websites can be a good place to begin. In the UK, the Burt Report uncovered a number of instances of 'unconscious bias' that resulted in less representation, less visibility, and less overall integration of women into the messaging and images portrayed on government-funded business support websites (Burt, 2015). This form of subtle bias and exclusion can unintentionally perpetuate gendered bias towards women's entrepreneurship. Another relatively easy intervention is the assessment of gender balance in government-sponsored panels, presentations, and publications related to entrepreneurship. This could be done by assessing whether women are visible as active participants and panelists (at the podium and in the audience) at all entrepreneurship-related events and not only for specific interventions that target women entrepreneurs.

In this chapter, we focus on the need for better data. To date, much of the data on women entrepreneurs are limited and/or outdated. No uniform definition for growth-oriented women entrepreneurs exists which hampers further comparative research as what does not get measured does not get counted or addressed. From a public policy perspective, collecting sex disaggregated data is the first step towards change. A critical starting point should focus on collecting gendered statistics for entrepreneurship on the existing beneficiaries of all government-funded initiatives related to entrepreneurship development. These data would provide valuable insights as to the gender breakdown of program participants in order to identify whether bottlenecks for women's participation in entrepreneurship programs exist. Most countries do not collect this basic form of data.

In addition, the following key areas would also benefit from gendered data collection:

- *Pre start-up phase:* It is important to assess the depth of coverage and visibility of women entrepreneurs in the media. For example: How often and in what ways are successful women entrepreneurs being portrayed in the mass media? Are women more likely to be portrayed as entrepreneurs engaged in only a few female-dominated sectors? Are there only a few female entrepreneurs that get media coverage?
- *Business start-up phase:* Are women starting businesses at a similar rate to men? Are women making use of government-funded entrepreneurship programs as well as of incubators and accelerators at a similar rate to men? In some cases, specific programs targeting women entrepreneurs may be needed but women should also be fully integrated into existing gender-neutral entrepreneurship programs. Are women and men acting at a similar level as leaders, instructors, facilitators, and mentors in government-funded entrepreneurship programs? In other words, more rigorous assessments of gender-funding parity for entrepreneurship needs to be conducted for governments, international organizations, and corporations in order to ensure there are no gendered impediments at this stage of entrepreneurship development.
- *Business growth phase:* In this final stage it is important to collect sex disaggregated data on the use of external financial resources such as bank loans, informal investors, and venture capital. In addition, it is important to know if women are participating at a similar rate to men in all government-sponsored programs geared towards business growth.

The next step is just as critical: commitment to developing a gender balance in entrepreneurship in terms of participation, presentation, and perception. Initiatives by both the government and the corporate sector to address the glass ceiling are needed.

NOTES

1. Especially in popular women's monthly magazines such as *Oprah* (in the US) and *Eve* (in the UK).
2. Designated as companies listed on the national stock exchange.
3. Calculations are based on the Women Business and the Law database, World Bank World Development Indicators database, and World Bank Enterprise Surveys.

4. Increased numbers of women have loans in economies that grant women the same property rights as men (World Bank, 2014).
5. In the US, in 2013, the ratio of women's to men's median annual earnings was only 78.3 percent for full-time, year-round workers (Hegewisch and Hartmann, 2014).
6. Businesses with a woman on the executive team are more likely to have higher valuations at both first and last funding (64 percent higher and 49 percent higher, respectively) (Brush et al., 2014).
7. In contrast, men experience a double advantage over women in perceived leadership ability since leadership is perceived as fulfilling both the male stereotype and incorporating ideal male behaviors (Eagly and Karau, 2002).
8. A minimum of ten employees is used in order to avoid distortions that could occur for firms with very few employees.
9. The study was based on Global Entrepreneurship Monitor (GEM) data.
10. For further discussion, see Aidis and Weeks (2016).
11. This definition is based on the question for growth-oriented start-up used by the GEM's annual survey.
12. This definition is also based on the question for growth-oriented start-up used by the GEM's annual survey.
13. Examples of privileged entrepreneurs are often found among the siblings, in-laws, and children of the ruling elite. An example of a US-based privileged entrepreneur is Ivanka Trump, daughter of real-estate entrepreneur and US president Donald Trump. Privileged entrepreneurs also include celebrities such as reality show star Kim Kardashian (USA), supermodel Gisele Bunchen (Brazil), and actress Jessica Alba (USA).
14. For example, in India, a recent study found that caste had the greatest impact on Hindu women entrepreneurs. Upper caste women faced significantly more gendered restrictions than scheduled castes which are the lowest group in the caste hierarchy (Field et al., 2010).
15. For a description of the methodology used to calculate the Gender Business Growth Gap, please refer to Aidis et al. (2015).

REFERENCES

Aidis, R. (2014). 'The Melting Middle: Unleashing the Full Potential of Entrepreneurship through Public Policy,' working paper, Research Gate, retrieved from: https://www.researchgate.net/publication/285590263_The_Melting_Middle_Unleashing_the_Full_Potential_of_Entrepreneurship_through_Public_Policy.

Aidis, R. (2016a). 'Female Occupational Crowding and Entrepreneurial Outcomes: Implications for Female Entrepreneurship Success,' Chapter 3 in C. Brush, E. Ljunggren, F. Welter, and C. Diz Garcia (eds), *Women's Entrepreneurship Global and Local Contexts*, Cheltenham, UK and Northampton, MA: Edward Elgar Publishing, pp. 43–62.

Aidis, R. (2016b). 'Three Faces of Innovation: The Gendered Realities for Female Entrepreneurs in Latin America,' Chapter 4 in G. Alsos, U. Hytti, and E. Ljunggren (eds), *Research Handbook on Gender and Innovation*, Cheltenham, UK and Northampton, MA: Edward Elgar Publishing, pp. 72–90.

Aidis, R. and Weeks, J. (2016). 'Mapping the Gendered Ecosystem: The Evolution of Measurement Tools for Comparative High-Impact Female Entrepreneur Development,' *International Journal for Gender and Entrepreneurship*, 8(4), 330–352.

Aidis, R., Weeks, J., and Anacker, K. (2015). 'The Global Women Entrepreneur Leaders Scorecard 2015: From Awareness to Action,' executive report, ACG

Inc., retrieved from: https://www.dell.com/learn/us/en/vn/corporate~secure~en/documents~2015-gwel-scorecard-executive-summary.pdf.

Audretsch, D. (2012). 'Determinants of High-Growth Entrepreneurship,' Report prepared for the OECD/DBA International Workshop on 'High-Growth Firms: Local Policies and Local Determinants,' Copenhagen, retrieved from: https://www.oecd.org/cfe/leed/Audretsch_determinants%20of%20high-growth%20firms.pdf.

Bank of America (2016). 'Spotlight on Women,' survey results, retrieved from: http://newsroom.bankofamerica.com/files/press_kit/additional/2016_Women_Small_Business_Owner_Spotlight_Infographic.pdf.

Brooks, A., Huang, L., Kearney, S., and Murray, F. (2014). 'Investors Prefer Entrepreneurial Ventures Pitched by Attractive Men,' *Proceedings of the National Academy of the Sciences*, 111(12), 4427–4431.

Brush, C., Greene, P., Balachandra, L., and Davis, A. (2014). 'Bridging the Gender Gap in Venture Capital,' report, Babson College, retrieved from: http://www.babson.edu/Academics/centers/blank-center/global-research/diana/Documents/diana-project-executive-summary-2014.pdf.

Burt, L. (2015). 'The Burt Report: Inclusive Support for Women in Enterprise,' retrieved from: https://www.gov.uk/government/uploads/system/uploads/attachment_data/file/403004/BIS-15-90_Inclusive_support_for_women_in_enterprise_The_Burt_report_final.pdf.

Catalyst (2014). *Women on Boards 2014*, retrieved from: http://www.catalyst.org/knowledge/women-boards.

Crunchbase (2016). 'Women in Venture Capital and Their Effect on Female Founders,' report, retrieved from: https://info.crunchbase.com/2015/09/infographic-female-founders-on-an-upward-trend-2/.

De Bruin, A., Brush, C., and Welter, F. (2007). 'Advancing a Framework for Coherent Research on Women's Entrepreneurship,' *Entrepreneurship Theory and Practice*, 31(3), 323–339.

Eagly, A. (1987). *Sex Differences in Social Behavior: A Social-Role Interpretation*, Hillsdale, NJ: Erlbaum.

Eagly, A. and Karau, S. (2002). 'Role Congruity Theory of Prejudice Toward Female Leaders,' *Psychological Review*, 109(3), 573–585.

Eddleston, K., Ladge, J., Mitteness, C., and Balanchandra, L. (2016). 'Do You See What I See? Signaling Effects of Gender and Firm Characteristics on Financing Entrepreneurial Ventures,' *Entrepreneurship, Theory and Practice*, 40, 489–514.

Eikhof, D., Carter, S., and Summers, J. (2013). 'Women Doing Their Own Thing: Media Representations of Female Entrepreneurship,' *International Journal of Entrepreneurship Behaviour and Research*, 19(5), 547–564.

Field, E., Jayachandran, S., and Pande, R. (2010). 'Do Traditional Institutions Constrain Female Entrepreneurship? A Field Experiment on Business Training in India,' *American Economic Review Papers and Proceedings*, 100(May), 125–129, retrieved from: http://scholar.harvard.edu/files/field/files/sewa_bt_pp.pdf?m=1360040249.

Girardet, E. (2009). 'In Afghanistan, An Entrepreneur Thrives,' *Forbes*, 12 October, retrieved from: http://www.forbes.com/2009/10/12/afghanistan-women-hassina-syed-forbes-woman-entrepreneurs-mega-finance.html.

Gompers, P. and Wang, S. (2017). 'Diversity in Innovation,' NBER Working Paper No 23082, retrieved from: http://www.nber.org/papers/w23082.

Grant Thornton International Business Report (IBR) (2014). Retrieved from:

https://www.grantthornton.global/en/insights/articles/Women-in-business-class room-to-boardroom/.

Grant Thornton International Business Report (IBR) (2015). Retrieved from: http://www.grantthornton.global/en/insights/articles/women-in-business-2015/.

Hegewisch, A. and Hartmann, H. (2014). 'The Gender Wage Gap: 2013,' Institute for Women's Policy Research, retrieved from: http://www.iwpr.org/publications/pubs/the-gender-wage-gap-2013#sthash.eozokWT6.dpuf.

Jennings J. and McDougald, M. (2007). 'Work–Family Interfaces and Coping Strategies: Implications for Entrepreneurship Research and Practice,' *Academy of Management Review*, 32(3), 747–760.

Labaton, V. (2014). 'Five Myths about the Gender Pay Gap,' *The Washington Post*, 25 July, retrieved from: https://www.washingtonpost.com/opinions/five-myths-about-the-gender-pay-gap/2014/07/25/9e5cff34-fcd5-11e3-8176-f2c941cf35f1_story.html.

Morris, R. (2012). 'The 2011 High-Impact Entrepreneurship Global Report,' sponsored by Ernst and Young, Endeavor, and the Global Entrepreneurship Monitor, retrieved from: http://www.gemconsortium.org/docs/download/295.

Nolasco, J. (2016). 'Female Founders Grab Record VC Deals,' Pitchbook, retrieved from: https://pitchbook.com/news/articles/female-founders-grab-record-vc-deal-sharebut-still-just-18-datagraphic.

North, D. (1990). *Institutions, Institutional Change and Economic Performance*, Cambridge, UK: Cambridge University Press.

OECD (Organisation for Economic Co-operation and Development) (2007). *Eurostat-OECD Manual on Business Demography Statistics*, Paris: OECD.

Sydell, L. (2016). 'Is There a Double Standard When Female CEOs in Tech Stumble?,' *All Things Considered*, National Public Radio (NPR), 3 August, retrieved from: http://www.npr.org/sections/alltechconsidered/2016/08/03/488569884/is-there-a-double-standard-when-women-ceos-in-tech-stumble.

Teare, G. and Desmond, N. (2016). 'The First Comprehensive Study on Women in Venture Capital and their Impact on Female Founders,' TeleCrunch, 19 April, retrieved from: https://techcrunch.com/2016/04/19/the-first-comprehensive-study-on-women-in-venture-capital/.

Tinsley, C., Wade, J., Main, B., and O'Reilly, C. (2014). 'Progress on Gender Diversity for Corporate Boards: Are we Running in Place?,' paper, retrieved from: https://pdfs.semanticscholar.org/fbbc/ae73fec9765f935ff30a54ca99715410bb38.pdf?_ga=1.51072169.1445137648.1475430789.

Tracy, S. (2011). 'Accelerating Job Creation in America: The Promise of High Impact Companies,' research report commissioned by the US Small Business Administration, No 381.

US Federal Glass Ceiling Commission (1995). 'A Solid Investment: Making Full Use of the Nation's Human Capital,' retrieved from: https://www.dol.gov/dol/aboutdol/history/reich/reports/ceiling2.pdf.

Welter, F. and Smallbone, D. (2011). 'Institutional Perspectives on Entrepreneurial Behavior in Challenging Environments,' *Journal of Small Business Management*, 49(1), 107–125.

World Bank (2014). *Women Business and the Law Report 2014*, retrieved from: http://wbl.worldbank.org/~/media/FPDKM/WBL/Documents/Reports/2014/Women-Business-and-the-Law-2014-FullReport.pdf.

World Values Survey (2015). *World Values Survey*, database, retrieved from: http://www.worldvaluessurvey.org/wvs.jsp.

5. Indigenous entrepreneurship: Māori female entrepreneurs in the tourism industry and constraints to their success

Alina Zapalska and Dallas Brozik

Over thousands of years and across a great range of continents, countries, and environments, indigenous peoples have displayed an ability to adapt, change, and prosper. Each group has its own distinctive identity, resilience, and set of cultural, managerial, and technical skills, but indigenous people around the globe continue to be socially and economically disadvantaged in today's developed world (Anderson et al., 2006; Hokowhitu, 2010). Despite substantial financial investment by government authorities in indigenous peoples' education, health, and housing programs, in many countries indigenous people suffer from poor health, inadequate education, and chronic poverty (Broderstad, 2010). The status of indigenous women differs from one community to another and from one region to another since men and women have different gender roles and responsibilities and often have different needs, desires, and interests (Birley, 1989). The experiences and challenges facing indigenous women throughout the world are often similar in terms of poverty, human rights violations, lack of access to education, health care, and socio-economic development. Indigenous women face harsher multiple-discrimination on the basis of race, ethnicity, language, culture, religion, and class.

Indigenous female entrepreneurs are a cultural asset and provide entrepreneurial capital that contributes to economic development and growth (Burke et al., 2002). Some Māori indigenous entrepreneurial women enjoy their social position, and their status is not low in comparison to non-Māori women. Those Māori women have been permitted to hold exclusive land rights and inherit ancestral properties. They are heavily involved in ventures within the tourism industry in New Zealand (Hudson, 2002; Zapalska et al., 2003). They have embraced both commercial development and cultural values and managed to maximize their economic and cultural sustainability and improve the well-being of their communities (Jones, 2007). It is critical to understand their entrepreneurial traits and to identify factors that impede and enhance their entrepreneurial undertakings. This chapter focuses on a case study of ten Māori female-owned and operated entrepreneurial businesses within the tourism industry and identifies female entrepreneurial elements of sustainability which are based on cultural, natural, and environmental fundamentals.

This chapter identifies four categories as significant contributors or barriers to female entrepreneurial success (Hindle and Moroz, 2010): (i) the cultural and social environment; (ii) entrepreneurial capacity, organizational drivers, and constraints; (iii) land and resources; and (iv) institutional infrastructure available to entrepreneurs. The chapter illustrates that the ethnic and cultural characteristics of their products and services have positively affected their entrepreneurial success. The unique characteristics of Māori female entrepreneurial activities were considered as positive factors affecting their success. The chapter also underlines several barriers that inhibited growth and success of indigenous entrepreneurial activities included in this study.

BACKGROUND ON MĀORI ENTREPRENEURSHIP

Māori, the indigenous people of New Zealand, arrived in New Zealand as part of the migration and settlement of Polynesian peoples throughout the Pacific almost 5000 years ago. The first settlement of Māori in New Zealand was documented around 1350 (King, 1975, 2003). Māori are distinctive but not unique among indigenous peoples in their ability to create and innovate, apply traditional knowledge to new challenges, and draw on the assets of their traditions in their search for a better future. These settlers brought skills and resources and adapted to a new environment. Prior to the European arrival to New Zealand in 1642 (King, 2003), Māori explored the territories, settled, and established laws to protect their land, natural resources, and tribal relations (Ngata, 1940; Dyall, 1985). By the end of the 1600s, Māori's Polynesian society became a unique cultural identity characterized by hierarchical family-based communities and a productive and innovative agricultural sector (O'Sullivan and Dana, 2008). Māori communities also specialized in boat construction and entrepreneurial practices which facilitated trade with Australia, Britain, and continental Europe (Petrie, 2006).

Over the years, Māori society evolved into communities governed by a chief with decision-making authority and access to the most skilled labor, productive resources, and fertile land. The prevailing Māori organization that was established also included a hierarchical tribal structure that brought economic independence and self-governing communities (O'Sullivan and Dana, 2008). Māori managed to produce a great number of successful innovations, and Māori entrepreneurial skills formed a successful commercial structure and a highly productive agricultural sector.

The impact of British colonization on indigenous Māori tribes in New Zealand was damaging to their culture, values, customs, and tradition, but Māori stayed open to many of the new ideas that came with this new British settlement. Māori managed to contribute to the British colonies in both New Zealand and Australia as the Māori tribal structure facilitated trade with Britain and European countries (Petrie, 2006). The first Māori involvement in tourism was reported around the North Island about 1850 where Māori became involved in lodge operations as the popularity of spas and hot springs brought tourists from Australia, Europe, and North America (Taylor, 1998). Successful Māori entrepreneurs not only provided tourist accommodation but also developed products and services that relied on Māori culture and customs (Ngata, 1940; Petrie, 2006).

The Treaty of Waitangi of 1840 recognized Māori ownership of land and other properties and provided Māori with the rights of British citizenship. In the late 1840s, as a consequence of the increasing British need for land and political control, the British colonists began ignoring Māori rights, traditions, and laws. The British government took actions that removed land, water, and other resources from Māori ownership without proper agreements or compensations (Sinclair, 1959). For years, Māori culture was suppressed with strict policy execution that positioned Māori tribes with no freedom to practice their culture and deprived them of spiritual and religious freedom and economic rights (Mead, 2003; Frederick and Henry, 2004). By 1900, Māori became devastated by conflicts, disease, and poverty. Throughout the first half of the twentieth century, the continued disregard of Pakeha (colonists) for Māori pushed them to live in rural and tribal isolation. Māori communities moved into disarray, and their leadership was stripped of its land (whenua) and prestige (mana). This dark and dreadful time for Māori marked almost a 90 percent loss of the ownership of their land and properties.

After World War II, Māori began moving to cities in search of work in the factories. By settling in urban ghettos, Māori people were able to live beside Pakeha. There was also an increase in migration of indigenous women, in search of employment, to cities where they faced the danger of exploitation and inhumane treatment. Forced displacement led to destruction of indigenous lifestyles and compounded the problems faced by indigenous women. The next few decades were marked by waves of protests and demands for the Treaty of Waitangi to be acknowledged and for

Māori grievances to be heard. In particular, the young and educated urban Māori who were moved away from their tribal communities became a generation of angry and discordant activists fighting for their rights. In the 1970s, the New Zealand government agreed that the loss of Māori rights to land and other resources was unmerited, bringing poverty and unequal rights for Māori descendants (Buck, 1987). In 1975, the Waitangi Tribunal was established to consider rights of Māori and remove the prejudice and provide compensation (Maaka, 1997).

Since the late 1980s, there has been an unparalleled revival in Māori identity, pride, and development. Māori have been taking charge of their land, language, and culture, and entrepreneurship is one of the skill sets that is facilitating this process. New Zealand's government has encouraged Māori to get involved in entrepreneurial activities and strongly supported the preservation, production, and trade of products and services that were based on Māori cultural heritage (Nana et al., 2011). As a result, recent years have seen many positive changes in Māori engagement and establishment of entrepreneurial businesses and a move to higher-skilled employment (NZIER, 2005).

Successful Māori entrepreneurs have provided tourist accommodation and developed products and services that have relied on Māori culture and customs (Ngata, 1940; Petrie, 2006). Traditional music and dance festivals, educational artistic shows, and traditional cuisine continue to be the most noteworthy characteristics in the tourism products and services run by Māori (Mead, 2003). Māori females have placed a special emphasis on the need to encourage entrepreneurial activity, overcome barriers of race, gender, and bureaucracy, and fight corruption and establish respect for standards and rules of law. Government initiatives geared towards Māori female entrepreneurs helped foster their entrance into the marketplace without the baggage of prejudice or inhibitions. Supporting a new generation of Māori female entrepreneurs required strategies, infrastructure, and policies of a proactive government that could successfully expand capacity through political, societal, and economic changes (NZIER, 2005).

Studies conducted by Dana et al. (2005) and Broderstad (2010) indicate that indigenous peoples, especially women, have been considered to be the most socially, economically, and culturally disadvantaged groups around the world. They have suffered greatly from unequal rights that led to chronic poverty, lower education level, and poor health (Peredo and Chrisman, 2006; Cahn, 2008). As the disadvantaged position of indigenous females has been perceived to be problematic, government policies in developed countries promoted development of indigenous entrepreneurial activities (Dana and Anderson, 2011). Pearson (1999) argued that stimulation of indigenous entrepreneurship in the Australian economy had the potential to repair the prior damage. Creation of an entrepreneurial culture based on the foundations of cultural and traditional norms empowers indigenous people and in particular females to start entrepreneurial endeavors.

Jones (2007) argued that the difference between Māori and non-Māori entrepreneurs is in the entrepreneurial process since Māori consider their communities and profits as the aim of their operations. Māori entrepreneurs embrace a holistic view of their goals taking into account the well-being of others and applying distinctive cultural values at the governance and management level within a marketplace (Durie, 2003; Jones, 2007). Despite those characteristics, some authors argue that Māori indigenous entrepreneurship can be categorized largely as innovative but without capitalist elements that are generally included in prevailing definitions of entrepreneurship (Baumback, 1992; Shane, 2003). Henry (2007) and Frederick and Chittock (2005) argued that entrepreneurs generally operate in an environment of risk and require the flexibility to capitalize on opportunities and develop new innovations without being constrained by community decision-making processes and shared ownership of resources. The authors compared Māori entrepreneurship to social entrepreneurship because Māori entrepreneurial activities are based on social objectives to improve the wealth and well-being of their communities rather than the individual. As a result, Māori entrepreneurship is not individualistic or capitalist (profit-based), but it is conducted with social, cultural, or ecosystem objectives (Peredo and Chrisman, 2006) in order to create balance and well-being within their communities.

A formal framework for entrepreneurship research has been based on a model of indigenous entrepreneurship developed by Hindle and Moroz (2010). The model (Figure 5.1) focuses on four major themes of entrepreneurship that include cultural and social norms, entrepreneurial capacity, organizational drivers and constraints, and land and resources to analyze entrepreneurial characteristics and factors that enhance and curb entrepreneurship. The goal is to identify the primary factors that contributed or enhanced success of Māori female indigenous entrepreneurship activities within tourism industry in New Zealand.

METHODOLOGY

Data for this study were collected through online interviews. Data were collected from ten Māori female small business owners. A data collection instrument in the form of an online interview guide was used to collect data about each case. The design of the interview guide followed the structure of successful entrepreneurship proposed in a study by Zapalska

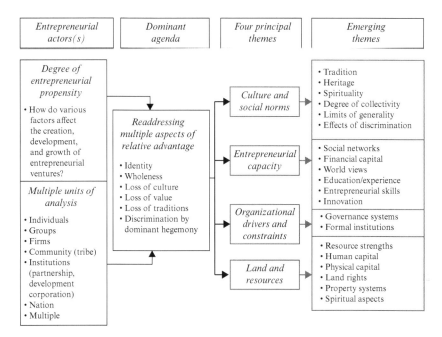

Entrepreneurial actors(s)	Dominant agenda	Four principal themes	Emerging themes

Degree of entrepreneurial propensity

• How do various factors affect the creation, development, and growth of entrepreneurial ventures?

Multiple units of analysis

• Individuals
• Groups
• Firms
• Community (tribe)
• Institutions (partnership, development corporation)
• Nation
• Multiple

Readdressing multiple aspects of relative advantage

• Identity
• Wholeness
• Loss of culture
• Loss of value
• Loss of traditions
• Discrimination by dominant hegemony

Culture and social norms

Entrepreneurial capacity

Organizational drivers and constraints

Land and resources

• Tradition
• Heritage
• Spirituality
• Degree of collectivity
• Limits of generality
• Effects of discrimination

• Social networks
• Financial capital
• World views
• Education/experience
• Entrepreneurial skills
• Innovation

• Governance systems
• Formal institutions

• Resource strengths
• Human capital
• Physical capital
• Land rights
• Property systems
• Spiritual aspects

Source: Developed by the authors, based on Hindle and Moroz (2010).

Figure 5.1 Entrepreneurship research framework

et al. (2003). The interview guide was kept flexible to permit the capture of rich qualitative data in an effort to understand the female Māori entrepreneurs. The interviews were semi-structured so that the follow-up interview captured the articulation of the entrepreneurs' thoughts. The use of in-depth online interviews provided insights and understanding of the personal and sensitive topics.

The ten Māori female entrepreneurial businesses included in this study were located in areas that included Auckland, Waikato, Rotorua, Taranaki, and Taupo. They were selected in areas with the largest concentration of Māori population, diversity of the tourism sector, and representation of Māori entrepreneurs who operate in the tourism industry. A list of Māori respondents was provided by the New Zealand Māori Council. The research was undertaken between September 2015 and January 2016. Respondents were asked to describe the working environment within their organizations and their working relationships with their employees, local authorities, and national government as well as other pertinent questions. The interview questions and the research results were grouped into four constraint categories that included culture and social norms, entrepreneurial capacity, organizational drivers and constraints, and land and resources.

Basic Characteristics of Māori Female Entrepreneurship

Ten cases of Māori female business owners operating entrepreneurial tourism businesses were studied. At the time of the study all the cases had survived the first critical years of small businesses. According to respondents, the mortality of Māori female small businesses in general has been high, particularly in the first three years of operation, and the odds for survival improve as the firms grow older. This result is consistent with other studies such as Baumback (1983). This continuation of business activities of minimum three years can be taken as a criterion for success (Littunen et al., 1998). As a result, all ten entrepreneurial firms in the study can be considered successful. According to all female respondents, indigenous Māori women traditionally have always been respected by indigenous Māori men and have had equal access to and control over collective land and natural resources. With the gradual loss of collective ownership of lands and other natural resources and the introduction by dominant outsiders of institutions of private property, Māori women progressively lost their traditional rights to lands and natural resources. One of the respondents expressed that:

> Regaining rights to my family's land was more than a blessing not only to my family but to my tribal community as I was able to provide work, income, happiness, and most importantly mana . . .

Respondents started small and grew over the years within the tourism industry by expanding their services, strategies, and markets. Their business expansion was steady since funding was limited. Substantial changes were made to the range of products and services offered since the mid 2000s due to changes in governmental policies. Respondents were more educated than the typical female in their own communities. A young and energetic Māori woman and entrepreneur stated:

> Growth of our small but important community was limited for years but new entrepreneurial undertakings brought big positive changes and hope for the future . . .

Activities of Māori women cover a wide spectrum of tourism products and services. Diversification of tourism products and services was greatly influenced by demographic and geographic changes in the tourists' interests. New and hybrid occupations reflect the nature of the new trends in products and services.

A list of the ten Māori female entrepreneurial businesses included in this study is provided in Table 5.1. According to Māori female entrepreneurs, their priority is focused on how land is utilized and the impact of economic activity on environmental consequences. The ecosystem, as an element

Table 5.1   Māori female entrepreneurial businesses based on type and sustainability

Māori	Name of business	Emphasis on sustainability	Type of business
Case 1	Māori cuisine and B&B	Accommodation, cultural, and ecological food	Wellness tourism
Case 2	Māori backpacker tour company	Tours, cultural, and nature oriented	Sport and adventure tourism, cultural tourism
Case 3	Cultural tours and entertainment	Catering, transport, tour guide	Sport and adventure tourism, cultural tourism
Case 4	Māori cultural ecotourism	Hiking, cycling, fishing, rafting, canoeing and kayaking, and Māori cuisine	Wellness tourism, ecotourism
Case 5	Cultural tours	Tours, cultural, traditional music, and dancing	Cultural tourism
Case 6	Take-away food and catering company	Cultural music and traditional Māori dancing and food	Wellness tourism
Case 7	Tour, music, and dance company	Cultural and traditional music, art studying, tours, and entertainment	Cultural tourism
Case 8	Arts and crafts enterprise	Learning and doing Māori arts and crafts, music, and dancing	Art tourism, cultural tourism
Case 9	Fishing and culture-tourism business	Tours, cultural, ecological, and natural environment	Sport and adventure tourism, cultural tourism, ecotourism
Case 10	Accommodation, tour, and entertainment company	Ecological and cultural tours with Māori artistic activities	Sport and adventure tourism, cultural tourism, ecotourism

of sustainability, is an important element of well-being incentive. A market share or high profits that are classic characteristics of non-Māori businesses are not considered to be objectives of Māori's entrepreneurial success. Success is also founded on moral values, ethical norms, culture, and tradition. The respondents' strategies that produced new and innovative products and services are based on the formation of a sustainable or ecosystem tourism industry within cultural and traditional norms. Māori entrepreneurs like to adopt natural resources as a strategy for optimal growth and employment of their businesses and balance the allocation of their resources to achieve efficiency and to maximize the benefits for their communities.

The background of the entrepreneurs in this study is typical of what has been established through studies of female business owners. Māori female entrepreneurs come from specialized areas, have had some tertiary education, and only begin to obtain business experience from their own business. The lack of business education did not stop the Māori women from getting into business and from developing businesses that had survived beyond the first three years. Although economic necessity has pushed Māori females into business, there is also a pull factor associated with the rewards of business ownership. This is about status (mana).

Drivers and Constraints to Māori Female Entrepreneurial Businesses

The women in this study went into business for the possibility of making more money for the family, making business a livelihood strategy, and protecting their communities. All the cases perceived the entrepreneurial environment to be extremely competitive and unfair. In this environment, the firm's survival was seen to be under continuous threat. As a result, Māori women entrepreneurs said they worked hard and kept searching for opportunities. The most important constraints to Māori female entrepreneurial growth and development are listed in Table 5.2.

The Cultural and Social Norms

Cultural and social patterns prescribe the characteristics of women entrepreneurs worldwide. For example, Māori entrepreneurial culture and tradition has had an enormous impact on the products and services that respondents were able to provide. Māori females benefited from sharing their ethnicity, customs, and culture with their customers. Crafts and arts design, music and dance, and cuisine based on Māori entrepreneurial culture made Māori tourist products and services increasingly popular in New Zealand's tourism industry. As one of the respondents stated:

Table 5.2   Constraints to Māori female entrepreneurial growth and development

Constraints	1990s	2010s
Culture and social norms		
Tradition	10	0
Heritage	10	0
Spirituality	10	0
Societal acceptance	10	4
Effects of discrimination	10	8
Entrepreneurial capacity		
Social networks	10	0
Financial capital	10	8
World views	10	0
Education/experience	10	4
Entrepreneurial skills	10	1
Innovation	10	0
Organizational drivers		
Governance systems	10	5
Formal institutions	10	4
Land and resources		
Resource weaknesses	10	5
Human capital	10	3
Physical capital	10	4
Land rights	10	8
Property systems	10	5
Capital utility	10	3
Spiritual aspects	10	10

Development of a special relationship and interaction with my clients provided an alternative to the western-style cultural experience which was valuable to the success of my small bed and breakfast operation . . .

All respondents also believed that traits such as tradition, heritage, and spirituality contributed to the long-term viability and competitiveness of their enterprises. Based on responses, sustainable development of Māori female entrepreneurships is founded on natural resources, tradition, natural ecosystem, and the social, traditional, and cultural fundamentals of the Māori way of life. All respondents desired to generate business with no harmful impact on Māori environment, communities, and culture.

According to Table 5.2 – *culture and social norms* – tradition, heritage, and spirituality were considered to be critical constraints to business growth and development until the beginning of the new millennium. Respondents affirmed that the uniqueness of their ethnicity and way of life have been crucial to New Zealand's tourism industry. This is supported by the studies conducted by Butler and Hinch (1996), Keelan (1996), Taylor (1998), and Cahn (2008). Māori respondents are interested in preserving a command of their resources with an objective for tourism development of their communities. Māori female respondents still believe that the effects of discrimination are the most critical barriers to the success of Māori businesses as some non-Māori still continue to undermine Māori culture and elements of heritage despite new anti-discriminatory government rules. The oldest respondent stated that:

> We Māori women have often been named third-class citizens because of our inferior status in relation to Pakeha, a non-indigenous group of people.

While the Māori female entrepreneurs acknowledge societal attitudes towards females in general, they do not allow this perception to drive them out of business. Again, the oldest respondent stated that:

> Societal attitudes towards females continue to be very negative, especially towards Māori females but it was critical to take it as an opportunity to prove that we females are capable.

This attitude is reflected in Māori women's business practices that reveal determination and ability to grow their firms. A strong desire to see the venture succeed is an attribute shared by the entire group of female entrepreneurs.

Today the entrepreneurial goal of Māori females is to continue creation of local employment, preservation of culture, and conservation of the environment. Tradition, heritage, and spirituality are no longer considered to be constraints. Forty percent of respondents believe that there is still a problem accepting Māori within New Zealand's society. Respondents also believe that resources must be allocated in such a way as to continue providing traditional education about family values, Māori tradition, and culture. They perceive that today's tourism industry must be responsible for providing support to younger Māori generations with a full acceptance of Māori tradition within all levels of society. This finding supports the general claim (Zapalska et al., 2003) that institutional practices and entrenched social values mean that despite the New Zealand government's broad commitments to gender equality Māori women remain disadvantaged.

~

The Entrepreneurial Capacity

Social networks and world views are no longer to be considered constraints to the growth of Māori businesses. As soon as the new government policies were implemented and assistance was provided to Māori tribes, they were able to develop the business skills that were required to run their entrepreneurial businesses. Only four females were not satisfied with their current education and skills. Māori tourism entrepreneurs established a network of relationships and strategic alliances after 2010. Respondents stated that forming strategic alliances with Māori organizations represents a sense of unity and cooperation with other Māori involved in tourism. This collaboration and mutual support enhanced their business opportunities and success. According to respondents' responses, 40 percent of females would like to gain more education in order to improve their entrepreneurial operations and become more competitive.

The availability of financial capital has been considered to be the most critical factor to maintain the growth of their activities. Financial capital has been considered the biggest impediment to female Māori entrepreneurial endeavors during both the first stages of development and most importantly throughout all the years in operation. The level of investment among Māori businesses has been low relative to non-Māori male businesses. These results were expected as all female entrepreneurs face this problem worldwide. All respondents stated that banks perceived a lack of precision, accounting practices, and marketing and management skills in Māori female business practices and especially towards young Māori females despite the fact that some had undergraduate college education. Their businesses had limited access to financial support and varying access to non-financial resources.

Organizational Drivers

The main observation made is that female entrepreneurs were strong in entrepreneurial competence but faced obstacles that made it difficult for them to grow their businesses. New Zealand's government policies that provide self-sufficiency and economic freedom in support of entrepreneurship development are vital to produce indigenous economic growth and reduce reliance on welfare programs. Respondents complained that some government systems and formal institutions and organizational drivers are not allowing them to use initiative, limiting their businesses' growth. This result is confirmed by Foley (2000, 2006) and Furneaux (2007), who argued that too much government regulation has a tendency to inhibit entrepreneurial behavior where there is a lack of cultural sensitivity and poor management of entrepreneurship intervention.

Māori institutions also played an important role in the development and survival of the Māori people. Over centuries, there developed social structures based on association and hierarchical relationships. One of the main social institutions was the Iwi tribal style that provided rules of conduct and norms for living arrangements. While the traditional Iwi structure of the eighteenth century was indispensable to Māori societies, the same institutional structure is important and critical for success in the twenty-first century. However, contemporary Māori must embrace new characteristics of a modern society. Māori development is based on private enterprise and the unleashing of entrepreneurial talents and needs to continue embracing modernity and the open society while maintaining heritage and Māori's mana. The government of New Zealand and local organizations should assist in the promotion of Māori entrepreneurial ventures and provide programs that would enhance their operations and improve their competitiveness in a global economy. As one of the respondents stated:

> Organizational planning should be based on understanding this wider system and the underlying principles that enable life on earth to function. To enter the Māori world, to understand its values and beliefs, is to enter the world of objectivity and sensitivity to driving forces of human lives. Our drive comes from Māori belief and spirituality. We are strong when our beliefs and spirituality are respected and observed . . .

Land and Resources

For Māori, the physical world is based on land that is measured as the creation of higher powers with critical elements that include food, culture, spirit, energy, identity, the sky, and the living elements. Cultural well-being involves the knowledge and approaches to people, behavior, and ceremonies. Spiritual well-being provides the foundation for healing of the spiritual and physical well-being of all creatures, the wisdom that is reinforced through oral history, and care of the homeland expressed through the laws and their maintenance and embraced by social well-being. As a result, the direction and strategies of respondents were founded on Māori values, ethical norms, and tradition. The strategies that produced new and innovative products and services were created on the formation of a sustainable tourism industry. They use culture and natural resources as a strategy for optimal employment of their limited assets. They carefully and responsibly balance allocation of their resources to achieve efficiency and to maximize the benefits for their communities. One of the respondents acknowledged that:

> Māori philosophy is interwoven within a complex of beliefs, attitudes, traditions, customs, and wisdom of Māori Iwi (tribe) communities. Māori behavior

in a contemporary life and workplace must continue to be founded in the spiritual needs of individuals within their communities and believe in making a difference in their communities by empowering members of their communities
. . .

By supporting and acting in care of cultural and environmental connections and awareness of their communities and surroundings, Māori women believe that their spiritual well-being empowers and preserves their heritage, cultural richness, and mana. Social well-being embraces a wide variety of relationships such as the power and authority that guarantee actions that lead to spiritual, cultural, environmental, and economic well-being in Māori communities. Both environmental well-being and economic well-being ensure that Māori entrepreneurial decisions are relevant to Māori cultural norms, values, and aspirations.

According to respondents, preservation of the indigenous land and the protection of intellectual property rights are critical. The traditional lands and resources of indigenous people constitute an integral part of the drive towards economic freedom and self-sufficiency of individuals, families, and communities (Anderson et al., 2006). Māori females are concerned that a commercialization of their culture causes its misinterpretation and oversimplification and a loss of their spirituality. Respondents also confirmed a relationship between Māori traditions and entrepreneurship and expressed that they have been proud of their model of entrepreneurship that has always been part of Māori society. Māori historically were removed from embracing cultural principles, values, and expressions. Their disadvantaged positions in New Zealand's society brought a lack of control and the ability to promote their image and culture. Those results are supported by Pihama and Penehira (2005), Whitehead and Annesley (2005), and O'Sullivan and Dana (2008).

CONCLUSIONS

Māori females have been considered to be the most entrepreneurial indigenous group in the world (Nana et al., 2011). This study confirms that Māori indigenous females have their own distinctive identity, resilience, and set of cultural and technological skills. Māori females demonstrated an ability to adapt, change, and prosper. They also maintained their family links to flora and fauna through a complex set of beliefs and rituals designed to protect and sustain their environment that is reflected through the orientation of their operations. The core beliefs of the traditional Māori female focused on the complementarities of gods, humans, and spirituality. Māori indigenous women face significant challenges to the full enjoyment of their human rights. They still experience multiple forms of discrimination, lack access to quality education, and in some cases access to ancestral lands.

This chapter identified characteristics of the tourism industry based on interviews with ten Māori female entrepreneurs. The framework advanced in this research shows that the orientation of Māori tourism products and services is based on maintaining cultural integrity, environmental sustainability, and community-based development. Entrepreneurship conducted by Māori females is conducted primarily for the benefit of their communities and protection of natural resources where there is a strong mutual agreement that economic independence is the path towards preserving all aspects of Māori community. Māori entrepreneurial businesses are distinct from the mainstream tourism industry. The New Zealand government should continue assisting and delivering strategies that promote and protect a diversified culture and traditions of Māori society that contribute to the prosperity of local communities and benefit global cultural tourism. Māori females were encouraged to develop new and existing facilities, services, and communal spaces that promote their tribal culture and values. Engaging tradition, culture, and art enhances the ability to deepen the quality of visitor interaction with local communities. Māori culture and heritage have been increasingly recognized as unique in the tourism industry.

Obstacles that Māori women entrepreneurs face are similar to problems that women face worldwide. They include a lack of financial capital, inadequate human capital potential, and lack of adequate network structures (Bitler et al., 2001). The sustainable tourism sector requires the achieving of a balance between ensuring financial success, providing satisfaction to customers, protecting the physical and ecological environment, and supporting the development and growth of local communities. Creating educational tactics for improving women's human capital potential is fundamental for entrepreneurial growth and an essential component for producing women entrepreneurs who can enter and survive in the entrepreneurial world. Finally, access to financial capital is seen as a major criterion for entrance and survival.

Female entrepreneurs face challenges and constraints when developing and running their firms. A sustainable tourism sector requires that businesses are financially profitable and able to reinvest in their business and attract and retain the skilled workforce they need. There is a need to sustain initiatives for entrepreneurial development on sound cultural principles. Governmental policies need to continue supporting female entrepreneurial initiatives and provide resources, networks, and legal foundations.

Financial institutions should not dismiss small female entrepreneurs as poor sources of income and high lending costs and risks. Financial institutions and micro-finance providers, incubator centers, and other services must support development policies that focus on micro-enterprises as they provide jobs and alleviate poverty.

REFERENCES

Anderson R., Dana, L., and Dana, T. (2006). Indigenous land rights, entrepreneurship, and economic development in Canada: 'Opting-in' to the global economy. *Journal of World Business*, 41(1), 45–55.

Baumback, C.M. (1983). *Basic Business Management*. New York: Prentice Hall.

Baumback, C.M (1992). *Small Business Management*. Englewood Cliffs, NJ: Prentice Hall.

Birley, S. (1989). Female entrepreneurs: are they really any different? *Journal of Small Business Management*, 27(1), 32–37.

Bitler, M.P., Robb, A.M., and Wolken, J.D. (2001). Financial services used by small businesses: evidence from the 1998 survey of small business finances. *Federal Reserve Bulletin*, 87, 183–205.

Broderstad, E. (2010). Promises and challenges of indigenous self-determination: the Sami case. *International Journal: Canada's Journal of Global Policy*, 66, 893–907.

Buck, P. (1987). *The Coming of the Māori* (2nd edn). Wellington, New Zealand: Whitcoull Limited for the Māori Purposes Fund Board.

Burke, A., FitzRoy, F., and Nolanm M. (2002). Self-employment wealth and job creation: the roles of gender, non-pecuniary motivation and entrepreneurship ability. *Small Business Economics*, 19(3), 255–270.

Butler, R. and Hinch, T. (eds) (1996). *Tourism and Indigenous People*. London: International Business Press.

Cahn, M. (2008). Indigenous entrepreneurship, culture and micro-enterprise in the Pacific Islands: case studies from Samoa. *Entrepreneurship and Regional Development*, 20(1), 1–18.

Dana, L. and Anderson, R. (2011). Indigenous entrepreneurship as a function of cultural perceptions of opportunity. In L. Dana (ed.), *World Encyclopedia of Entrepreneurship*. Cheltenham, UK and Northampton, MA: Edward Elgar Publishing, p. 249.

Dana, L., Dana, T., and Anderson, B. (2005). A theory-based empirical study of entrepreneurship in Iqaluit, Nunavut. *Journal of Small Business and Entrepreneurship*, 18(2), 143–151.

Durie, M. (2003). *Ngā kahui pou: Launching Māori Futures*. Wellington, New Zealand: Huia.

Dyall, J. (1985). *Māori Resources: A Handbook on Māori Organisations*. Christchurch, New Zealand: J.R. Dyall.

Foley, D. (2000). *Successful Indigenous Australian Entrepreneurs: A Case Study Analysis*. S. Ulm, I. Lilley, and M. Williams (eds). Brisbane: Aboriginal & Torres Strait Islander Studies Unit, UQ.

Foley, D. (2006). Indigenous Australian entrepreneurs: not all community organizations, not all in the outback. Discussion Paper No 279, Centre for Aboriginal Economic Policy Research, Australian National University.

Frederick, H. and Chittock, G. (2005). *Global Entrepreneurship Monitor Aotearoa New Zealand (GEM)*. Unitec New Zealand's Centre for Innovation and Entrepreneurship Research Report Series, 4(1). Auckland, New Zealand: Unitec New Zealand.

Frederick, H.H. and Henry, E. (2004). Innovation and entrepreneurship among Pākeha and Māori in New Zealand. In C.H. Stiles and C.S. Galbraith (ed.), *Ethnic Entrepreneurship: Structure and Process (International Research in the Business Disciplines, Volume 4)*. Bingley, UK: Emerald Publishing, pp.115–140.

Furneaux, C. (2007). Indigenous entrepreneurship: an analysis of capital restraints. In *AGSE 2007*. Melbourne: Swinburne University of Technology, pp.669–682.

Henry, E. (2007). Kaupapa Māori entrepreneurship. In L. Dana and R. Anderson (eds), *International Handbook of Research on Indigenous Entrepreneurship*. Cheltenham, UK and Northampton, MA: Edward Elgar Publishing, pp.536–548.

Hindle, K. and Moroz, P. (2010). Indigenous entrepreneurship as a research field: developing a definitional framework from the emerging canon. *International Entrepreneurship and Management Journal*, 6(4), 357–385.

Hokowhitu, B. (2010). A genealogy of indigenous resistance. In B. Hokowhitu, N. Kermoal, C. Andersen, A. Petersen, M. Reilly, I. Altamirano–Jimenez, and P. Rewi (eds), *Indigenous Identity and Resistance: Researching the Diversity of Knowledge*. Dunedin, New Zealand: University of Otago Press, pp.207–225.

Hudson, S. (2002). *Sport and Adventure Tourism*. New York, London, and Oxford: The Haworth Hospitality Press.

Jones, S. (2007). *Te Whakamana Umanga: Enhancing Māori Business Success in Hawke's Bay*. Unpublished research report, Eastern Institute of Technology, Taradale, New Zealand.

Keelan N. (1996). Maori heritage: visitor management and interpretation. In C.M. Hall and S. McArthur (eds), *Heritage Management in Australia and New Zealand: The Human Dimension*, 2nd edn. Melbourne: Oxford University Press, pp.195–201.

King, M. (ed.) (1975). *Te Ao Hurihuri: The World Moves On – Aspects of Māoritanga*. Wellington, New Zealand: Hicks Smith and Sons.

King, M. (2003). *The Penguin History of New Zealand*. Auckland, New Zealand: Penguin.

Littunen, H., Storhammar, E., and Nenonen, T. (1998). The survival of firms over the critical first three years and the local environment. *Entrepreneurship and Regional Development*, 10, 189–202.

Maaka, R. (1997). The politics of diaspora. Paper given at the 'Treaty of Waitangi: Māori political representation future challenges' conference. Māori Economic Development Panel: Discussion Document. Wellington, New Zealand: Te Puni Kokiri and Ministry of Economic Development.

Mead, H. (2003). *Tikanga Māori: Living by Māori Values*. Wellington, New Zealand, Huia Publishers.

Nana, G., Stokes, F., and W. Molano (2011). *The Māori Economy, Science and Innovation*. Wellington, New Zealand: Te Puni Kokiri, BERL and Māori Economic Taskforce.

Ngata, A. (1940). Tribal organization. In I.L.G. Sutherland (ed.), *The Māori People Today*. Wellington, New Zealand: New Zealand Council for Educational Research, pp.155–181.

NZIER (New Zealand Institute of Economic Research) (2005). Māori business and economic performance: a summary report. New Zealand Institute of Economic Research.

O'Sullivan, J. and Dana, T. (2008). Redefining Māori economic development. *International Journal of Social Economics*, 35(5), 364–379.

Pearson, N. (1999). Rebuilding communities. ABC Video Commercial, Australian Broadcasting Corporation, Brisbane Institute.

Peredo, A. and Chrisman, J. (2006). Toward a theory of community-based enterprise. *Academy of Management Review*, 31(2), 309–328.

Petrie, H. (2006). *Chiefs of Industry: Māori Tribal Enterprise in Early Colonial New Zealand*. Auckland, New Zealand: Auckland University Press.

Pihama, L. and. Penehira, M. (2005). *Building Baseline Data on Māori, Whanau Development and Māori Realizing Their Potential: Literature Review – Innovation and Enterprise*. Auckland, New Zealand: International Research Institute for Māori and Indigenous Education.

Shane, S. (2003). *A General Theory of Entrepreneurship: The Individual Opportunity Nexus*. Cheltenham, UK and Northampton, MA: Edward Elgar Publishing.

Sinclair, K. (1959). *A History of New Zealand*. London: Penguin.

Taylor, J. (1998). Consuming identity: modernity and tourism in New Zealand. *Research in Anthropology and Linguistics, No. 2*. Wellington, New Zealand: Department of Anthropology, University of Auckland.

Whitehead J. and Annesley, B. (2005). *The Context for Māori Economic Development*. Wellington: NZ Treasury.

Zapalska, A., Perry, G., and Dabb, H. (2003). Māori entrepreneurship in the contemporary business environment. *Journal of Developmental Entrepreneurship*, 8(3), 219–235.

6. Women entrepreneurs in South Africa: maintaining a balance between culture, personal life, and business

Bridget Irene

Research on women's entrepreneurial motivation reveals that the need for flexibility and maintaining a balance between work and family makes entrepreneurship a viable career option for women. According to Brush et al. (2006), women are more likely than men to venture into business ownership for the purpose of achieving work–life balance. This is a view that is supported by researchers such as Boden and Nucci (2000) and Lombard (2001), who argue that most of the women venturing into entrepreneurship do so with the aim of developing more flexible schedules that provide the opportunity for them to balance work and family demands. According to Caputo and Dolinsky (1998) and Robinson and Sexton (1994), children and marriage have also been found to be among the most influential reasons for women venturing into entrepreneurship. Nevertheless, some women find that the presence of children poses a different set of challenges (Irene, 2016c), therefore Williams (2004) suggests that for many women having children is synonymous with distractions and an inability to give 100 percent to a business while for men, on the other hand, having children represents a source of motivation and fulfilment. In most societies (developed or developing), the responsibility of childcare is considered primarily as women's. This, therefore, requires women to possess multi-tasking skills as this responsibility in no way detracts from other responsibilities such as work or business. While men can compartmentalize their work and family life, women choose entrepreneurship for flexibility as the career option that enables them to manage marriage and children (Wilmerding, 2007). This choice, however, often leads to conflict, as striving to fit business with family obligations is often 'a difficult position for most women especially those with children' (ibid., p. 149). Women often must make difficult choices in trying to be successful in a career or business while fulfilling family obligations, often to the detriment of their health as this puts an enormous strain on them physically and psychologically. To this end, Jacobs and Gerson (2004) suggest that there are negative consequences arising from the combination of work tensions and family responsibilities. Fels (2004) also argues that women's entrepreneurial skills are enriched by engaging in both spheres of life, mainly because they are both demanding areas of life to deal with. Notwithstanding the personal and family challenges that women are faced with, greater pressure is placed on them by societal norms and beliefs in both developed and developing countries alike. There are gender-specific roles regardless of the culture or society, and, according to Baughn et al. (2006), women's career choices are often influenced by these societal expectations.

WORK–LIFE BALANCE AND WOMEN ENTREPRENEURS IN SOUTH AFRICA

The work–life issue has sparked a lot of scholarly attention within mainstream research on women's entrepreneurship in various developed and industrialized societies such as the USA, the UK, Sweden, and Canada (Ahl, 2006; Brush, 2006; Caputo and Dolinsky, 1998; DeMartino and Barbato, 2003). The discussion is further influenced by the gender perspective in this regard, particularly as it relates to cultural views, family responsibilities, and reproductive works (factors which are considered as vital to the success of women entrepreneurs). Although work and family are two of the most important areas of life for both men and women, in many societies, family obligations are presumed to be women's primary responsibility while men are considered the breadwinners (Brush, 1992). Therefore, work and family present a different set of priorities and challenges for both men and women, especially in the African societies. One major motivation for women engaging in entrepreneurial activities has been the need for flexibility and the desire to create a balance between work and family (Baughn et al., 2006; Buttner and Moore, 1997; Carter et al., 2003). According to Brush et al. (2006), women are more likely than men to start their own business for the purpose of achieving work–life balance. A number of researchers suggest that the majority of women venturing into entrepreneurship do so to develop more flexible schedules that provide them with the opportunity to balance work and family demands (Boden and Nucci, 2000; Lombard, 2001) and allow them to work from home, thereby reducing the burden of finding childcare (Boden and Nucci, 2000). DeMartino and Barbato (2003) found that while the major motivating factor for men to go into new venture creation was for financial gains or profit, for women it was mostly for flexibility and consideration of children and marriage (Caputo and Dolinsky, 1998; Robinson and Sexton, 1994).

Maternal responsibilities also pose a different set of challenges for women. Williams (2004) found that for many women the presence of children is associated with distraction and supervision issues, as childcare is primarily a woman's responsibility, particularly in Africa. The findings from research on 1050 female entrepreneurs in South Africa by this researcher in 2016 found that most women believe their performance is impacted greatly by the presence of children and the constant need to achieve a balance between family and business demands (Irene, 2016a). This could imply that women are endowed with multi-skills which make them effective in multi-tasking and become evident in their ability to manage the business and look after the family, while men, on the other hand, can compartmentalize their work and family life. In South Africa, as with other African cultures, the woman's primary function is that of the home-maker, and women who choose entrepreneurship as a career pact mostly do so to have flexibility and achieve success in balancing the demands of their married life and children (Wilmerding, 2007), but this choice is not an easy one and sometimes leads to conflict and feelings of unfulfilment. Fitting business with the family obligation is often 'a difficult position for most women especially those with children' (Wilmerding, 2007, p. 149). The findings of a recent study on South African small, medium and micro-sized enterprise (SMME) operators indicate that although most women consider their efforts as essential in order to care for and provide for their families, they also consider it sacrificial and inhibiting. They suggest that being a 'woman' limits their business performance as family demands mean they cannot network effectively like the men, and family obligations limit the hours they spend outside the home, contrary to men whom they believe have no such constraints (Irene, 2016b). This means that in order to succeed in fulfilling business and family demands, women have to work twice as hard, and this also has some health implications. According to Jacobs and Gerson (2004), negative and psychological consequences arise from the combined primary pressure of managing business and family, while Fels (2004) contends that managing work and family responsibilities provides sufficient prospects for growth and development as women's participation in both spheres of life enriches their entrepreneurial skills.

Besides family and personal challenges experienced by women entre-preneurs, culture further increases the pressure on women in developed and developing countries alike. This is because culture delineates societal values which in turn impacts certain expectations from people and defines gender-specific roles. These values and expectations often affect the career choices of women (Baughn et al., 2006). As stated earlier, in South

Africa as with other African cultures, women are perceived primarily as care-givers and home-makers, therefore entrepreneurship is considered a career option to gain greater flexibility and manage family obligations rather than a career in a traditional corporate job. This, however, impacts the performance and success of women-owned businesses as they are unable to give full attention to their businesses. According to Ahl (2007), domestic responsibilities and unequal distribution of domestic work between men and women make it difficult for women to compete equally with men on a professional level, particularly in the African society where women have subservient roles. This view is consistent with the findings of Fels (2004) and Irene (2016c) that women are defined by their roles, which present a real challenge in women's entrepreneurial endeavors. Therefore, Mirchandani (1999) contends that it is important to understand the mediating factors of women's entrepreneurship and determine the extent to which these factors influence the success of women entrepreneurs. While most of the literature cited above are from studies undertaken mostly from Western countries, they are consistent with the findings of Irene (2016c), which were undertaken using samples drawn from South Africa. Not much research has been focused on the work–life conflict in cultural settings of South Africa as it relates to women entrepreneurs; the focus, rather, has largely been on the work–life balance of female employees and has only given the perspective of organizationally employed persons. The literature that addresses women entrepreneurs' perception of the work–life balance phenomenon, especially exploring the challenges they face in achieving balance and the strategies they use to balance work and family obligations, are necessary and vital in understanding success in the context of women's entrepreneurship. Therefore, this research contributes to an already established discourse in the field of women's entrepreneurship.

METHODOLOGY

The methodological framework proposed for this study is largely based on a positivist and realist approach to research. The researcher assumes that what exists in the social world is real and can be largely measured and described just as physical scientists measure and describe the physical world. According to Lin (1998), positivists seek to identify details with propositions that can be tested by identifying causal relationships present in a data set with some degree of probability. The positivist approach involves trying to decipher which pieces of information in the data sets are associated with one another and assesses the strength of the association by counterfactual thinking and problems of reliability and representativeness.

However, positivism cannot easily explain how the mechanism implied by the causal relationship works or interacts. The works of the interpretivists, on the other hand, can produce detailed examinations of causal mechanisms in specific cases and explains how particular variables interact. The combination of both modes of logic adds more functional content which neither positivism nor interpretivism can produce alone, and gives more additional confidence to our conclusions.

Data Collection and Analysis

A 'mixed-method' approach, conducted in two parts, was adopted for this study. Study 1 was qualitative, involving 50 individual interviews with 50 female entrepreneurs. Ten focus group discussions with 78 entrepreneurs were completed. The purpose was to identify gender (female) and context (South African) specific issues relating to work–life balance and their impact on the success of women entrepreneurs.

The second aspect of this study was quantitative and involved 785 entrepreneurs completing a six-part questionnaire. Data collection and preliminary assumption testing involved defining the psychometric elements of the dependent variables and covariates. The sample consisted of female entrepreneurs from four different South African provinces. The survey instrument was a structured questionnaire.

The method of data collection for the qualitative aspect of this study was mostly based on communication by means of face-to-face interaction with participants. Personal interviews were conducted with female entrepreneurs over a period of five months, after which focus group discussions were conducted (with female entrepreneurs). The information gathered from these interviews and discussions was then used to formulate the questionnaire used for the quantitative study. Samples for the quantification study were randomly selected by means of simple random sampling. This method was considered appropriate for this study, given that simple random sampling allows for statistical analysis to be conducted on the samples and, due to its representativeness (it provides an equal opportunity for every member of the population to be selected), generalizations can also be made from the results of the sample back to the population. The secondary data were obtained from the review of the literature.

Given that the data collected in this current study comprised both qualitative and quantitative data, the analysis of the data was also done qualitatively and quantitatively. The qualitative data were tape-recorded and transcribed by professional transcribers to ensure accuracy and precision of the transcript. The quantitative data were captured into SPSS 12.0.1. Thematic analysis was conducted on the qualitative data while regression was done on the quantitative data by building a one-factor congeneric model.[1]

FINDINGS AND DISCUSSIONS

Race has always played a historic role in economic inequality in South Africa. The findings from this study consisted of the data from STATS-SA that suggested that African or black women are the largest self-employed group in the population but are largely engaged in informal businesses, like hawking, the trading of goods, and the services sector. There are over 1 million African female entrepreneurs (approximately 1 021 059) compared to 119 671 from the white population group. The African (black) women entrepreneurs are largely engaged in SMMEs, employing between one and four people, while the white female entrepreneurs are engaged in small and medium-sized enterprises (SMEs), employing between 5 and 20 people. The African female entrepreneurs are only just beginning to move up the business ladder and engage in activities like franchising, printing, manufacturing, hospitality, and property agencies.

The findings also showed that in South Africa there are a large number of entrepreneurs involved in the economic process and according to previous researchers, this is greatly significant and important (Thomas, 1994). Women constitute 59 percent of the South African national population and the mobilization and development of these women entrepreneurs have posed a major challenge (ibid.). This challenge is further heightened by high unemployment levels, particularly among women who have little education or skills and consider self-employment as a source of survival. The South African government views entrepreneurship as critical to successful self-employment efforts, thereby making the mobilization and involvement of individuals in entrepreneurship more critical (especially among women).

In a 2011 study by Carol Mantwa Rasego (2011), it was revealed that female entrepreneurs rated the following motivating factors: (i) the desire for wealth; (ii) the need for independence; (iii) the need for flexibility; (iv) the need for a challenge; (v) self-fulfilment; (vi) the desire to pursue a hobby; (vii) insufficient family income; and (viii) the need to ensure high job security. This is also consistent with the findings from this study, which also revealed that female entrepreneurs are also affected by fear of failure and their perceived inequality of access to credit in their business start-up. Furthermore, female entrepreneurs in South Africa who participated in this study reveal that family pressures persistently affect them according to their perceived traditional roles (at home and in the society) and a lack of awareness of or access to business support structures. Despite this traditional role bias, there are more female than male entrepreneurs in South Africa (this could also be because women make up 59 percent of the South African population). Furthermore, the only group in which there are fewer male entrepreneurs than females is the black group. The high female-to-male ratio could also be attributed to the fact that more men from the other racial groups have a higher education and favor white-collar jobs to entrepreneurship (Gender Statistics, 2011).

Demographic Profiles of South African Women Entrepreneurs

A review of the census data from Statistics South Africa reveals two categories of business owners: (i) self-employed, that is, a person who works for profit or for a fee at his/her own corporation or profession with no employees, who is not employed by any entity; and (ii) employer, that is, a person who works for profit or for a fee at his/her own corporation or profession with one or more employees working for him/her.

The findings of this study also corroborate the literature, which suggests that unemployment impacts negatively on entrepreneurship (Viviers et al., 2001) and that a high rate of unemployment gives rise to a large number of 'necessity' entrepreneurs embarking on entrepreneurship as a means of survival (Dollinger, 2008; Wickham, 2001). It was evident from the findings of this research that more than 75 percent of the participants in this study confirmed that they embarked on their entrepreneurial journey out of necessity. This, coupled with the low levels of education and skills among South African women suggested by Dollinger (2008) and Wickham (2001), creates undue competition as more people become entrepreneurs, scrambling for a share in a market that is limited (most of them in the retail or services sector). The highest level of qualification of the participants in the qualitative aspect of this study is indicated in Figure 6.1, which shows that 40.16 percent of the participants did not have a tertiary education (below matriculation, that is, less than Grade 12, and matriculation, that is, at Grade 12), 59.84 percent had a tertiary education (National Diploma consisting of 2–3 years of study and a bachelor's degree consisting of 3–4 years of study), and only 8 percent of the total number of participants have a postgraduate degree.

Previous studies have shown that South African male and female entrepreneurs operate in two distinct sectors: the formal or traditional mainstream sector, and the informal or marginalized sector. Therefore, it was not surprising to find that most of the participants in the quantitative aspect of this study operated in the informal sector. While the men operate more in the formal sector, the women operate largely in the informal sector (Botha et al., 2006). According to Verheul et al. (2005), the informal sector

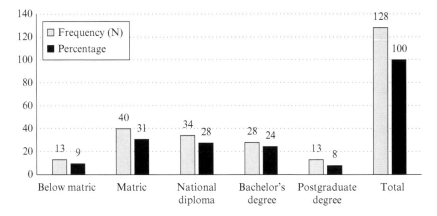

Source: Irene (2016b).

Figure 6.1   Educational level of participants in the current qualitative research

has a certain appeal to female entrepreneurs because of the relative ease of start-up and proximity to home, enabling combined entrepreneurial and household duties. As highlighted from the review of the literature, this offers greater flexibility, which is a major motivational factor for female entrepreneurs. Most female-owned and -managed businesses are in the service sector, in line with the traditional perception of women's role in society and their perceived area of employment (as shown in Figure 6.2).

Business Success in the Context of Women-owned Businesses in South Africa

Measuring business success in relation to SMEs has been a controversial issue. While some researchers propose measuring business success using only financial indicators (such as profit, sales turnover, increase in market share and return on investment), more recent studies suggest that non-financial indicators (personal satisfaction, personal growth, and development, skills acquisition and improvement, flexibility with time and lifestyle, business survival, and staff and customer retention, as well as career progress) can be used to measure business success (Simpson et al., 2004; Walker and Brown, 2004; Watson, 2003).

During the interviews and focus group discussions in this current research, participants were asked: 'How do you measure business success?'. The responses from the participants were compared with the propositions

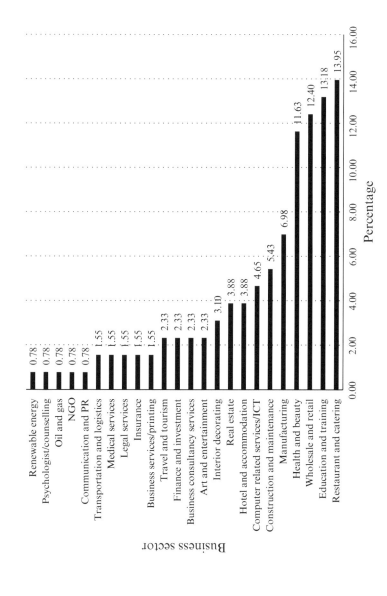

Source: Irene (2016b).

Figure 6.2 Business sub-sector of respondents in the current research

in the literature (such as examples proposed by Buttner and Moore, 1997; Cooper, 1993; Walker and Brown, 2004; and Watson, 2003). The answers were clustered into four groups proposed by Walker and Brown (2004) and Reichel and Haber (2005): (i) monetary measures; (ii) daily life conditions; (iii) societal obligation criteria; and (iv) customer retention. Business success was summarized by two of the entrepreneurs who participated in this study as:

> Success means freedom for me to express who I am and also for me to uplift and support others. (Renewable energy consultant)

> Success means having a venture that I can be proud of, so then it has to be a venture that has integrity and is sustained by my values and those of my partners. (Legal practitioner)

This study adopted four dimensions for measuring business success and all items in the four dimensions were retained in all the sample sets. All dimensions for the business success construct were subjected to the measurement process that was adopted and they are illustrated in Table 6.1. While 13 business success indicators were identified by the women entrepreneurs who participated in this study, the scores for the indicators that reflected familism[2] were higher (79 percent and 56 percent). This is also consistent with the literature on women's entrepreneurship, which suggests that success for men and women means different things. Therefore, it is necessary to reconsider women's entrepreneurship as not just an agent for financial emancipation but also as an agent for social and cultural change. For women, entrepreneurship offers greater flexibility to manage their obligations in contrast with the constraints of a traditional corporate job. However, some women consider their success to be hindered since their first priority (given societal views and obligations) will always be family and not the business. Therefore, the ability to maintain a balance between family and business obligations has become a major source of concern due to the unequal distribution of domestic work. This makes it difficult for women to compete equally with men on professional grounds where the societal mind-set reckons a woman's business to be secondary to her husband's work and family. The notion of women's role as primary caregiver poses a real challenge in women's entrepreneurial endeavors. However, previous research does not address the women entrepreneurs' perception of the work–life balance phenomenon, especially exploring the challenges women face in achieving balance and the strategies they use to balance work and family obligations.

Table 6.1   Business success indicators identified by participants in this study

Business success indicator	Base: all respondents in this study Total participants (%)
Customer retention and goodwill****	14%
Financial stability*	13%
Bringing value to other people around**	29%
Contentment/self-satisfaction**	35%
Work and family life balance**	79%
Growth*	11%
Bottom-line/profit*	27%
Job creation (particularly for other women)***	36%
Staff retention***	17%
Ability of the entrepreneur to develop skills/ competencies**	14%
Promote integrity and good values**	19%
Creating a lasting legacy for family**	56%
Increased market share*	11%

Notes:
* Financial indicators;
** lifestyle criteria;
*** social responsibility criteria;
**** customer retention criteria.

Sources: Criteria proposed by Walker and Brown (2004) and Reichel and Haber (2005).

CONCLUSIONS

The findings of this study of female entrepreneurs are consistent with the findings of previous researchers that women were concerned with achieving a better work–life balance. Many did not want success at the expense of family life (either their own family or the families of their employees). They wanted to still have time to see and look after their families. Nevertheless, female entrepreneurs were also inclined towards business success and raised a concern for their customers, suppliers, and other stakeholders and the continuous assessment of their own progress via multi-tasking to achieve their objectives. The results showed that behaviors that reflected 'familism' were considered very important to female entrepreneurs. Female entrepreneurs indicated that family support was vital to their success and they showed concern for the family members of their employees. Also, many of the female South African entrepreneurs considered the personal competency vital to success and felt the need for self-development in order to succeed in a society that still undermines and doubts the abilities of women to effectively manage a business. Therefore, the behaviors associated with personal competencies were highlighted as crucial for the success of female South African entrepreneurs.

The main limitation of this chapter is that while there are numerous researches on the work–life balance of mainstream female employees, there is little on work–life balance of women entrepreneurs (owner-managers). This chapter, therefore, relies on the perceptions of participants and the findings from this research could only be compared with the findings from research focused on career women in mainstream employment.

This research fills a gap in the literature by focusing on women entrepreneurs, increasing understanding of entrepreneurial behaviors related to balancing personal responsibilities and achieving professional objectives (DeMartino and Barbato, 2003; Shelton, 2006).

NOTES

1. The fitting of a one-factor congeneric measurement model was to maximize the reliability of the composite scores. For a one-factor congeneric measurement model, the factor score (FS) regression coefficients represent the estimated bivariate regression of the factor on all observed indicator variables.
2. 'Familism' refers to an affection for family structure that drives daily activities and, according to Park (2003, p. 8–9), it is manifested in the way 'family members support each other by sharing resources and co-operating with each other to achieve common goals.'

REFERENCES

Ahl, H. (2006), 'Why research on women entrepreneurs needs new directions,' *Entrepreneurship Theory and Practice*, 30(5), 595–621.

Ahl, H. (2007), 'Sex business in the toy store: a narrative analysis of a teaching case,' *Journal of Business Venturing*, 22(5), 673–693, available at: https://doi.org/10.1016/j.jbusvent.2006.10.007.

Baughn, C., B.-L. Chua, and K.E. Neupert (2006), 'Normative, social and cognitive predictors of entrepreneurial interest in China, Vietnam and the Philippines,' *Journal of Developmental Entrepreneurship*, 11(1), 57–77.

Boden, R.J. and A.R. Nucci (2000), 'On the survival prospects of men's and women's new business ventures,' *Journal of Business Venturing*, 15(4), 347–362.

Botha, M., G.H. Nieman, and J.J. Van Vuuren (2006), 'Evaluating the women entrepreneurship training program: a south study,' *The International Indigenous Journal of Entrepreneurship, Advancement, Strategy and Education*, 2(1), 479–493.

Brush, C.G. (1992), 'Research on women business owners: past trends, a new perspective and future directions,' *Entrepreneurship Theory and Practice*, 16(4), 5–14.

Brush, G.C. (2006), 'Women entrepreneurs: a research overview,' in A. Basu, M. Casson, N. Wadeson, and B. Yeung (eds), *The Oxford Handbook of Entrepreneurship*, Oxford: Oxford University Press, available at: www.oxfordhandbooks.com, doi: 10.1093/oxfordhb/9780199546992.003.0023.

Brush, C.G., N.M. Carter, E.J. Gatewood, P.G. Greene, and M.M. Hart (2006), 'The use of bootstrapping by women entrepreneurs in positioning for growth,' *Venture Capital*, 8(1), 15–31.

Buttner, E. and D. Moore (1997), 'Women's organizational exodus to entrepreneurship: self-reported motivations and correlates with success,' *Journal of Small Business Management*, 35(1), 34–46.

Caputo, R.K. and A. Dolinsky (1998), 'Women's choice to pursue self-employment: the role of financial and human capital of household members,' *Journal of Small Business Management*, 36(3), 8–17.

Carter, N.M., W.B. Gartner, K.B. Shaver, and E.J. Gatewood (2003), 'The career reasons of nacent entreprenuers,' *Journal of Business Venturing*, 7, 295–316.

Cooper, A.C. (1993), 'Challenges in predicting new firm performance,' *Journal of Business Venturing*, 8(3), 241–253.

DeMartino, R. and R. Barbato (2003), 'Differences between men and women MBA entrepreneurs: exploring family, flexibility and wealth creation as a career motivators,' *Journal of Business Venturing*, 18(6), 815–832.

Dollinger, B. (2008), 'Problem attribution and intervention: the interpretation of problem causations and solutions in regard of Brickman et al. "Problemattribution und intervention: Die interpretation von problemursachen und problemlösungen nach Brickman ua",' *European Journal of Social Work*, 11(3), 279–293.

Fels, A. (2004), 'Do women lack ambition?' *Harvard Business Review*, 82(4), 50–56, available at: https://www.europeanleadershipplatform.com/assets/downloads/infoItems/71.pdf (accessed on 15 August 2015).

Gender Statistics (2011), Gender Statistics in South Africa, 2011/Statistics South Africa, available at: http://www.statssa.gov.za/publications/Report-03-10-05/Report-03-10-052011.pdf (accessed on 12 June 2014).

Irene, B.N.O. (2016a), 'A cross-cultural review of the impact of entrepreneurial motivation on the success of female SMMEs operators in South Africa,' *International Journal of Current Advanced Research*, 5(7), 1122–1130.

Irene, B.N.O. (2016b), 'Women entrepreneurs: a cross-cultural study of the impact of the commitment competency on the success of female-owned SMMEs in South Africa,' *International Journal of Sciences: Basic and Applied Research (IJSBAR)*, 27(2), 70–83.

Irene, B. (2016c), 'Gender and entrepreneurial success: a cross cultural study of competencies of female SMEs operators in South Africa,' PhD thesis, Cardiff Metropolitan University.

Jacobs, J.A. and K. Gerson (2004), *The Time Divide: Work, Family, and Gender Inequality*, Cambridge, MA: Harvard University Press.

Lin, A.C. (1998), 'Bridging positivist and interpretivist approaches to qualitative methods,' *Policy Studies Journal*, 26(1), 162–180.

Lombard, K. (2001), 'Female self-employment and demands for flexible, non-standard work schedule,' *Economic Inquiry*, 39(2), 214–237.

Mirchandani, K. (1999), 'Feminist insight on gendered work: new directions in research on women and entrepreneurship,' *Gender, Work & Organization*, 6(4), 224–235.

Park, T.H. (2003), 'The influence of familism on interpersonal trust in South Korea,' Hawaii International Conference of Social Sciences, Honolulu, USA.

Rasego, C.M. (2011), 'A comparative study between white and black women entrepreneurs in selected areas in South Africa,' North-West University, MBA dissertation.

Reichel, A. and S. Haber (2005), 'A three-sector comparison of the business performance of small tourism enterprises: an exploratory study,' *Tourism Management*, 26(5), 681–690.

Robinson, P.B. and E.A. Sexton (1994), 'The effect of education and experience on self-employment success,' *Journal of Business Venturing*, 9(2), 141–156.

Shelton, L. (2006), 'Female entrepreneurs, work–family conflict, and venture performance: new insights into work–family interface,' *Journal of Small Business Management*, 44(2), 285–297.

Simpson, M., N. Tuck, and S. Bellamy (2004), 'Small business success factors: the role of education and training,' *Education and Training*, 46(8/9), 481–491.

Thomas, W.H. (1994), 'Promoting entrepreneurship among Black South Africans,' in W.B. Vosloo (ed.), *Entrepreneurship and Economic Growth*, Pretoria: HSRC, pp. 373–383.

Verheul, I., L. Uhlaner, and R. Thurik (2005), 'Business accomplishments, gender and entrepreneurial self-image,' *Journal of Business Venturing*, 20(4), 483–518.

Viviers, S., S. Van Eeden, and D. Venter (2001), 'Identifying small business problems in the South African context for proactive entrepreneurial education,' Proceedings of the 11th Global IntEnt-Conference, 2–4 July 2001, Kruger National Park, South Africa.

Walker, E. and A. Brown (2004), 'What success factors are important to small business owners?' *International Small Business Journal*, 22(6), 577–594.

Watson, J. (2003), 'Failure rates for female-controlled businesses: are they any different?' *Journal of Small Business Management*, 41(3), 262–277.

Wickham, P.A. (2001), *Strategic Entrepreneurship: A Decision-Making Approach to New Venture Creation and Management*, 2nd edn, Harlow, UK: Financial Times, Prentice Hall.

Wilmerding, G. (2007), *Smart Women and Small Business: How to Make the Leap from Corporate Careers to the Right Small Enterprise*, Oxford: John Wiley.

Williams, D.R. (2004), 'Effects of childcare activities on the duration of self-employment in Europe,' *Entrepreneurship Theory and Practice*, 28, 467–485, doi: 10.1111/j.1540-6520.2004.00058.x.

FURTHER READING

Adler, N.J. (1997), *International Dimensions of Organizational Behavior*, Cincinnati, OH: South-Western College Publishing.

Ahl, H.J. (2002), *The Making of the Female Entrepreneur: A Discourse Analysis of Research Texts on Women's Entrepreneurship*, Jönköping: Jönköping International Business School/Parajett AB.

Allen, I.E., N. Langowitz, and M. Minniti (2006), 'Global entrepreneurship report on women and entrepreneurship,' Global Entrepreneurship Monitor (GEM), London: Babson College and London Business School.

Bartlett, C.A. and S. Ghoshal (1997), 'The myth of the generic manager: new personal competencies for new management roles,' *California Management Review*, 40(1), 92–116.

Berrell, M., P. Wright, and T. Thi Van Hoa (1999), 'The influence of culture on managerial behavior,' *Journal of Management Development*, 18(7), 578–589.

Bosma, N. and J. Levie (2009), 'Global Entrepreneurship Monitor global report,' Global Entrepreneurship Monitor.

Botha, M. (2006), 'Measuring the effectiveness of the women's entrepreneurship program, as a training intervention, on potential, start-up and established women entrepreneurs in South Africa,' PhD thesis, University of Pretoria.

Botha, M., G. Nieman, and J. Van Vuuren (2007), 'Measuring the effectiveness of women entrepreneurship program on potential, start-up and established women entrepreneurs in South Africa,' *South African Journal of Economic and Management Sciences*, 10(2), 163–183.

Brohman, J. (1996a), *Popular Development: Rethinking the Theory and Practice of Development*, Oxford: Blackwell.

Brohman, J. (1996b), 'New directions in tourism for third world development,' *Annals of Tourism Research*, 23(1), 48–70.

Brush, C.G., N.M. Carter, E.J. Gatewood, P.G. Greene, and M.M Hart (2006), *Growth-Oriented Women Entrepreneurs and Their Businesses: A Global Research Perspective*, Cheltenham, UK and Northampton, MA: Edward Elgar Publishing.

Carter, N.M. and C.G. Brush (2004), 'Gender: demographic characteristics of the entrepreneur,' in W.B. Gartner, C.G. Brush, N.M. Carter, E.J. Gatewood, and P.G. Greene (eds), *Handbook of Entrepreneurial Dynamics*, Thousand Oaks, CA: Sage, pp. 12–25.

Carter, S. (2000), 'Improving the numbers and performance of women-owned businesses: some implications for training and advisory services,' *Education and Training*, 42(4/5), 326–334.

Carter, S., S. Anderson, and E. Shaw (2001), 'Women's business ownership: a review of the academic, popular and internet literature,' Small Business Service Research.

Dia, M. (1991), 'Development and cultural values in sub-Saharan Africa,' *Finance and Development*, 28(4), 10–13.

Drakopoulos, S.A. and A.D. Karayiannis (2004), 'The historical development of hierarchical behavior in economic thought,' *Journal of the History of Economic Thought*, 26(3), 363–378.

Dreisler, P., P. Blenker, and K. Nielson (2003), 'Promoting entrepreneurship changing attitudes or behavior?' *Journal of Small Business and Enterprise Development*, 10(4), 383–392.

Gbadamosi, G. (2004), 'Academic ethics: what has morality, culture and administration got to do with its measurement?' *Management Decision*, 42(9), 1145–1161.

Greene, P.G., M.M. Hart, E.J. Gatewood, C.G. Brush, and N.M. Carter (2013), 'Women entrepreneurs: moving front and center: an overview of research and theory,' Coleman White Paper Series, available at: www.usasbe.org/knowledge/whitepapers/greene2003.pdf (accessed on 23 January 2015).

Hofstede, G. (1980), 'Culture and organizations,' *International Studies of Management and Organization*, 10(4), 15–41.

Jalbert, S.E. (2000), 'Women entrepreneurs in the global economy,' Paper presented at the 2nd international conference for women entrepreneurs, June, Washington, DC: Center for International Private Enterprise.

Kehler, J. (2013), 'Women and poverty: the South African experience,' *Journal of International Women's Studies*, 3(1), 41–53.

Kunene, T.R. (2008), 'A critical analysis of entrepreneurial and business skills in SMEs in the textile and clothing industry in Johannesburg, South Africa,' PhD Thesis, University of Pretoria.

Lee, S.M., S.-B. Lim, R.D. Pathak, D. Chang, and W. Li (2006), 'Influences on students' attitudes toward entrepreneurship: a multi-country study,' *The International Entrepreneurship and Management Journal*, 2(3), 351–366.

Ligthelm, A.A. and M.C. Cant (2002), *Business Success Factors of SMEs in Gauteng*, Pretoria: University of South Africa.

Maas, G. and M. Herrington (2006a), 'Global Entrepreneurship Monitor, South Africa report,' University of Cape Town, South Africa: The UCT Center for Innovation and Entrepreneurship.

Maas, G. and M. Herrington (2006b), 'Global Entrepreneurship Monitor report,' Global Entrepreneurship Monitor.

Mahadea, D. (2001), 'Similarities and differences between male and female entrepreneurial attributes in manufacturing firms in the informal sector in the Transkei,' *Development Southern Africa*, 18(2), 189–199.

Mayrhofer, A.M. and S.L. Hendriks (2003), 'Service provision for street-based traders in Pietermaritzburg, KwaZulu-Natal: comparing local findings to lessons drawn from Africa and Asia,' *Development Southern Africa*, 20(5), 595–604.

McClelland, D.C. (1987), 'Characteristics of successful entrepreneurs,' *Journal of Creative Behaviour*, 21(3), 219–233.

Mead, R. and T.G. Andrews (2009), *International Management*, Chichester, UK: John Wiley.

Minniti, M. and P. Arenius (2003), 'The entrepreneurial advantage of nations: women in entrepreneurship,' Paper presented at a United Nations Symposium, 'The Entrepreneurial Advantage of Nations: Women in Entrepreneurship,' Kansas City, MO: United Nations Symposium.

Minniti, M. and W.A. Naudé (2010), 'What do we know about the patterns and determinants of female entrepreneurship across countries?' *European Journal of Development Research*, 22(3), 1–17.

Minniti, M., P. Arenius, and N. Langowitz (2005), 'The 2004 Global Entrepreneurship Monitor special topic report: women in entrepreneurship,' Babson Park MA: Center for Women Leadership, Babson College.

Mitchell, B. (2004), 'Motives of entrepreneurs: a case study in South Africa,' *Journal of Entrepreneurship*, 12(2), 167–193.

Mueller, S.L. and A.S. Thomas (2001), 'Culture and entrepreneurial potential: a nine country study of locus of control and innovativeness,' *Journal of Business Venturing*, 16(1), 51–75.

Mukhtar, S. (1998), 'Business characteristics of male and female small and medium enterprises in the UK: implications for gender-based entrepreneurialism and business competence development,' *British Journal of Management*, 9(1), 41–51.

Naser, K., W.R. Mohammed, and R. Nuseibeh (2009), 'Factors that affect women entrepreneurs: evidence from an emerging economy,' *International Journal of Organizational Analysis*, 17(3), 225–247.

Nieman, G. (2006), *Small Business Management: A South African Approach*, Pretoria: Van Schaik.

Nieman, G. and C. Nieuwenhuizen (2009), *Entrepreneurship: A South African Perspective*: Van Schaik.

Orford, J., M. Herrington, E. Wood, and N. Segal (2003), 'Global Entrepreneurship Monitor: South Africa executive report,' University of Cape Town.

Pretorious, M. and J. Van Vuren (2003), 'Critical evaluation of two models for entrepreneurial education: an improved model through integration,' *South African Journal Educational Management*, 19(5), 413–427.

Reynolds, P.D., W.D Bygrave, E. Autio, L.W. Cox, and M. Hay (2002), 'The entrepreneur next door: characteristics of individuals starting companies in America: an executive summary of the panel study of entrepreneurial dynamics,' Executive report, Babson College/London Business School, available at: SSRN 1262320.

Rwigema, H. and R. Venter (2004), *Advanced Entrepreneurship*, Oxford: Oxford University Press.

Shapero, A. and L. Sokol (1982), 'The social dimensions of entrepreneurship,' *Encyclopedia of Entrepreneurship*, pp. 72–90, available at SSRN: https://ssrn.com/abstract=1497759 (accessed 18 June 2015).

Shim, S. and M.A. Eastlick (1998), 'Characteristics of Hispanic female business owners: an exploratory study,' *Journal of Small Business Management*, 36(3), 18–34.

Stanger, A.M.J. (2004), 'Gender-comparative use of small business training and assistance: a literature review,' *Education and Training*, 46(8/9), 464–473.

Stewart Jr, W.H., J.C. Carland, J.W. Carland, W.W. Watson, and R. Sweo (2003), 'Entrepreneurial dispositions and goal orientations: a comparative exploration of United States and Russian entrepreneurs,' *Journal of Small Business Management*, 41(1), 27–47.

Stoyanovska, A. (2001), 'Jobs, gender and small enterprises in Bulgaria', SEED Working Paper No 20, Series on Women's Entrepreneurship Development and Gender in Enterprises, Geneva: International Labour Organization.

Themba, G., M. Chamme, C.A. Phambuka, and R. Makgosa (1999), 'Impact of macro-environmental factors on entrepreneurship development in developing countries,' in L. Kinunda-Rutashobya and D.R. Olomi (eds), *African Entrepreneurship and Small Business Development*, Dar es Salaam: University of Dar es Salaam, pp. 103–119.

Thomas, A.S. and S.L. Mueller (2002), 'A case for comparative entrepreneurship: assessing the relevance of culture,' *International Business Studies*, 31(2), 287–301.

Verwey, I.V. (2005), 'A comparative analysis between SA and USA women entrepreneurs in construction,' MBA Dissertation, University of Pretoria.

Vosloo, W.B. (1994), 'The African experience,' in W.B. Vosloo (ed.), *Entrepreneurship and Economic Growth*, Pretoria: HSRC, pp. 109–127.

7. How vague entrepreneurial identities of Swedish women entrepreneurs are performed by government financiers

Aija Voitkane, Jeaneth Johansson, Malin Malmström and Joakim Wincent

Although often merely implied rather than explicitly studied or stated, financiers have different perceptions of women and men entrepreneurs (Becker-Blease and Sohl, 2007), which affect finance distribution to ventures (Ahl, 2006) and ultimately lead to the undercapitalisation and long-term underperformance of women entrepreneurs (Carter and Williams, 2003). Research on women's entrepreneurship has indicated that financiers' investment decisions in entrepreneurship might be influenced by the myth of women's underperformance (Marlow and McAdam, 2013). Accordingly, governmental financiers' role in ensuring gender equality in entrepreneurship is crucial. Governmental financiers aim to support venture growth based on equality criteria, that is, fostering equality via the public policy vehicles of law, regulation, programming, and budget allocation (Ahl and Nelson, 2015; Jennings and Brush, 2013). However, there is limited knowledge regarding governmental financiers' role as financial support providers. Interestingly, Ahl and Nelson (2015) showed that the underlying message of the discourse surrounding women's entrepreneurship policy in Sweden and the United States is not of equalising women's role in entrepreneurship but instead of putting women in second place. Given the proven controversy between the intention of such policies and their actual application, it causes us to question perceptional differences among financiers as they assess women's versus men's ventures.

Sweden has gained global attention for its progressive stance on gender-equality issues compared to other countries. Evidence of this progressive viewpoint can be seen in the *Global Gender Gap Report 2015* (Schwab et al., 2015), the number of Swedish non-governmental organisations involved in gender-equality issues, and Sweden's high governmental involvement in this pivotal area. Indeed, Sweden's official website proclaims that 'Gender equality is one of the cornerstones of Swedish society'. However, despite regulations and policies intended to boost women's entrepreneurship in Sweden, the number of women entrepreneurs is less than one-third. Accordingly, we study Swedish governmental financiers' social interactions during decision-making meetings where the major focus is on performing entrepreneurial identity. By doing so, we offer a new approach for studying myths – namely, how myths are constructed in financiers' natural environment.

Previous studies in entrepreneurial finance have typically ignored conceptualising social mechanisms and exploring their underlying processes, which can in turn have a major impact on nurturing and perpetuating gendered norms and power structures that constrain women entrepreneurs from fully exploiting their entrepreneurial and business potential (cf. Marlow and McAdam, 2013). Prior research has mostly focused on the individual entrepreneur rather than on organisations or individuals who actually perform myths. We believe that research exploring the social mechanisms in governmental financiers' decision-making can provide fruitful insights for the question of gender in access to finance.

Myths are closely related to culture and are reflected through social interactions. To gain a deeper understanding of the social mechanisms behind the underperformance myth, we employ Butler's (1988) theory of identity and study how gender is performed through social interactions. Accordingly, we focus on socially constructed gendered processes to explore the mechanisms behind the myth of women's underperformance (Ahl and Marlow, 2012). We outline the processes whereby governmental financiers 'position people as "men" and "women" within business practices and as "entrepreneurs" within gender practices' (Bruni et al., 2004, p. 410). Furthermore, we embrace and extend Gherardi's (1994) research by identifying ceremonial and remedial rituals in the venture-assessment process. The ceremonial rituals are based on rules embedded in governmental financiers' culture, which define how accepted patterns of performing gender are maintained, reproduced, and culturally transmitted. On the other hand, the remedial rituals restore well-accepted norms and ways of performing gender if and when they break down (Gherardi and Poggio, 2001; van den Brink et al., 2016). Our design, which includes unique access to governmental financiers' practices, allows us to contribute to the field of entrepreneurial finance by providing insights into the contextual performance of myths.

We collected data by participating in Swedish governmental financiers' financial decision-making meetings, which occurred behind closed doors where gender was actively performed in the financiers' natural environment. The Swedish context makes our study especially interesting due to the Swedish culture's worldwide reputation of gender equality and the country's beneficial welfare regime (see, for example, Ahl and Nelson, 2015). Swedish governmental financiers represent the closest link between the regulatory system and the practical reality of equality for women's entrepreneurship. All meetings were recorded and transcribed to enable discourse analysis, which prior research has proven to be especially useful when studying gender embeddedness of myths (see, for example, Ahl, 2006; Bourdieu, 1980; Jännäri and Kovalainen, 2015).

THEORETICAL BACKGROUND

Butler's (1988) theory of identity and performativity is carried out through language, with the relationship between language and the practice of an identity being defined by the social structure and practices of the particular community to which the speaker feels he or she belongs (Cameron, 1998). According to this view, the way gender is performed in the context of this study is a result of the relationship between language and the governmental financiers' practice of language when performing entrepreneurial identity. Discourse forms legitimate semantic and social meanings in a given community and determines symbolic value, which is consequently continually reproduced (Bourdieu, 1980). Butler's (1990) concepts of 'performance' and 'performativity' (closely linked to Austin's (1962) speech-act theory) consider acting to be central to the theory. According to Butler, 'masculine' and 'feminine' are what we *do* rather than what we *are*. Performance implies 'acting' (that is, performing a gender identity), which also comprises 'being' (being a gender identity). In other words, acting creates what it describes. Performativity implies performing acts of identity as an ongoing creation of social and cultural performances rather than as the expression of a prior identity. As such, gender identity is not stable, not pre-existing, and not clearly articulated; it is performativity constituted and based on formalised repetitive acting in accordance with social expectations in discourses that secure the illusion of an identity (Butler, 1990). Butler's (1988) performativity notion of gender implies that individuals and organisations create gender through the stylisation of repeated acts.

Performing Language

Scholars emphasise the social importance of language and the role of linguistic exchanges in the act of doing gender in relation to entrepreneurial identity as a part of the notion of 'performativity' (see, for example, Butler, 1998; Cameron, 2001; Mannheim, 1995; Mühlhäusler and Harré, 1990; Romaine, 1999, 2000). The performance of language represents consistent ways of doing gender in financial decision-making, where cultural assumptions and aspects of everyday reality are taken for granted. From such a viewpoint, financiers construct convergent and widely shared descriptions and explanations through their discourses (Phillips et al., 2004). The social mechanisms in the prevailing performance of language determine what is considered right or wrong, good or bad, and true or false among the financiers during the venture-assessment process (Hardy and Maguire, 2016). Indeed, language is central to how individuals enact gendered identities (Bergvall, 1999; Cameron, 1998; Eckert and McConnell-Ginet, 1992), with embedded linguistic choices turning attention to the culturally shaped and conditioned performance of language and its impact on action, such as further investment decisions. For this reason, it is essential to study dominant discourses to comprehend the institutionalised practice of performing language around gender identities. Doing so can provide fruitful insights into the social mechanisms behind myth construction (Hardy and Maguire, 2010).

Positioning

The performative character also offers possibilities for challenging established identities (Butler, 1988). It emphasises the productive force of language in constituting identity rather than identity being a pre-given construct that is reflected in language use. Here, it is of interest to understand the performance enacted, the binary understanding of male and female for enabling the enactment of alternative performances that can transform and change the prevailing gender order (Jeanes, 2007; Phillips and Knowles, 2012; Pilgeram, 2007; Pullen and Knights, 2007). This socially guided reciprocal positioning of gendering processes involves perceptions, interactions and actions that lay the groundwork for gender identities (Davies and Harré, 1990; West and Zimmerman, 1987).

Rituals in Social Acts

Organisations 'do gender' and create symbolic gender ordering through ceremonial and remedial rituals (Gherardi, 1994). Butler (1990) argued that identities are a product of ritualised social performatives calling the subject into being and being 'sedimented through time'. Ceremonial rituals, based on rules and organisational culture, ensure that gender identity is maintained, reproduced and culturally transmitted. Remedial rituals, on the other hand, restore the symbolic gender identity following norms of what is culturally accepted and expected (Gherardi, 1994). Ceremonial acting involves language as a discursive activity that enables the visualisation of practices (for example, such rituals may be expressed through greetings and compliments when socially accepted), and expected norms impact the way women and men talk and act (Gherardi and Poggio, 2001).

As such, we use a symbolic–interpretative lens (Gherardi, 1995) to understand the men and women in the financier organisation who produce interpretations and attribute meanings to gender relationships in their assessment work, and we explore how these interpretations may give rise to interactions within the financiers' own organisation and with ventures applying for finance. This approach enables us to explore the hidden dimensions of organisational practice and the procedures the financiers use in everyday practice (Bruni et al., 2014; Gherardi and Poggio, 2001).

METHOD

Prior studies exploring discourses of 'doing gender' (that is, performing gender) have predominantly adopted interview data as their primary source for analysis. We embrace Jännäri and Kovalainen's (2015) criticism that this method puts limitations on the potential interpretations available for analysing the conceptual idea of 'performing gender'. Instead, our study offers a new approach for uncovering the social mechanisms underlying gender performance, enabling us to better capture an actual performance of gender and thus reveal how myths are constructed (cf. Gherardi and Poggio, 2001). To accomplish this goal, we became an invisible part of several official closed-door meetings where financial decision-making took place among a group of Swedish governmental financiers. To the best of our knowledge, no other studies in the field have explored the social mechanisms behind these myths while allowing the discourse to emerge as naturally as it did in this study. Our observations of these governmental financiers' meetings enable us to investigate cultures and discourses taking place in financiers' performance of entrepreneurial identities and thus myth construction.

The Sample

The study was conducted in Sweden and is based on one year's worth of longitudinal data gathered from one group of nine governmental financiers (four women and five men) and their assessments of financial applications from 30 women- and 30 men-owned ventures. The ventures were randomly selected and are located all over Sweden. Swedish governmental organisations must follow explicit mandatory requirements regarding gender equality when distributing venture finance. The organisational policy is to equally support ventures owned and led by women and by men. Our longitudinal approach, which included several rounds of data collection, allowed us to identify patterns of ceremonial and remedial rituals in the presentations and discussions of venture applications. The procedure and language used for each round of data collection remained consistent. Through this research design, we identified that ceremonial rituals maintained and reproduced gender identities and also triggered remedial rituals to act in accordance with accepted norms. Language performances through discourse during the meetings were recorded and later transcribed. Further analyses were carried out after coding and categorising the transcribed data.

Data Analysis

To maintain distinction between the first-order, second-order and third-order analyses (Gioia and Chittipeddi, 1991; van Maanen, 1979), our data analysis was conducted (and is now presented) in several steps.

First step
We began first-order categorisation by entering the transcribed data into the qualitative data analysis software NVivo10. We manually scanned each discourse to identify common patterns revealing the underlying categories of performing gender. After discussing and agreeing on these categories as a research group, we started manual coding. The identified patterns in the discourse fell into six categories: passive/active, positive/negative, general/detailed, amplifying/underestimating the performance of an entrepreneur, prescribing titles, and contributors.

Second step
Second, we followed Miles and Huberman's (1994) suggestion and looked for relationships between the first-order categories. This allowed us to organise first-order themes in two larger constructs, or second-order themes, in performing gender: language and positioning. These two categories are in line with several authors who have indicated that the way gender is positioned in entrepreneurship is constructed through language, which reflects the socially constructed identities of women and men in the entrepreneurial context (Ahl, 2006; Bruni et al., 2004).

Third step

In the third step, we looked for the financiers' overall agreement/disagreement in venture assessments, which reflects the foundation of financial decision-making. We captured this category by comparing financiers' discourses and observing whether they agreed or disagreed with each other's opinions. This approach gives additional depth to our understanding of the social mechanisms underlying gender performance among a group of financiers from a broader perspective, which fortifies the gender structures in financiers' performance of language.

FINDINGS

Performing and Performative Mechanisms

Our analyses are theoretically grounded in Butler's (1988) conceptualisation of gender identity as a performativity act. Accordingly, this grounded theory provides a conceptualisation of the social mechanisms underlying the performance of gender structures in financial decision-making, thus enabling a new perspective on myths. The performative structures were captured through both participating women and men financiers performing gender through discourses. Our results portray the social machinery involved in performing gender, including performing and performative mechanisms (see Figure 7.1). *Performing mechanisms* construct gender identity partly through narratives of spoken words revealing the related traits associated with women and men in an entrepreneurial context and partly through positioning, which reveals the role actively prescribed to women and men during the narrating. Examples of these performing mechanisms are provided in Table 7.1. The table shows that the performance of an entrepreneurial identity is gendered and that financiers perform simplified dichotomies by categorising and distinguishing women business owners. On the other hand, *performative mechanisms* reflect gender performance executed in 'sets of repeated acts', revealing habitual practices in the financiers' discourses, norms and inner culture. This mechanism contributes to the perseverance of gender differences in the performance of entrepreneurial identity. These interactive mechanisms are shaped and reshaped in the context of established structures, which we explain below and illustrate in Figure 7.1.

1) *Performing identity traits* involves four underlying forces of dual character:

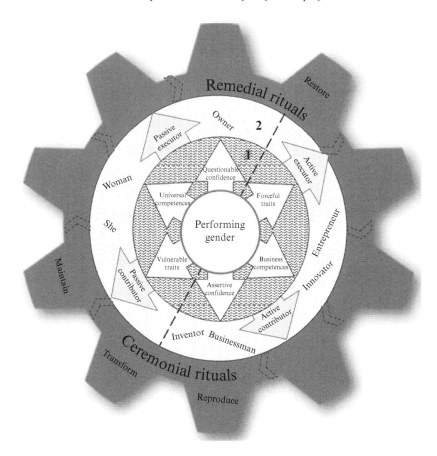

Figure 7.1   The social machinery of performing gender

i)   *Performing intrinsic traits: vulnerable versus forceful.* The financiers often described entrepreneurs in relation to their characteristics. Women were portrayed as 'emotional', 'difficult' and in other ways 'weak'. At the same time, men's intrinsic traits were in line with the traditional perception of entrepreneurship: 'serious', 'practical' and 'powerful'.

ii) *Performing confidence: questionable versus assertive.* Another observation is how confidently financiers expressed themselves about women and men entrepreneurs and thereby how they performed the confidence of an entrepreneurial identity. Even when both women and men were described with the same adjectives (for example, competent, broad networked, skilful,

Table 7.1 *Performing forces of social mechanisms*

Second order	First order	Performing female entrepreneurial identity	Performing male entrepreneurial identity
Attribute performing forces	*Performing intrinsic traits* vulnerable vs forceful	*Vulnerable intrinsic traits* • Emotional • Difficult • Nagging • Cute • To be pitied • Weak • Dependent • Flighty	*Forceful intrinsic traits* • Aggressive • Calm • Clever • Competent • Stimulating • Powerful • Solid • Serious
	Performing confidence questionable vs assertive	*Questionable confidence* • Is ok • Probably knows what she's doing • Probably quite ok • Knows some people • Has some ideas that might have potential • Most likely doesn't have experience with business activities • Probably doesn't know how to act • Seems inexperienced	*Assertive confidence* • Really good at doing business • A world-class entrepreneur • Huge social network • Does it extremely well • Done a really great job in managing the venture • Really impressive • Knows what he's doing 110% • Will make a fortune
	Performing entrepreneurial competence universal vs business	*Universal competences* • Speaks many languages • Has some experience • Been doing this for some years • Has education	*Business-related competences* • Knows the market • Takes risks • Impressive network • Knows customers well

Table 7.1 (continued)

Second order	First order	Performing female entrepreneurial identity	Performing male entrepreneurial identity
			Performing male entrepreneurial identity • Takes opportunities • Is a good salesman • Knows the industry
		• Has an academic background • Versatile (too many things) • Risk averse	
Positioning performing forces	*Performing executor passive vs active*	*Passive executor* • Takes part in many different things • Has a well-known surname • The company is led by a woman • Waiting for an offer • Accompanied by her husband • Barely manages • Hopes for the best	*Active executor* • Engages actively • Takes on a lot • Takes opportunities • Utilises his network • Starts and runs businesses • Markets himself • Acts professionally
	Performing the contributor orientation internal contribution performance vs external contribution performance	*Internal contribution performance* • Interested in these things • Venturing enables her to fulfil her dreams • Started the business to enjoy herself • Needed something to do	*External contribution performance* • Offers a unique service • Has a unique concept • Is an innovator • Provides opportunities
	Performing titles informal vs formal	*Informal titling* • She • Business owner • The woman • Name in use	*Formal titling* • The entrepreneur • Multi-entrepreneur • Engineer • Businessman • Innovator • Inventor

educated, etc.), men were described with amplifiers, whereas women were described with understatements. Discourse analysis revealed that the discourse about women involved insecurity as well as expressions performing questionable confidence of their entrepreneurial identities: 'probably knows what she's doing', 'has some experience', and 'most likely doesn't have experience with business activities'. Interestingly, such insecurity was observed despite equal amounts of documented evidence for decision-making for both the men and the women. At the same time, it was common that financiers were strongly assertive about men: 'he's really good at doing business', 'huge social network', and 'really impressive'.

iii) *Performing entrepreneurial competence: universal versus business.* Another observation entails how financiers picture entrepreneurs' competences through their discourses. Interestingly, even when some women and men entrepreneurs had comparatively equal competences, the financiers' discursive content differed: 'she is educated' versus 'he has a good education, an engineering degree' or 'she has been doing this for some years' in contrast to 'he knows how to sell'. In addition, men's competences were discussed with specific details, whereas women's competences were mentioned as something unspecific and broad. For example, 'he knows the market', 'he knows his customers', and 'he takes risks'. At the same time, women were described as follows: 'she speaks many languages', 'she is versatile', and 'has an academic background'. Interestingly, women's competences were rarely related to the entrepreneurial context.

2) *Performing positioning traits* expresses structures that reveal how governmental financiers identify, address, and position women and men entrepreneurs in the entrepreneurial context. The performing forces in positioning involve two underlying forces, which are also dualistic.

i) *Performing executer: passive versus active.* Women were not performed in terms of being actively involved in what they were doing. Women entrepreneurs were described more often within a passive context, whereas men were most often viewed through active forms or in line with the typical entrepreneur. Active performance of language clearly shows who is in charge and performs the action and also who is important for the company. Passive performance of language, on the other hand, neglects or decreases the importance of the actor. For example, 'she takes a part in many different things' and 'the company is led by a woman' in contrast to 'he engages actively' and 'he utilises his network'.

ii) *Performing contributor orientation: internal contribution orientation versus external orientation.* Women were described mostly with internally oriented contributions, or in other words, 'they do it for themselves'. However, externally oriented contributions were more often prescribed to men and related to novelty or benefit to a broader society. For example, 'uniqueness' was only discussed for men's entrepreneurship: 'a unique service', 'unique technology' and 'unique concept'. Women were discussed in terms of, for example, 'fulfilling her own dreams' or 'having something to do'.

iii) *Performing titles: informal titling versus external titling.* A great difference was revealed in how women and men entrepreneurs were being identified and addressed in governmental financiers' discourse. Men were assigned identities like 'entrepreneur', 'businessman', 'innovator' and 'inventor'; for example: 'he is a real entrepreneur' and 'very smart businessman'. Generally, women entrepreneurs were simply assigned the identity 'she'. A few times women were assigned an identity with the epithet 'business owner'. Women were never given the epithets 'an entrepreneur' or an 'inventor'.

3) *Performative mechanisms* represent the ongoing continuous performance of identity through formalised and repetitive acting executed through ceremonial and remedial rituals. Ceremonial rituals maintain and reproduce gender identities. The group of financiers has a long history of working together with an established culture and discourse patterns. The meetings and discourses follow the same procedures during each meeting and for every decision taken. One financier presents the entrepreneur's financial application, then the group discusses the application, and they finally agree on a decision to finance or not. Performance of entrepreneurial identity takes the main role in their discourse. When the financiers agree with each other and support each other's opinions, they strengthen the stereotypical picture of gender identity. Expressions like 'mhm, yes, I agree' or adding information in the same discursive way were observed during the meetings. The nature of the discourse was stable in the identity performance, and the same expressions and wordings constantly recurred in the discussions during the meetings throughout the year.

Remedial rituals were also identified because according to policies, the financiers were asked to go beyond gender stereotyping to avoid the repetitive performance of gender identities. However, despite the request, active discussions showed no sign of considering gender equality in the matter. This pattern of performing gender became invisible and unconscious due to the repetitive characteristics of the venture-assessment process, which in turn contributed to restoring the invisible symbolic gender identity. The financiers' remedial rituals were based on social expectations and beliefs within the group of financiers, and their acting became repetitive, thereby creating mechanisms that endure.

DISCUSSION

This chapter provides new insights into constraints associated with women entrepreneurs' exploitation of business potential, that is, constraints in access to critical resources for fully taking advantage of business potential. We examined discussions to explore how gender identities are being performed by governmental financiers; in doing so, we showed how social mechanisms enable the construction of the women's underperformance myth. We suggest that bias in distributing finance may be caused by a vague understanding and an 'own' categorisation in the decision group when performing gender identities. Furthermore, we explain the role of language in establishing a culture for how financiers categorise the gender identity of women entrepreneurs.

This chapter contributes a conceptualisation of gender in finance to an understudied part of the entrepreneurial support system – namely, governmental financiers' performance of gender and their construction of an underperformance myth. We contribute with a model that draws upon the ideas of several authors who indicate that gender and entrepreneurship positioning are undertaken through discourses, practices, norms, languages and values reflecting the socially constructed identities of women and men in entrepreneurship (Ahl, 2004; Bruni et al., 2004). We extend research by Gherardi (1994) by showing how ceremonial and remedial rituals are practised when constructing the gender identity of women entrepreneurs in the culturally embedded context of governmental financiers' financial decision-making. We found that entrepreneurship positioning through gender is undertaken through performing language that reflects norma-tive images of women and men entrepreneurs (Ahl, 2004; Bruni et al., 2004). The embedded choices the governmental financiers made when performing women and men entrepreneurs' identities in their assessment work reflect the culturally shaped and conditioned traits in the financiers' social mechanisms. In turn, the dominant language performance tends to reveal unconsciously accepted norms and standards as well as reflect institutionalised practices of performing gender in the financiers' language (Hardy and Maguire, 2010, p. 1367).

Consistent with Butler's (1990) concepts of 'performance' and 'performativity', we found that the financiers did not have a clear perception of women's entrepreneurial identity in entrepreneurship, standing in contrast to men entrepreneurs, which can be categorised as having a very clear entrepreneurial identity. This finding is also in line with Bruni et al. (2004), who showed that women entrepreneurs are performed as passive, adaptive and flexible, whereas men entrepreneurs are performed as active and proactive. The performing of gender and the performing of entrepreneurship are culturally embedded in tacit knowledge that constrains actions such that the man entrepreneur is performed as the norm and the woman entrepreneur is performed as 'the other' – namely, a vague, featureless, inexplicit entrepreneur. The clear, favourable entrepreneurial identity assigned to men entrepreneurs aligns well with the big picture of gender in access to finance provided by the research on performance of research, including studies from across the globe showing that women entrepreneurs are under-represented and have difficulties obtaining financial support (Bellucci et al., 2010; Brush et al., 2009; Lewis, 2006; Muravyev et al., 2009). Social boundaries assert and defend the performance of gender in accordance with accepted and expected norms, thereby perpetuating and spreading the myth about women's entrepreneurship.

In addition, we observed herding behaviour among the financiers, which also reflects the inner culture, providing an additional explanation for this myth survival. The high level of agreement and lack of debates and second opinions when performing gendered identities can cause the biased distribution of finance. Social mechanisms stimulate repeated interaction between gender perceptions and gender performance in the decision-making process. Thus, social mechanisms lay a foundation for gender differences in distributing finance.

CONCLUSIONS

Social mechanisms are powerful in shaping perceptions of gender identities when the inherited culture for financial behaviour provides the necessary condition for unconscious myth construction. Financiers tend to apply pragmatic rules that govern the performance of language as well as specify differences in performing women's and men's entrepreneurial identities. The shared values of entrepreneurial identity attached to a group of women and men financiers can undermine the financiers' inner culture that accordingly sets expectations for how disputants should construe and communicate entrepreneurial identity. Both women and men financiers belong to the same culture with embedded social norms, values, meanings and expectations in how they 'do gender', and it is in this culture that gender-positioning is institutionalised through continuous processes performed through rituals (cf. Gherardi and Poggio, 2001).

IMPLICATIONS

The study we presented in this chapter has several implications. Obviously, by performing vague identities for women entrepreneurs when assessing their abilities to succeed with their business endeavours, the governmental financiers' work process itself causes them to doubt women entrepreneurs' abilities to succeed. Such performance of gendered identities influences associated decision-making outcomes and thus the way finance is distributed between women and men entrepreneurs. This finding has implications for the undercapitalisation and subsequent underperformance of businesses run by women entrepreneurs. A lack of access to finance hinders women entrepreneurs trying to exploit growth ambitions and may even severely damage their business development. Furthermore, governmental financiers are the closest link to policy execution among the different types of financiers and thus have the responsibility to work toward reaching gender equality in entrepreneurship. Policies and regulations are calling for gender equality, but even though awareness is present, understanding how to perceive women is unclear for many; hence, acting in accordance with policy becomes unclear. If such underlying structures are not corrected, it will be impossible to ensure gender equality in entrepreneurship through policies and regulations.

REFERENCES

Ahl, H. (2004). *The Scientific Reproduction of Gender Inequality: A Discourse Analysis of Research Texts on Women's Entrepreneurship*. Copenhagen: CBS Press.

Ahl, H. (2006). Why research on women entrepreneurs needs new directions. *Entrepreneurship Theory and Practice*, 30(5), 595–621.

Ahl, H. and Marlow, S. (2012). Exploring the dynamics of gender, feminism and entrepreneurship: advancing debate to escape a dead end? *Organization*, 19(5), 543–562.

Ahl, H. and Nelson, T. (2015). How policy positions women entrepreneurs: a comparative analysis of state discourse in Sweden and the United States. *Journal of Business Venturing*, 30(2), 273–291.

Austin, J.L. (1962). *How to Do Things with Words*. Oxford: Clarendon Press.

Becker-Blease, J.R. and Sohl, J.E. (2007). Do women-owned businesses have equal access to venture capital? *Journal of Business Venturing*, 22, 503–521.

Bellucci, A., Borisov, A. and Zazzaro, A. (2010). Does gender matter in bank–firm relationships? Evidence from small business lending. *Journal of Banking and Finance*, 34(12), 2968–2984.

Bergvall, V.L. (1999). Toward a comprehensive theory of language and gender. *Language in Society*, 28(2), 273–293.

Bourdieu, P. (1980). Structure, habitus, practices. In P. Bourdieu, *The Logic of Practice*. Stanford, CA: Stanford University Press, pp. 52–65.

Bruni, A., Gherardi, S. and Poggio, B. (2004). Doing gender, doing entrepreneurship: an ethnographic account of intertwined practices. *Gender, Work and Organization*, 11(4), 406–429.

Bruni, A., Gherardi, S. and Poggio, B. (2014). *Gender and Entrepreneurship: An Ethnographic Approach*. New York: Routledge.

Brush, C.G., De Bruin, A. and Welter, F. (2009). A gender-aware framework for women's entrepreneurship. *International Journal of Gender and Entrepreneurship*, 1(1), 8–24.

Butler, J. (1988). Performative acts and gender constitution: an essay in phenomenology and feminist theory. *Theatre Journal*, 40(4), 519–531.

Butler, J. (1990). *Gender Trouble: Feminism and the Subversion of Identity*. New York: Routledge.

Butler, J. (1998). Subjects of sex/gender/desire. In A. Phillips (ed.), *Feminism and Politics*. Oxford: Oxford University Press, pp. 273–294.

Cameron, D. (1998). *The Feminist Critique of Language: A Reader*. London: Routledge.

Cameron, D. (2001). *Working with Spoken Discourse*. London: Sage.

Carter, N. and Williams, M. (2003). Comparing social feminism and liberal feminism. In J. Butler (ed.), *New Perspectives on Women Entrepreneurs*. Greenwich, CT: IAP, pp. 25–41.

Davies, B. and Harré, R. (1990). Positioning: the discursive production of selves. *Journal for the Theory of Social Behavior*, 20(1), 43–63.

Eckert, P. and McConnell-Ginet, S. (1992). Think practically and look locally: language and gender as community-based practice. *Annual Review of Anthropology*, 21, 461–490.

Gherardi, S. (1994). The gender we think, the gender we do in our everyday lives. *Human Relations*, 47(6), 591–610.

Gherardi, S. (1995). *Gender, Symbolism and Organizational Cultures*. London: Sage.

Gherardi, S. and Poggio, B. (2001). Creating and recreating gender order in organizations. *Journal of World Business*, 36(3), 245–259.

Gioia, D.A. and Chittipeddi, K. (1991). Sensemaking and sensegiving in strategic change initiation. *Strategic Management Journal*, 12(6), 433–448.

Hardy, C. and Maguire, S. (2010). Discourse, field-configuring events, and change in organizations and institutional fields: narratives of DDT and the Stockholm Convention. *Academy of Management Journal*, 53(6), 1365–1392.

Hardy, C. and Maguire, S. (2016). Organizing risk: discourse, power, and 'riskification'. *Academy of Management Review*, 41(1), 80–108.

Jännäri, J. and Kovalainen, A. (2015). The research methods used in 'doing gender' literature. *International Journal of Gender and Entrepreneurship*, 7(2), 214–231.

Jeanes, E.L. (2007). The doing and undoing of gender: the importance of being a credible female victim. *Gender, Work and Organization*, 14(6), 552–571.

Jennings, J.E. and Brush, C.G. (2013). Research on women entrepreneurs: challenges to (and from) the broader entrepreneurship literature? *The Academy of Management Annals*, 7(1), 663–715.

Lewis, P. (2006). The quest for invisibility: female entrepreneurs and the masculine norm of entrepreneurship. *Gender, Work and Organization*, 13(5), 453–469.

Mannheim, B. (1995). Introduction. In D. Tedlock and B. Mannheim (eds), *The Dialogic Emergence of Culture*. Urbana, IL: University of Illinois Press, pp. 1–32.

Marlow, S. and McAdam, M. (2013). Gender and entrepreneurship: advancing debate and challenging myths; exploring the mystery of the under-performing female entrepreneur. *International Journal of Entrepreneurial Behavior and Research*, 19(1), 114–124.

Miles, M. and Huberman, M. (1994). *Qualitative Data*. Thousand Oaks, CA: Sage.

Mühlhäusler, P. and Harré, R. (1990). *Pronouns and People: The Linguistic Construction of Social and Personal Identity*. Oxford: Blackwell.

Muravyev, A., Talavera, O. and Schäfer, D. (2009). Entrepreneurs' gender and financial constraints: evidence from international data. *Journal of Comparative Economics*, 37(2), 270–286.

Phillips, M. and Knowles, D. (2012). Performance and performativity: undoing fictions of women business owners. *Gender, Work and Organization*, 19(4), 416–437.

Phillips, N., Lawrence, T.B. and Hardy, C. (2004). Discourse and institutions. *Academy of Management Review*, 29(4), 635–652.

Pilgeram, R. (2007). 'Ass-kicking' women: doing and undoing gender in a US livestock auction. *Gender, Work and Organization*, 14(6), 572–595.

Pullen, A. and Knights, D. (2007). Editorial: undoing gender – organizing and disorganizing performance. *Gender, Work and Organization*, 14(6), 505–511.

Romaine, S. (1999). *Communicating Gender*. Mahwah, NJ: Lawrence Erlbaum.

Romaine, S. (2000). *Language in Society: An Introduction to Sociolinguistics*. Oxford: Oxford University Press.

Schwab, K., Samans, R., Hausmann, R., Zahidi, S., Bekhouche, Y., Ugarte, P.P., Ratcheva, V. (2015). *The Global Gender Gap Report 2015*. Switzerland: World Economic Forum. Retrieved from http://www3.weforum.org/docs/GGGR2015/cover.pdf (19 February 2016).

Van den Brink, M., Holgersson, C., Linghag, S. and Deé, S. (2016). Inflating and down playing strengths and weaknesses: practicing gender in the evaluation of potential managers and partners. *Scandinavian Journal of Management*, 32(1), 20–32.

Van Maanen, J. (1979). The fact of fiction in organizational ethnography. *Administrative Science Quarterly*, 24, 539–550.

West, C. and Zimmerman, D.H. (1987). Doing gender. *Gender and Society*, 1(2), 125–151.

FURTHER READING

Ainsworth, S. and Hardy, C. (2012). Subjects of inquiry: statistics, stories, and the production of knowledge. *Organization Studies*, 33(12), 1693–1714.

Alsos, G.A., Isaksen, E.J. and Ljunggren, E. (2006). New venture financing and subsequent business growth in men- and women-led businesses. *Entrepreneurship Theory and Practice*, 30, 669–686.

Alvesson, M. and Kärreman, D. (2000). Taking the linguistic turn in organizational research challenges, responses, consequences. *The Journal of Applied Behavioral Science*, 36(2), 136–158.

Brush, C.G., Carter, N.M., Gatewood, E.J., Greene, P.G. and Hart, M.M. (2006). *Growth-Oriented Women Entrepreneurs and their Businesses: A Global Research Perspective*. Cheltenham, UK and Northampton, MA: Edward Elgar Publishing.

Carter, S. and Rosa, P. (1998). Indigenous rural firms: farm enterprises in the UK. *International Small Business Journal*, 16(4), 15–27.

Carter, S., Shaw, E., Lam, W. and Wilson, F. (2007). Gender, entrepreneurship, and bank lending: the criteria and processes used by bank loan officers in assessing applications. *Entrepreneurship Theory and Practice*, 31, 427–444.

Coleman, S. (2000). Access to capital and terms of credit: a comparison of men- and women-owned small businesses. *Journal of Small Business Management*, 38, 37–52.

Down, S. (2006). *Narratives of Enterprise: Crafting Entrepreneurial Self-Identity in a Small Firm*. Cheltenham, UK and Northampton, MA: Edward Elgar Publishing.

Ennew, C. and McKechnie, S. (1998). *The Financial Services Consumer: Consumers and Services*. Chichester, UK: John Wiley, pp. 185–207.

Foucault, M. (1980). *Language, Counter-Memory, Practice: Selected Essays and Interviews*. Ithaca, NY: Cornell University Press.

Jaffe, A. (1999). *Ideologies in Action: Language Politics on Corsica* (Vol. 3). Berlin: Walter de Gruyter.

Lins, E. and Lutz, E. (2016). Bridging the gender funding gap: do female entrepreneurs have equal access to venture capital? *International Journal of Entrepreneurship and Small Business*, 27(2–3), 347–365.

Marlow, S. and Patton, D. (2005). All credit to men? Entrepreneurship, finance, and gender. *Entrepreneurship Theory and Practice*, 29(6), 717–735.

Pennycook, A. (2004). Performativity and language studies. *Critical Inquiry in Language Studies: An International Journal*, 1(1), 1–19.

Riding, A.L. and Swift, C.S. (1990). Women business owners and terms of credit: some empirical findings of the Canadian experience. *Journal of Business Venturing*, 5(5), 327–340.

Roper, S. and Scott, J.M. (2009). Perceived financial barriers and the start-up decision: an econometric analysis of gender differences using GEM data. *International Small Business Journal*, 27(2), 149–171.

Schatzki, T.R. (2001). Introduction: practice theory. In T.S. Schatzki, K. Knorr-Cetina and E. Von Savigny (eds), *The Practice Turn in Contemporary Theory*. New York: Routledge, pp. 1–14.

8. Socially constructed masculine domination: officials' perception of female entrepreneurs in Kerala, India

Roshni Narendran

Many earlier works on female entrepreneurship have been based on the liberal feminist view that treats women as equals with men, and thus assumes that barriers lead to the women's underperformance. Researchers have stressed the importance of researching men and women as separate entities and the need to move beyond victim blaming, that is, the belief that women should be held accountable for their circumstances (Ahl and Marlow, 2012). The paucity of studies addressing feminist theories of female entrepreneurship has led to the call for incorporating post-structural feminist research, which considers social constructs through history, geography and culture (Ahl and Marlow, 2012; Foss, 2010). Post-structural feminism in female entrepreneurship research gained popularity in the late 2000s; researchers have used Foucault's work, which argued that discourse analysis is necessary to understand social practices (Ahl, 2006). Social practices in a society are 'created through discourses, which can be defined as how something is presented or regarded' (ibid., p. 597). By adopting this view, the present chapter explores the perception of agents in implementing programmes that facilitate female entrepreneurship, to clarify gender relations in the current Indian societal structure. Furthermore, this chapter aims to help to establish some preliminary assumptions regarding the gender gap in reforms for female entrepreneurs in Kerala, India, by integrating feminist theory into the female entrepreneurial ecosystem.

An ecosystem is a biological community of interacting organisms and their physical environment (Stam, 2015). It encompasses a comprehensive set of resources among actors (ibid.). Isenberg (2011) and Mason and Brown (2014) developed an entrepreneurship ecosystem model that includes policy, finance, culture, support, human capital and markets. However, Mazzarol (2014) noted that all components of the entrepreneurial ecosystem are related to government policies and legal authority. In this study, an ecosystem is considered as an interactive, physical environment in which female entrepreneurs exist due to the extensive public policy changes in Kerala, and assumes that the government is the primary actor within Kerala's ecosystem. Additionally, many publications encourage authors to address policy implications, though these become void if there is an apparent misalignment between the perceptions of officials and the assistance required for female entrepreneurs. Therefore, learning about officials' perceptions would help to determine the existence of gendered assumptions affecting female entrepreneurship. Marlow and McAdam (2013, p. 120) suggest the need for 'far greater reflexive critical interrogation of the assumptions which form the foundation of knowledge in the entrepreneurial domain'. This chapter strives to review the assumptions of gender in Indian society by reviewing the perceptions of the officials. In the next section, the literature on entrepreneurial ecosystems is reviewed, followed by an explanation of the study's methods and findings. Next, a discussion on female entrepreneurship in Kerala is provided. Finally, the policy implications and limitations of the study are discussed.

ENTREPRENEURIAL ECOSYSTEM AND FEMALE ENTREPRENEURSHIP

Moore (1993) introduced the term 'business ecosystem' to encompass multiple factors, such as the birth, expansion, leadership, self-renewal or decline of businesses. Moore's article focused mainly on the influence of company leadership and their strategies to coexist in the ecosystem. In later years, the term 'ecosystem' gained a different connotation with the emphasis shifting to the interconnected relationships between multiple actors facilitating entrepreneurial activities. Isenberg (2011) developed an entrepreneurial ecosystem model comprising six interconnecting variables: policy, markets, human capital, supports, culture and finance. Stam (2015) recently extended the model to address the role of the entrepreneurial ecosystem in creating value.

Public policy is a key component of the entrepreneurial ecosystem (Hechavarria and Ingram, 2014). Hechavarria and Ingram (ibid.) critically analysed policies and businesses in the United States and argued the importance of innovation for large businesses. There have been many debates on the suitability of 'entrepreneurial policies'. Through the lens of female entrepreneurs, Yousafzai et al. (2015) used the Global Entrepreneurship Monitor data to demonstrate the positive influence of regulatory institutions on the vision for female entrepreneurship. In a more micro analysis, in Finland, women depend on government-provided family services such as day care to balance work and family commitments (Koreen, 2000). Some nations, including the US, Spain, Italy, the Netherlands and Portugal, introduced a Nanny Tax, that is, tax incentives for women for their contribution to household chores (Mayoux, 2001). However, Marlow (2002) considered such incentives to reaffirm that it is women's duty to be involved in household duties.

Recently, Pettersson et al. (2017) analysed the assumptions that the government holds in developing female entrepreneurship policies. The study concluded that the policies promoting female entrepreneurship in Scandinavian countries adopt a neoliberal approach that emphasises economic growth; that is, the policy considers women to be an untapped and not fully utilised resource. Furthermore, the study concluded that the policies of Scandinavian countries did not reflect the gender equality that they are reputed for and did not recognise the problematic gender–power relations within their policies. Although the current study does not analyse these policies, it uses the perception of officials in Kerala to analyse the discourses of officials to determine the power relations.

Women Entrepreneurs in Kerala

From 1817, the ruling monarch of Kerala implemented measures to change the social status of women by providing them with basic education (Drèze and Sen, 2002), which increased Kerala's literacy rate. Later, in 1957, when the communist party came into power, the Kerala government encouraged education, provided affordable health care, and initiated progressive public action measures in the agrarian sector in an effort to mobilise class-based divisions (Kurien, 2000; Singh, 2010). Changes in people's welfare started to be reflected in the sex ratio and literacy. The sex ratio in Kerala is 1084 women per 1000 men, and its literacy rate is 94 per cent (Kerala State Planning Board, 2016). These figures are much higher than those of India as a whole, and many will assume a higher status of women in Kerala. In contrast to expectations, in 2014–2015, 11 061 crimes were reported against women in Kerala, among which domestic violence is the most common (Department of Economics and Statistics, 2016). Domestic violence could be the result of the patriarchal nature of the society. Patriarchy is widely practised in Kerala, although some communities practise a matrilineal system. The matrilineal system is where children are considered to be the members of the mother's family rather than their father's (Ramachandran, 1997). The matrilineal system is considered the reason why women in Kerala enjoy certain privileges such as education; however, others argue the matrilineal system to be a form of sexual permissiveness (Kodoth and Eapen, 2004). To sustain the empowerment of women, Duflo (2012) argues for a continuous policy commitment to equality. The present chapter argues that a continuous policy commitment is not possible unless we study officials' attitude towards women business owners.

Although women in Kerala have fared better than women in other Indian states, female entrepreneurs in Kerala encounter the same problems as other female entrepreneurs, such as securing funds for their businesses, poor market access, family responsibilities, mobility constraints (lack of infrastructure and harassment), and negative social perceptions (Abraham, 2000; D'Cruz, 2003; Narendran, 2012; Navaprabha, 2000). D'Cruz (2003) highlighted the lack of awareness of various support agencies. Many studies conducted in Kerala are related to self-help groups; a prominent one is Kudumbasree, a poverty alleviation programme. However, researchers have argued against using poverty alleviation programmes to encourage entrepreneurship, as highlighted by Marlow (2002), since such programmes unintentionally perpetuate the subordination of women. To understand the inherent problems of the programmes, it is essential to analyse the perceptions of officials to understand the gender and power relations of agents involved in programme implementation.

METHODS

This study aims to use post-structural feminist theory to investigate gender constructs among government officials in Kerala. In post-structural feminism, social reality is constructed through discourses (Ahl and Nelson, 2015). To facilitate this discourse and to explain the social reality of female entrepreneurs in an open dialogue, this study investigates the officials implementing and disbursing support programmes for women. Ahl and Marlow (2012) and more recently Henry et al. (2016) advocate for qualitative and exploratory approaches to investigate female entrepreneurship.

The participants were informed that the study's objective is to gain insight into the challenges and solutions to increase the participation of female entrepreneurs. From 15 questions, the current chapter includes the responses to the following: (i) Please state your opinion of women business owners; (ii) In your opinion, what are the barriers faced by female entrepreneurs in Kerala?; and (iii) What changes do you recommend to improve the programmes? Data were collected from the government officials in Trivandrum, the capital of Kerala, who provide assistance to help women business owners. Second, a directory of non-government organisations (NGOs), published by the All India Women's Education Fund Association, was sourced. The directory comprises a list of NGOs in every state in India, from which NGOs in Trivandrum were identified. These NGOs were contacted by phone to verify whether they provide assistance to female-owned industries. Out of the 18 NGOs in Trivandrum, only six were short-listed. Others were excluded on the basis that either they do not provide assistance for female-owned industries or they could not be contacted. The data presented in this study were developed through field research conducted in Kerala over two months using in-depth interviews as the primary data collection method. The researcher interviewed 16 high-ranking officials from the NGOs and autonomous government bodies assisting women-owned businesses in Trivandrum.

FINDINGS

Challenges Faced by Female Entrepreneurs

Six types of perceived barriers for female entrepreneurs were identified from compiling the responses of the officials, which include (i) lack of venture-creation skills; (ii) lack of financial literacy; (iii) mobility constraints; (iv) family socialisation and dependency; (v) social constraints; and (vi) miscellaneous barriers.

Lack of venture-creation skills The interviewed officials consistently perceived barriers to market products. About half of the participants recognised that finding suitable market outlets is a difficult task for female entrepreneurs. The marketing barrier was acknowledged mostly by the female officials. One female official discussed the predicament at length. She was apprehensive about the impact of branded products on the Indian market and claimed that increasing competition and the arrival of many multinational companies in the Indian economy decreased the opportunities for female entrepreneurs. She added that products from multinational companies had higher demand compared to locally produced products. Competition from multinational companies can be argued to be a gender-neutral problem not specific to women. Women respondents were confident that women in Kerala are capable of effectively managing the businesses. Such a positive response was not evident from a male official. His response revealed the patriarchal nature of the society. His views are as follows:

> Men can be sterner, so their marketing and cash collection is more effective than that of women. Also, a male supervisor has more respect among the employees compared to a woman supervisor. (Official 8)

Lack of financial literacy   In response to the perceived financial barriers for female entrepreneurs, a female official responded to the question with an example from her experience. She narrated the story of a female entrepreneur who received assistance from the government. This particular entrepreneur established a tailoring business with a number of employees and machines. She puts it thus:

> A woman had started a stitching unit with assistance from the government. She had a number of machineries and employees. Thus, with the available inventory, she started a stitching unit for women. To attract customers, she started to sell the clothes at a lower cost compared to her competitors. Without the owner's awareness, these low-priced items created losses in her business. When the business incurred these losses, the owner did not have the finances to sustain the business. Eventually, the woman had to sell the machinery and close down the unit. (Official 11)

Agreeing with this official, another female NGO official expressed the opinion that women lack financial management and planning. She concurred that a woman's attitude was 'go to the bank, take a loan, and do something'. She argued that the lack of financial management has adversely affected these businesses and their sustainability. This reflected on Ahl and Marlow's (2012) argument that people tend to blame the victims.

Moreover, a government official added that most of the women in Kerala initiate businesses with fewer financial resources than men do and that female entrepreneurs cannot afford to employ professionals. Thus, their businesses find it difficult to survive while lacking skilled labourers.

Mobility constraints   Mobility constraints are the result of the epidemic in societies like India where women are sexually harassed in public places. Only a portion of the officials highlighted mobility constraints as a barrier. According to two officials, a male and a female, Kerala is not a suitable province for women to work late at night. These officials emphasised that travel is a major impediment to the development of female-owned businesses. Additionally, fear of acting against social norms is an important contributor to mobility constraints. A female government official who works for a poverty alleviation programme recalled that when the government holds product fairs or exhibitions of products from women participants, female entrepreneurs are hesitant to leave the fair after dark. One official commented:

> In Kerala, there are no specific barriers for women except that they find it difficult to work late at night. (Official 3)

Even though the official did not elaborate the reason for women finding it difficult to work late at night, the sexual harassment endured by women in public places has been widely reported (see *The Hindu*, 2016).

Family socialisation and dependency   About half of the officials (three government and two NGO officials) identified family and family responsibility as major barriers for female entrepreneurs. The officials' main concern was that they believed that multi-tasking compromised female entrepreneurs' efforts. Female NGO officials noted that family responsibilities are an inevitable component in the lives of women. One female NGO official summarised this view in a single phrase: 'double burden'. The double burden describes the multi-tasking required to manage the responsibilities in both the household and the business. Past studies have confirmed that women have domestic responsibilities, especially in terms of raising children and looking after elderly family members entrusted to them (Bradley, 2002; Marlow, 2002).

Another female NGO official agreed and elaborated that a woman is the nucleus of the family. Consequently, family difficulties will affect women the most. Thus, complex family problems will adversely affect a woman's business. Supporting the view of the female NGO officials, a female government official also indicated family responsibility as a barrier to entrepreneurship. In contrast to the opinions of the female officials, a male government official believed that women should treat family and business responsibilities as two separate entities. He critically observed that many female entrepreneurs are incapable of differentiating between family and business responsibilities.

A male official working in women's development had a different view and indicated that family responsibility is embedded in a woman's life by society. He added that society requires women to take care of their children and household, so a woman's priority shifts predominantly to the family's welfare and not towards career development. He supported his view by stating that such a mentality would compel women to establish a business on the premises of her home and that this will, in turn, affect the performance of the business. He states:

> Society expects women to look after the children and household. Thus, women's priority turns out to be their family. This, in turn, leads women to establish a business where they can manage family and business. (Official 7)

Social constraints   This section on societal constraints is broad because in Indian society, with its embedded values, there are many reflections of social perceptions. The discussions on family socialisation and mobility constraints also involve the social views of women as entrepreneurs. This section discusses some of the additional comments relevant to social perceptions.

A government official points out that the people in Kerala encourage others to work for someone else rather than establish a business and to be one's own boss. The official stated that Kerala does not have an industrial culture:

> In Kerala, people want to be employed with the government, or they migrate to other parts of India or outside India for a job. Thus, the people of Kerala lack an industrial culture. (Official 2)

A male official added that even if a woman starts a business, society misinterprets her intentions and does not accept an independent woman. He added that if a female entrepreneur spends a considerable length of time within a government office, she becomes the subject of gossip. Thus, the society will question women's reputations. The official stated:

> Society has no respect for women. Society misinterprets women's independence. Especially when they visit government officials and when they have to wait at the office for a long time. People start to badmouth the women, and this affects their reputations. (Official 2)

In line with the comments above, a female official also highlighted the discouraging attitude of society. Society, particularly men, try to demotivate women in their attempts to run a business. The officials elaborate:

> People think women are hopeless and helpless. They say that women cannot complete a task. Men discourage and humiliate women who go for work. Men ask women, 'Where are you going? Will something work out?' (Official 12)

> There are women masons. People are not willing to entrust the construction of their house to these women. People would rather make these women fix toilets rather than build the whole house. (Official 11)

Miscellaneous barriers   Lastly, some government officials (two male government officials) raised two particular concerns that other respondents did not mention. First, a government official reported that risk-averse behaviour was another major barrier among women business owners. Second, the other male government official pointed out that a business could succeed only if the business owners could rebuild a business despite failures.

Overall, the above discussion highlighted the six perceived barriers to the female entrepreneurs identified by the government and NGO officials who took part in the survey. The following section will examine the responses of the officials related to various policies and programmes available for the female entrepreneurs.

Methods to Increase Female Entrepreneurship

Respondents were asked for their recommendations to improve female entrepreneurship in Kerala. The government and NGO officials shared many ideas about how to promote the growth of female entrepreneurship. Only one government official believed that the government provides sufficient incentives and that women fail to utilise these incentives. The responses from the officials can be classified into four areas: (i) funding allocation; (ii) training programme implementation; (iii) market outlet facilitation; and (iv) additional government activities.

Funding allocation Half of the government officials were critical of the government's level of funding and their approach to handling these funds. A government official stated that the incentives for women target low-income groups, are very meagre, and are not sufficient to start and run a business. He explains:

> There are no attractive incentives for women. The government provides only small amounts as grants. A business is difficult to sustain with 10 000 to 20 000 rupees. Such a low grant is useful for small units. This leads to dwarfing of business units. Low grants force the units to be dwarfs. (Official 2)

Two officials criticised the government's funds disbursement. The funds did not reach deserving women. They stated that the loans were not used properly. A government official added that some women possibly mistake the loan as a grant and do not repay the funds. Most of the business units that accessed funds through the PMRY (Prime Minister's Rozgar Yojana) loan scheme have closed down, and there are only a handful of working units. The women involved in micro enterprises gradually quit the programmes, and eventually close their business units. Thus, fund disbursements for micro-enterprises are not as effective as the government had planned.

Training programme implementation Four of the government officials suggested that women should be trained to facilitate growth in female-owned businesses. All respondents had diverse suggestions to share. One official mentioned that education about business culture should start from within schools. Another official suggested that it is not the women who need education, but the government officials who need it in order to pass on the relevant information to women. He stated:

> Our employees are not knowledgeable. They can pass on the information to women and other members of the society only when they themselves are knowledgeable. Officials who lack awareness are also hindering the performance of business activities. (Official 5)

The government should be more careful about monitoring loan repayments, and should disburse loans only to beneficiaries who use the funds for their business. An official further elaborated that women require training and guidance to start a business. One suggestion proposed a databank of failed and successful businesses to provide information as guidance to entrepreneurs before they start a business. The government should allocate sufficient funds for training and training should use case studies from experienced entrepreneurs rather than general seminars and lectures.

Market outlet facilitation   Some officials recommended that the government should facilitate marketing outlets. One official from each group suggested that the government should conduct periodic fairs and exhibitions that allow women to sell their products and provide a suitable platform for women to attract customers.

In addition, one female official who was part of a women's development programme suggested that the government should try to collaborate with multinational companies to encourage these companies to outsource manufacturing to some female-owned enterprises. This would support female-owned businesses in India as well as solve problems related to product and services marketing. Thus, the government could take advantage of the new competition that would favour local industries.

Additional government activities   About half of the officials raised some concerns about the execution of the government programmes. All NGO officials were critical of the government's procedures. Three of the officials wanted transparency in the government's assistance and opposed the influence of political parties on government decisions. They noted that political parties interfere with government decisions and thus influence the government's financial assistance. As an official puts it:

> Political parties are a bad influence. The government officer listens to the party members, so it is difficult to allocate resources to those in need. (Official 12)

A male official also wanted more efficient interventions and criticised the communication system:

> Once there was an advertisement in the newspaper for NGOs to apply for funds. We sent in an application to receive the funds, and for days, we did not receive any reply. So, I contacted some people in Delhi to gather more information. They informed me that the government advertisement came long after the due date, so nothing could be done. (Official 15)

DISCUSSION

This chapter has considered the post-structural feminist approach, where the perceptions of the officials involved in developing and implementing programmes were analysed. The study aimed to explore the normative practices of providing policy implications in published studies without considering the agents involved in policy development and implementation. The responses from the government officials provided an insight into the perception of women in Kerala. It validates Marlow's (2002) claim that masculine identity overshadows entrepreneurial activity, that is, the gendered institutional norm treats men as superior to women. Indian society is apprehensive toward women's independence and considers men to be more efficient. In addition, some of the responses involved victim blaming, which Ahl and Marlow (2012) argued against. Women were blamed for not having sufficient skills to manage their finances and develop a business plan. In addition, a widely acclaimed constraint faced by women is their family responsibilities. This study affirmed society's expectation of women to manage household duties, which is not unique to India or other countries (see Abraham, 2000; D'Cruz, 2003; Navaprabha, 2000). Family and business responsibilities were mentioned to the study to have influenced business growth.

Furthermore, the chapter considered the safety issues encountered by women in India. Despite the many factors that contribute to a high literacy rate, better health-care system, and the high female–male sex ratio in Kerala, the women are vulnerable to physical and sexual harassment. Officials stressed the difficulties women faced when working late at night; women are susceptible to harassment when travelling at night. This is in accordance with the news reports on sexual harassment and is a reflection of the socially constructed reality of male hegemony. The social construct of the sexual domination of men over women affects women's perception of safety.

The chapter highlights gender subordination within the society. There is a common presumption among the officials that women are considered as the weaker sex. This perception of gender gap will adversely influence female entrepreneurs' ecosystem and will affect their business start-ups and growth. This study reaffirms the significance of post-structural feminism in understanding the inherent issues with policy formulation and program implementation.

IMPLICATIONS FOR POLICY-MAKERS AND FUTURE RESEARCHERS

The officials were asked to provide suggestions for increasing entrepreneurial activities among women. Their recommendations were as follows: The government should extend the loan limit since the current limit is inadequate to sustain a business. Additionally, officials could be provided with training to help them provide better services to female clients. The officials stressed the need to reduce excessive governmental regulations. They only provided suggestions to rectify the financial, managerial and marketing issues. Their observations are essential for rectifying social issues. However, further investigation is required to understand some of the male hegemonic responses to the issues faced by female entrepreneurs. Officials mentioned the need for support from men due to increasing reports of harassment among women. The response should be further investigated by the government agencies and researchers. This study also reaffirms prior research (see Ahl, 2006; Marlow, 2006), which suggests moving away from barrier-focused approaches, and focusing more on using post-structural feminism in the studies on female entrepreneurship. Researchers could also consider using other theories such as social identity theory to explore the influence of identity on the differences in perception. This is a preliminary study that highlights officials' inconsistent opinions, which can adversely affect the programme's success, and disrupt the entrepreneurship ecosystem. Hence, a remodelling of the entrepreneurial ecosystem is warranted.

LIMITATIONS

Although this study provides a few important outcomes, it has some limitations. The first is that this study interviewed only officials in a single state. Second, the sample size was small. Future studies should increase the sample size and include officials from other regions to provide a wider perspective. Third, the officials had some symmetrical and asymmetrical views to share; further research is required in this field to derive suggestions to assist female entrepreneurship and avoid any inconsistencies. Lastly, the officials should have been prompted to discuss the cultural issues in India, in particular the caste system and its influence on female entrepreneurship.

REFERENCES

Abraham, V.L. (2000). Factors influencing and shaping women entrepreneurship in Kerala. In K. Sasikumar (ed.), *Women Entrepreneurship*. New Delhi: Vikas Publishing House, pp. 181–190.

Ahl, H. (2006). Why research on women entrepreneurs needs new directions. *Entrepreneurship Theory and Practice*, 30(5), 595–621.

Ahl, H. and Marlow, S. (2012). Exploring the dynamics of gender, feminism and entrepreneurship: advancing debate to escape a dead end? *Organization*, 19(5), 543–562.

Ahl, H. and Nelson, T. (2015). How policy positions women entrepreneurs: a comparative analysis of state discourse in Sweden and the United States. *Journal of Business Venturing*, 30(2), 273–291.

Bradley, H. (2002). Gendered jobs and social inequality. In *The Polity Reader in Gender Studies*. Cambridge, UK: Polity Press, pp. 150–158.

D'Cruz, N.K. (2003). *Constraints on Women Entrepreneurship Development in Kerala: An Analysis of Familial, Social and Psychological Dimensions*. Thiruvananthapuram: Centre for Development Studies.

Department of Economics and Statistics (2016). *Gender Statistics 2014–15*. Viewed 25 March 2017, http://www.ecostat.kerala.gov.in/docs/pdf/reports/others/gender_statistics1415.pdf.

Drèze, J. and Sen, A. (2002). *India: Development and Participation*. New Delhi: Oxford University Press.

Duflo, E. (2012). Women empowerment and economic development. *Journal of Economic Literature*, 50(4), 1051–1079.

Foss, L. (2010). Research on entrepreneur networks: the case for a constructionist feminist theory perspective. *International Journal of Gender and Entrepreneurship*, 2(1), 83–102.

Hechavarria, D.M. and Ingram, A. (2014). A review of the entrepreneurial ecosystem and the entrepreneurial society in the United States: an exploration with the global entrepreneurship monitor dataset. *Journal of Business and Entrepreneurship*, 26(1), 1–35.

Henry, C., Foss, L. and Ahl, H. (2016). Gender and entrepreneurship research: a review of methodological approaches. *International Small Business Journal*, 34(3), 217–241.

Hindu, The (2016). Private buses unsafe for women in Kochi. Viewed 25 March 2017, http://www.thehindu.com/news/cities/Kochi/private-buses-unsafe-for-women-in-kochi/article5265757.ece.

Isenberg, D. (2011). *The Entrepreneurship Ecosystem Strategy as a New Paradigm for Economy Policy: Principles for Cultivating Entrepreneurship*. Babson Entrepreneurship Ecosystem Project, Babson Park, MA: Babson College.

Kerala State Planning Board (2016). *2015 Kerala Economic Review*. Viewed 25 March 2017, http://www.keralaplanningboard.org/.

Kodoth, P. and Eapen, M. (2004). Discrimination against women in Kerala engaging inductors and processes of well-being. Workshop report, Kerala's

Development: a feminist perspective, Thiruvananthapuram, Kerala, 23–25 March.

Koreen, M. (2000). Women entrepreneurs in SMEs: realizing the benefits of globalization and the knowledge-based economy: synthesis. Conference proceeding: OECD conference on 'Women entrepreneurs in SMEs: realising the benefits of globalisation and the knowledge-based economy', Paris, 29–30 November.

Kurien, J. (2000). The Kerala model: its central tendency and the 'Outlier'. In G. Parayil (ed.), *Kerala: The Development Experience: Reflections on Sustainability and Replicability*. London and New York: Zed Books, pp. 178–197.

Marlow, S. (2002). Women and self-employment: a part of or apart from theoretical construct? *International Journal of Entrepreneurship and Innovation*, 3(2), 83–91.

Marlow, S. (2006). Enterprising futures or dead-end jobs? Women, self employment and social exclusion. *International Journal of Manpower*, 27(60), 588–600.

Marlow, S. and McAdam, M. (2013). Gender and entrepreneurship: advancing debate and challenging myths; exploring the mystery of the under-performing female entrepreneur. *International Journal of Entrepreneurial Behavior & Research*, 19(1), 114–124.

Mason, C. and Brown, R. (2014). Entrepreneurial ecosystems and growth oriented entrepreneurship. OECD workshop paper. Viewed 10 November 2015, www.oecd.org/cfe/leed/entrepreneurial-ecosystems.pdf.

Mayoux, L. (2001). Jobs, gender and small enterprises: getting the policy environment rights. Working paper 15, Series on women's entrepreneurship development and gender in enterprise. Geneva: International Labour Organisation.

Mazzarol, T. (2014). Growing and sustaining entrepreneurial ecosystems: what they are and the role of government policy. Small Enterprise Association of Australia and New Zealand, SEAANZ white paper WP01-2014.

Moore, J.F. (1993). Predators and prey: a new ecology of competition. *Harvard Business Review*, 71(3), 75–83.

Narendran, R. (2012). Social risk and female entrepreneurs in Kerala, India: a preliminary assessment. *The Business Review, Cambridge*, 20(2), 51–58.

Navaprabha, J. (2000). Problems faced by women entrepreneurs in Alappuzha. In K. Sasikumar (ed.), *Women Entrepreneurship*. New Delhi: Vikas Publishing House, pp. 157–164.

Pettersson, K., Ahl, H., Berglund, K. and Tillmar, M. (2017). In the name of women? Feminist readings of policies for women's entrepreneurship in Scandinavia. *Scandinavian Journal of Management*, 33(1), 50–63.

Ramachandran, V.V. (1997). On Kerala development achievements. In J. Drèze and A. Sen (eds), *Indian Development: Selected Regional Perspectives*. Delhi: Oxford University Press, pp. 205–356.

Singh, P. (2010). We-ness and welfare: a longitudinal analysis of social development in Kerala, India. *World Development*, 39(2), 282–293.

Stam, E. (2015). Entrepreneurial ecosystems and regional policy: a sympathetic critique. *European Planning Studies*, 23(9), 1759–1769.

Yousafzai, S., Saeed, S. and Muffatto, M. (2015). Institutional theory and contextual embeddedness of women's entrepreneurial leadership: evidence from 92 countries. *Journal of Small Business Management*, 53(3), 587–604.

PART 3

Overcoming constrained performance: facilitating women entrepreneurs

9. Exploring alternative gendered social structures within entrepreneurship education: notes from a women's-only enterprise programme in the United Kingdom

Monique Boddington and Shima Barakat

Although there have been increases in recent years, women still lag behind men in terms of entrepreneurial activity (de Bruin et al., 2006; Jennings and Brush, 2013; Kelley et al., 2011). The low participation of women in comparison to men has raised concerns as an indicator of sexual inequality (Devos et al., 2003) and loss to the economy (Nixdorff and Rosen, 2010; Wilson et al., 2007). Within the high-tech sector women are represented in even lower numbers and despite 40 per cent of EU science, engineering and technology graduate students being female, only 15 per cent of high-tech businesses are women-owned (Marlow and McAdam, 2012). This chapter considers how learning interventions could contribute to engaging more women in entrepreneurship by addressing structural factors that affect women's entrepreneurial practice within an educational setting.

There is an ongoing debate about how, when, where, by whom and to whom entrepreneurship should be taught, and yet studies into the impact of entrepreneurship education and enterprise education have rarely considered how gender moderates impact and how enterprise education could be tailored for women. Measuring the impact of multiple programmes in the UK it has been shown that while enterprise education did equally increase entrepreneurial self-efficacy (a strong predicator for future entrepreneurial activity) of both men and women, post education intervention, women still displayed lower self-efficacy (Barakat et al., 2010). It has been suggested that entrepreneurship education has put women in a subordinate position, reaffirming the myth of women's underperformance and sustaining the male norm in entrepreneurship (Jones, 2015; Pettersson, 2012), leading to women being labelled as somehow at 'fault'. Education, though, can be an opportunity to develop a diversity of perspectives and act as a tool of empowerment and yet few papers have focused on gender within an entrepreneurial education context (Tegtmeier and Mitra, 2015). This chapter explores a women's-only entrepreneurial programme for post-doctoral researchers and PhD students at the University of Cambridge, UK. EnterpriseWISE aims to address the gender gap (that is, the lack of women's entrepreneurial practice compared to men's) in entrepreneurship by providing enterprise education tailored to the needs of women in science and engineering (WISE), including technology. Previous research indicated that EnterpriseWISE had a positive impact on participants' entrepreneurial self-efficacy and appetite for start-up (Barakat et al., 2012) and multiple participants have started their own enterprises. Although the programme did not have venture start-up as an objective, the realities were that ten ventures were set up from the 102 participants to date (2012–2016).

Entrepreneurship is, unquestionably, socially embedded (Davidsson, 2003; Steyaert and Katz, 2004), hence we need to consider the macro/meso environment. Cultural norms and the expectations of society are capable of limiting the exercise of choice for women entrepreneurs (Brush et al., 2009). The work of Bourdieu is used to understand the social dynamics and impact of EnterpriseWISE. In the context of habitus and reflexivity, this study explores the dynamic change facilitated by the EnterpriseWISE programme with the aim of understanding how women's-only enterprise education may help encourage more women to pursue entrepreneurial careers and further foster alternative gendered orders (for example practices associated with the feminine) within entrepreneurial practice.

ENTREPRENEURSHIP EDUCATION AND ENTERPRISEWISE

Entrepreneurship education is a growing phenomenon (Katz, 2008; Kuratko, 2005). There is no uniform approach (Neck and Greene, 2011; Vanevenhoven and Liguori, 2013) and a variety of different methodologies are used, often with different purposes and goals (Matlay, 2005; Solomon, 2007). Multiple studies have shown that women have lower entrepreneurial intentions (Chen et al., 1998; Gupta et al., 2008; Zhao et al., 2005), and lower entrepreneurial self-efficacy (Barakat et al., 2010; Boddington and Barakat, 2015; Wilson et al., 2007). Entrepreneurial self-efficacy (ESE) is an important antecedent to entrepreneurial action (Chen et al., 1998). ESE has been identified as playing an instrumental role in the new venture-creation process and a growing body of literature supports the idea that an individual's intention to start a company is formed in part by their perception of the expected outcome (Barbosa et al., 2007; Chen et al.,

1998; Zhao et al., 2005). Using ESE as a measurement of the impact of enterprise and entrepreneurship education illustrated that women demonstrated, compared to their male counterparts, lower ESE both before and after enterprise and entrepreneurship programmes (Barakat et al., 2010; Boddington and Barakat, 2015), illustrating a gap in the effectiveness of entrepreneurship education.

Designed for women and delivered completely by women, EnterpriseWISE was offered and delivered as a tailored entrepreneurship course with the express purpose of increasing skills, knowledge and confidence as well as intent in being more entrepreneurial in their approach to research and its commercial exploitation. The programme offered 36 hours of contact time spread over two weekends, one month apart, for researchers in science and technology. Sessions were delivered in both lecture style and smaller mentored groups. In terms of content, the programme covered both personal awareness and skills development as well as the key stages of the commercial exploitation of research. Gender sensitivity was sought and changes to more traditional course content were made. Entrepreneurial stereotypes and notions of success were explicitly challenged and discussion around how women can succeed in different contexts was addressed in most sessions. Alternative models of entrepreneurship and different role models were presented to the participants during the course. It has been shown that women are much more sensitive to the presence of same-gender role models (Laviolette et al., 2012). At the same time social capital development opportunities were offered.

Studies have shown that women-only programs have overwhelmingly positive outcomes for participants (Brown, 2000; Devos et al., 2003; Knight and Pritchard, 1994; Limerick et al., 1995; Ruderman and Hughes-James, 1998; Vinnicombe and Singh, 2003). For example, a survey of 1452 women in the UK showed that those who attended women-only management training, compared to mixed-sex courses, expressed their views more freely, felt more confident, trusting, comfortable, 'free to be myself', able to take risks and able to speak up. These impacts benefited more than 50 per cent of participants in each case, and in the case of confidence, 73.9 per cent said it made them feel more confident (Willis and Daisley, 2008).

It has often been reported that women-only training allows participants to feel 'safe', thereby allowing fuller participation, leading to increased gains from the course (Debebe, 2011; Limerick et al., 1995; Ruderman and Hughes-James, 1998). Unconscious gender patterns are delineated within a safe, women-only environment and may lead to the bypassing of certain traits of gender domination. Previous research into the impact of EnterpriseWISE indicated that it has a positive impact on women's ESE, more so when compared to women on other enterprise and entrepreneurship programmes (Barakat et al., 2012; Boddington and Barakat, 2015). Furthermore, there is clear indication that there is a real appetite for a women-only programme like EnterpriseWISE which has been consistently oversubscribed, whilst other programmes run within the same centre are consistently undersubscribed by women. What is it about EnterpriseWISE, as a learning intervention, that makes it more attractive to women and has a greater positive impact on women's ESE?

GENDER, FROM HABITUS TO REFLEXIVITY

An issue for women entrepreneurs, conceivably, is the structure of the social world. For Bourdieu (1985) the social world is defined by the structure and distribution of 'capital' arranged within a hierarchy. Capital is the different forms of power held by social agents, for example: economic, social, cultural, symbolic, linguistic, academic and corporeal (physical attractiveness). Women, according to Bourdieu, are not capital-accumulating subjects, instead women are capital-bearing objects whose value accrues relative to the primary group to which they belong (Lovell, 2000; Skeggs, 2004). The very concept of a female entrepreneur is contradictory to this claim (Adkins, 2000; Lawler, 2000; Skeggs, 1997). Despite criticisms, it is argued that Bourdieu's work reveals the relative autonomy of gender domination (Fowler, 2003).

Habitus is central to naturalizing gender domination. Habitus is the strategy-generating propensities which enable agents to deal with a situation and is an unconscious embodied phenomenon. This system of dispositions mediates an individual's actions which allows for symbolic violence, a form of domination upon a social agent, complicity (Bourdieu, 1992). The prominence of male role models and stereotypes has been cited as a reason for women lagging behind in terms of entrepreneurial activity (Gupta et al., 2009). Entrepreneurship discourse has been heavily criticized for its underlying masculine character (Bourne, 2010; De Bruin et al., 2006) and the stereotypical characterization of entrepreneurs as an embodiment of masculine traits (Ahl, 2006; Marlow et al., 2009). The unconscious embodiment of entrepreneurship as the masculine enforces a system of dispositions, which mediate an individual's actions. Women do not become entrepreneurs because they associate being an entrepreneur with the masculine: offering alternative role models may shift and open up the field.

Habitus contains a temporal element, as it is a result of the incorporation of regularities and tendencies of the world and of embodied practices which, by necessity are temporal, expressing and anticipating tendencies and regularities. Thus, within habitus there is a protention which allows for the potential of change (Bourdieu, 1992). Alternative models of entrepreneurship can cause a shift, which in turn may encourage more women to follow entrepreneurial career routes. However, the destabilizing of gender relations on one level may entrench other patterns (McNay, 1999) and habitus continues to work long after the reasons for its emergences have been dislodged (Bourdieu, 1990). Bourdieu forces us to be a realist in understanding the difficulties of change (Krais, 1993), though he always recognized that there are women who are 'lucid outsiders' who break through the habitus of the powerless female at whatever the cost (Fowler, 2003).

The detraditionalization of gender has occurred through the movement of feminine habitus into different fields of action (for example, the workplace), signalling an increasingly reflexive nature to gender identity (McNay, 1999). Reflexivity, in gender, arises through the negotiation of discrepancies in fields of action (Adkins, 2003), fields being the structured systems of individuals and institutions that are structured internally by power relations (Bourdieu, 1993). A women's-only programme, arguably, could allow a change in field by removing women from their day-to-day lives but further allowing certain norms of behaviour to be nullified through the women's-only nature of the programme and content. This process of renegotiation is not straightforward and may not lead to critical deconstruction of norms, habits and rules; reflexivity may not mean liberal freedoms but be tied to new arrangements of gender (Adkins, 2003). By giving women a safe and open place to explore alternative models of entrepreneurship it may allow for an alternative gendered order in entrepreneurship and in turn encourage them to consider entrepreneurial career paths. Reflexivity is a key element of this, 'as the ability to reflect with perspicuity upon the previous "givens" of all dimensions of social structure in relation to subjectivity, to the point of further substantiating transformative social change that makes such reflexivity possible' (Adams, 2006, p. 516). It has been asserted that reflexivity is increasingly a feature of self-identity in the late-modern era (Archer, 2012; Beck, 1992; Giddens, 1992). An increase in communication (Heelas, 1996) has led to a relativizing of cultural and individual practices as we are increasingly exposed to others (Gergen, 1991) and an ebbing-away of tradition and social structures (Beck and Beck-Gernsheim, 2002), though it is argued that this fails to account for the restraints on agency which persist in contemporary societies (Adams, 2006).

Bourdieu always insisted his theory of practice was not one of total determinism allowing that humans possess reflexivity (Fowler, 2003), for example at times of crises with the lack of a future, 'there is the relative autonomy of the symbolic order which in all circumstances, especially in periods where expectations and chances fall out of line, can leave a margin of freedom for political action aimed at reopening the space of the possible' (Bourdieu, 2000, p. 234). Habitus is a generative rather than determining structure and social action is thus neither fully determined nor fully willed (Crespi, 1989). In the literature, we see the emergence of a middle ground in which it is recognized that, through habitus, gender relations are controlled and restrained but that within modern society a reflexivity is becoming more prevalent that makes it possible to renegotiate gender relations, though this is clearly not straightforward and comes with many pitfalls. Within this framework, it is posited that by controlling the field of education, by creating a women-only environment, it is possible to allow for a greater amount of reflexivity and thus renegotiate habitus to present an alternative gendered order of entrepreneurial practice, at least within the classroom.

METHODOLOGY

EnterpriseWISE was delivered for women working in research and early career managerial positions in science, engineering and technology. EnterpriseWISE was advertised to women at the early stages of their academic careers, considering their career options, to come and find out more about entrepreneurship. The women who attended were not necessarily aspiring entrepreneurs. Twenty-three individuals attended the programme in 2012 and 30 in 2013. The majority of the individuals who attended the programme in 2012 and 2013 were graduate students or early career researchers at the University of Cambridge. Most of the women who applied had not shown interest or participated in other entrepreneurial programmes available through the centre and also displayed lower ESE than women on our other programmes (Barakat et al., 2012). To understand the impact of EnterpriseWISE, within the context of the work of Bourdieu's (1990) theory of practice and reflexivity (Archer, 2012), a qualitative approach was used. Semi-structured interviews were used to allow for an openness to responses (Wengraf, 2001).

A cross-sectional sample was selected across different subject areas, career stages and backgrounds. In total, six individuals (one postdoc, two PhD students, two master's students and one local business woman) who attended the 2012 programme and three postdocs who attended the 2013 programme were interviewed. Interviews were conducted primarily face to face. Skype was used on two occasions for the 2012 group when it was not possible to meet in person. All interviews were conducted roughly two months after the programme. A second set of interviews was conducted 14 months after the programme on participants of the 2012 programme, six individuals (two had previously been interviewed) who had taken part in the 2012 programme, roughly 14 months later; the aim of these interviews was to the gauge the more long-term impact of EnterpriseWISE.

The aim of the interviews was to understand and analyse the impact EnterpriseWISE had on individuals' understanding of entrepreneurship and future career plans, and personal reflections regarding EnterpriseWISE. All interviews were transcribed and analysed in NVivo using content analysis. Following Strauss and Corbin (1998), the transcripts were first open-coded and then reassessed during a second analytical phase to align common themes.

DATA ANALYSIS

Changing the Field

EnterpriseWISE was run by women for women. It was noted earlier that it has often been reported that women-only training allows participants to feel safe, thereby allowing fuller participation, leading to increased gains from the course. By allowing a change in field, by taking subjects out of the context of their daily life, it makes it possible to renegotiate gender relations, theoretically. An overarching theme of participants' reflections of EnterpriseWISE was how an open and safe environment was created, in which individuals felt comfortable; for example, participants could speak their mind:

> It promoted speech, you know, women talk all the time and this was a big opportunity for me to speak and you don't get these opportunities elsewhere, and this was an environment where you could speak your mind, you didn't have to mask it . . . One could bring up your issues, one could bring up new ideas, freely discuss them and, you know, these people were perfect strangers.

In a mixed environment: 'you have to act in certain way around men, when it was just women it was possible to be yourself'. Making the course women-only facilitated a change in the behaviour of individuals. For some women, this was a reason for choosing the course, because it would offer them an environment in which they did not feel the need to self-censor:

> . . . so I was doubting myself a lot due to my own personal experience, I wanted to find out in a very safe environment so EnterpriseWISE, I read through the description of the course and it seemed to offer the security that I needed to

explore myself so that the first reason, that was the reason why I chose the course.

Not all participants were originally attracted by the women's-only element of the course. Two of the individuals interviewed from the 2012 programme expressed how they had been cynical about this element of EnterpriseWISE. However, they found their worries unfounded and that the programme celebrated difference and individuality over a 'women against men' viewpoint: 'It made me, I think celebrate the fact that we are different individually and as women we can give'.

EnterpriseWISE also aimed to attract women to entrepreneurship by breaking certain stereotypical views of the subject. Even women who had already set up their own businesses struggled to view themselves as entrepreneurs:

> I have my own business, and it's not my first business I have set up, and it's not the first society I have set up, but before going on that course I did not think of myself as an entrepreneur.

Entrepreneurship was for the most part associated by participants with financially motivated men or sleek business professionals:

> Men who like to make lots of money, people who know things about business models and finance, things that I didn't necessarily know much about. And more sort of, ambitious money focus, wanting to grow a large company that will be worth millions.

Part of the course aims were to break away from stereotypical views of who entrepreneurs are and what they do. For example, at the most simplistic level, entrepreneurship is not just about financial gains: 'well I can have a business but we can still have a social part to it and if we wanted it doesn't have to be'.

EnterpriseWISE participants were introduced to multiple different women entrepreneurs with the aim of encouraging entrepreneurial intentions. Within a safe environment it was possible for these women to build new categories of entrepreneurship and a different understanding of what an entrepreneur is – one more aligned to themselves:

> I think that it is difficult, at least for me and maybe for women in general, to see ourselves as entrepreneurs, as business people, a lot of people that we see and a lot of people that we interact with and do that kind of thing are men and so the fact it was taught entirely by women as well was really valuable because it kind of makes you look at them, all these people are doing it and so maybe I am one of these people.

A Reflexive Space

The interviews identified certain *a priori* beliefs held by the participants. Individuals voiced a lack of self-confidence. Individuals felt they lacked business skills and the ability to set up their own enterprise. This was accompanied by a fear of being too inexperienced to move forward with an idea, a fear of taking a risk (which was connected to a fear of failure, though not necessarily connected to an expectation of failure), and also a fear of success and the burden of success. Within a women's-only environment, participants felt they could embrace their own talents and overcome *a priori* assumptions about themselves. EnterpriseWISE provided an open and safe environment in which they could be reflexive:

> It has the aspect of relating personality towards entrepreneurship . . . it gave me a sense that a person like me who has never stepped beyond serious research circles could actually come out and talk to people and create new ideas, it gave me that confidence.

Reflexivity enabled women in different ways. One individual used the skills she gained during EnterpriseWISE and her newfound confidence to ask for a raise to match the salaries of her male colleagues. Recognizing the value of their own skills was important in boosting confidence. The boost in entrepreneurial self-efficacy the women experienced on EnterpriseWISE helped the women deal with and overcome their fear of failure.

> I think before the course I was very much not the type to take the risk of an extremely novel product, now I think I am willing to take my chances. More of a gambler, it is not that, I would say I have become more of a reasonable gambler.

This may be symbolic of a delineating of gender norms as habitus is delineated due to this reflexive inward-looking. Providing a reflexive space and presenting alternative role models facilitated a turnaround in participants' attitudes towards themselves, and also towards entrepreneurship. Entrepreneurship became a tool of empowerment, giving women a strategy to achieve what they wanted:

> This had a totally different twist to it, it had the aspect of relating personality towards entrepreneurship and, you know for me take off the pressure. It was not business, it is a quality of mind that enables to you to do anything that you want. So I look at it from that perspective it is kind of quality that anybody should have irrespective of actually going on to a business or not, even doing research should have, the person should have entrepreneurial characteristics.

From Habitus to Reflexivity

Participants began EnterpriseWISE with certain preconceptions about themselves and entrepreneurship that had negatively impacted their confidence, their work and their entrepreneurial practice. The content and environment of the course were not solely responsible for the end results; participants were also driven by their own motivational factors and expertise in a wide remit of specialized areas. Table 9.1 details the *a priori* issues, motivational factors and impact the course had on the individuals interviewed from the EnterpriseWISE 2012 and 2013 cohorts. EnterpriseWISE acted like a catalyst boosting confidence and enabling participants to start moving forward in their entrepreneurial aims.

For EnterpriseWISE to truly be a success it needs to have a longer-term impact. Habitus is only ever realized within a particular context or field (McNay, 1999). A second set of interviews was conducted on the 2012 EnterpriseWISE cohort, 14 months after the programme to see if the programme had any lasting impact once the women went back into their daily lives. Confidence remained a major theme, for example the confidence to be more entrepreneurial in different contexts:

> I am more entrepreneurial in the approach that I take to my research – I take over initiatives, try and take new directions. You see confidence is not consistence in all levels. I feel confident about what I do.

Since the course, in practical terms, the individuals have continued to engage with entrepreneurship: one individual discussed setting up her second company; another discussed joining and becoming president of an entrepreneurship society; and another was intending to take part in another entrepreneurial education programme. Central to this was empowerment through recognizing their own skills.

Habitus is encoded with us, it is an embodied experience that we learn through socialization and the learning process, beginning in childhood, a process that is naturalized over history. Habitus is an open-ended system and reflexivity arises through the renegotiation of discrepancies in the field, provoked by conflict and tension. EnterpriseWISE provided women with a change of field which gave them the space to reflexively renegotiate their understanding of themselves and entrepreneurship to a great enough extent to delineate habitus sufficiently to have long-term impact. Despite many changes over the last decades, it is still difficult to dislodge entrenched gender relations (McNay, 1999). By creating an artificial field it was possible to delineate the impact of habitus. Each participant brought their own *a priori* assumptions which acted as barriers to entrepreneurial

Table 9.1 Examples of participant issues and motivations, and recognized results from participants of the Enterprise WISE 2012 and 2013 programme

	A priori issues	Motivational factors	End results
1	Over-think things, never getting in a productive direction. Fear of success – responsibility, life change.	Bring academic science to the public. Help other people do the same.	Reassessment of direction, look at things that need doing and start. Getting help putting together business plan, will be pitching for investment in next 6 months.
2	Lack of confidence impacting networking.	To work for self. Drive by creation, process of making an idea reality.	More networking. Talking to people about her business.
3	Lack of knowledge on business and business-averse. Inexperience.	Drive innovation in the Arab region. Social enterprise.	Less business-averse – more confidence in handling business affairs. Less fear of risk.
4	Issues with networking. Confidence meeting new people.	Applying science to business.	Running own business, changed pricing. Networking.
5	Lack of confidence. Fear from bad experiences.	Entrepreneurial intent. Social enterprise.	Confidence boost and change of outlook. Change of attitude and relationship with colleagues.

Table 9.1 (continued)

	A priori issues	Motivational factors	End results
6	Lack of experience. Lack of contacts.	Business application of science.	Thinking more creatively. Gaining experience for next steps. New contacts.
7	Associated entrepreneurship with men. Lack of confidence.	See particular things and want to make them happen.	Changing understanding of what an entrepreneur is. Taking self more seriously. Better idea how to start a business.
8	Issues with colleagues. Lack of confidence.	Explore ways to progress career. Make something out of research.	How to manage colleagues. Boost to confidence and self-esteem.
9	Association of business with men. Lack of knowledge on how to progress career.	Entrepreneurship or industry application of research.	New contacts. More effective in leadership role. More assertive.

activity. The women who attended EnterpriseWISE had significantly lower entrepreneurial self-efficacy compared to other women attending entrepreneurial programmes across Europe (Barakat ct al., 2012).

Misconceptions of what entreprenurship is, who entrepreneurs are and what entrepreneurs do stopped the women who attended EnterpriseWISE from thinking that entrepreneurship was for them. One can posit that this is the product of socialization through their shared experiences in academia. EnterpriseWISE participants, despite their research record and expertise had very low self-confidence, which could also be a pre-selection bias: a women's-only programme may attract certain individuals. For these individuals, EnterpriseWISE had the desired effect. The women's-only environment provided a change in field that allowed these women to renegotiate their understanding of entrepreneurship and themselves. Figure 9.1 draws together these findings: the *a priori* issues that attracted the women to the programme and blocked their own practice of entrepreneurship; the motivational factors that drive the women in their own careers and towards a renegotiation of entrepreneurship and the impact of EnterpriseWISE.

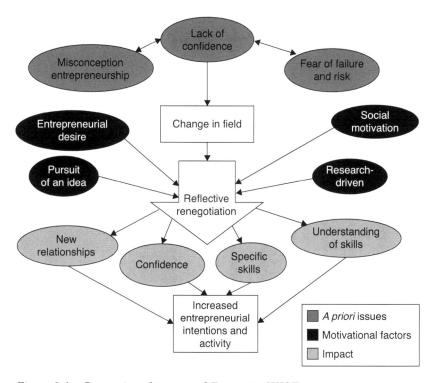

Figure 9.1   Dynamics of impact of EnterpriseWISE

Obviously a shift in habitus takes more than a single short programme delivered to a handful of women; however, it did allow these women enough of a separation to facilitate long-term impact. Living in a more reflexive age (Archer, 2012; Beck, 1992; Giddens, 1992) it is, arguably, possible for these women to work against social norms of habitus and also make for a more accepting society for women who are breaking social norms, especially since reflexivity makes further transformative social change possible (Adams, 2006). Programmes like EnterpriseWISE can only ever be part of the solution and there is always going to be a need for critical social change to allow for real assimilation.

CONCLUSIONS

EnterpriseWISE significantly increased the entrepreneurial self-efficacy of the women on the programme (Barakat et al., 2012) and reached a population that would not otherwise seek to engage with entrepreneurship or such a training course (indicated by the numbers of women attracted to the courses as compared to other entrepreneurial programmes). Ten ventures were set up from the 102 participants to date (2012–2016), three from the 2013 cohort alone. This research has sought to understand what caused this impact and to understand in greater depth how learning interventions could help more women to enter entrepreneurial careers. The three elements that appear to be key to this impact are: the creation of a safe environment within which women can be reflexive; providing alternative role models; and being for women, led only by women. This research does have certain limitations. Ideally, research into the impact of any enterprise education should use control groups, but on this occasion it was not practically possible. This research sampled a cross-section of participants from two cohorts; ideally, it would have been more robust to track all participants, but this was not possible for logistical reasons. The results here are based on a small sample size and from one programme which focused on a very specific demographic (that is, WISE researchers) and therefore it is not proven whether this type of programme would be impactful across different contexts. This research also highlights the need for much more practice-theory-driven research. Given the complexities of both the work of Bourdieu and self-efficacy, further research could address how social norms and self-efficacy relate to each other. Furthermore, one has to be careful in promoting women's education to, by association, support a viewpoint that somehow women are at fault and therefore need extra help. This was never the intention of the programme and it has been shown that for some women the programme was highly impactful.

This research illustrates a programme with high practical impact for women in science and engineering which education and training practitioners can draw inspiration from. The value of this is in adding to our understanding of the impact of educational interventions in terms of practice, which is ultimately the aim: to design, deliver and resource programmes that provide the desired result, in this case increasing the number of women in high-tech businesses. Clearly women's-only programmes are not the final answer in increasing the numbers of women entrepreneurs and should not be at a cost to women attending other programmes, economic activity and policy-making or allow us to forget the need for larger critical changes to culture to allow for changes to the configuration of gender relations. It is important to acknowledge and foster different gendered practices within entrepreneurship. Education has a key role in this, and in this context, by not questioning the social structure behind entrepreneurial practice, we are reaffirming the structure; and by not offering alternatives, we naturalize one dominant gendered order.

REFERENCES

Adams, M. (2006). Hybridizing habitus and reflexivity: towards an understanding of contemporary identity? *Sociology*, 40(3), 511–528.

Adkins, L. (2000). Objects of innovation: post-occupational reflexivity and re-traditionalizations of gender. In S. Ahmed, J. Kilby, M. McNeil and B. Skeggs (eds), *Transformations: Thinking through Feminism*. London: Routledge, pp. 259–272.

Adkins, L. (2003). Reflexivity: freedom or habit of gender? *Theory, Culture and Society*, 20(6), 21–42.

Ahl, H. (2006). Why research on women entrepreneurs needs new directions. *Entrepreneurship Theory and Practice*, 30(5), 595–621.

Archer, M.S. (2012). *The Reflexive Imperative in Late Modernity*. Cambridge, UK: Cambridge University Press.

Barakat, S., McLellan, R., Winfield, S., Ihasz, O. and Vyakarnam, S. (2010). *Same Programme, Different Students: Same or Different Self-efficacy Effects?* Proceedings of ISBE2010 Conference, London. Barnsley, UK: Institute for Small Business and Entrepreneurship.

Barakat, S., Rigozzi, M.K., Boddington, M. and McLellan, R. (2012). *Enterprise WISE: Making WISE Women More Enterprising?* Proceedings of ISBE2012 Conference, Dublin. Barnsley, UK: Institute for Small Business and Entrepreneurship.

Barbosa, S., Gerhardt, M. and Kickul, J. (2007). The role of cognitive style and risk preference on entrepreneurial self-efficacy and entrepreneurial intentions. *Journal of Leadership and Organizational Studies*, 13(4), 86–104.

Beck, U. (1992). *Risk Society*. London: Sage.

Beck, U. and Beck-Gernsheim, E. (2002). *Individualization: Institutionalized Individualism and its Social and Political Consequences*. London: Sage.

Boddington, M. and Barakat, S. (2015). Entrepreneurial self-efficacy as a measurement of entrepreneurship education: understanding programme affects and demographic variability. *Frontiers of Entrepreneurship Research*, 35(16), art. 7.

Bourdieu, P. (1985). The social space and the genesis of groups. *Theory and Society*, 14, 423–444.

Bourdieu, P. (1990). *The Logic of Practice*. Cambridge, UK: Polity Press.

Bourdieu, P. (1992). *An Invitation to Reflexive Sociology*. Cambridge, UK: Polity.

Bourdieu, P. (1993). *The Field of Cultural Production*. Cambridge, UK: Polity.

Bourdieu, P. (2000). *Pascalian Mediation*. Cambridge, UK: Polity.

Bourne, K.A. (2010). The paradox of gender equality: an entrepreneurial case study from Sweden. *International Journal of Gender and Entrepreneurship*, 2(1), 10–26.

Brown, R. (2000). Personal and professional development programmes for women: paradigm and paradox. *International Journal for Academic Development*, 5(1), 68–74.

Brush, C.G., de Bruin, A. and Welter, F. (2009). A gender-aware framework for women's entrepreneurship. *International Journal of Gender and Entrepreneurship*, 1(1), 8–24.

Chen, C.C., Greene, P.G. and Crick, A. (1998). Does entrepreneurial self-efficacy distinguish entrepreneurs from managers? *Journal of Business Venturing*, 13, 295–316.

Crespi, F. (1989). *Social Action and Power*. Oxford: Blackwell.

Davidsson, P. (2003). The domain of entrepreneurship research: some suggestions. *Advances in Entrepreneurship, Firm Emergence and Growth*, 6(3), 315–372.

Debebe, G. (2011). Creating a safe environment for women's leadership transformation. *Journal of Management Education*, 35(5), 679–712.

De Bruin, A., Brush, C.G. and Welter, F. (2006). Introduction to the special issue: towards building cumulative knowledge on women's entrepreneurship. *Entrepreneurship: Theory and Practice*, 30(5), 585–593.

Devos, A., Mclean, J. and O'Hara, P. (2003). The potential of women's programmes to generate institutional change. Unpublished conference paper, available at http://www.academia.edu/772383/The_potential_of_womens_programmes_to_genera te_institutional_change.

Fowler, B. (2003). Reading Pierre Bourdieu's *Masculine Domination*: notes towards an intersectional analysis of gender, culture and class. *Cultural Studies*, 17(3–4), 468–94.

Gergen, K. (1991). *The Saturated Self*. New York: Basic Books.

Giddens, A. (1992). *The Transformation of Intimacy*. Cambridge, UK: Polity Press.

Gupta, V.K., Turban, D.B. and Bhawe, N.M. (2008). The effect of gender stereotype activation on entrepreneurial intentions. *Journal of Applied Psychology*, 93(5), 1053–1061.

Gupta, V.K., Turban, D.B., Wasti, S.A. and Sikdar, A. (2009). The role of gender stereotypes in perceptions of entrepreneurs and intentions to become an entrepreneur. *Entrepreneurship Theory and Practice*, 33(2), 397–417.

Heelas, P. (1996). Detraditionalization and its rivals. In P. Heelas, S. Lash and P. Morris (eds), *Detradtitionalization*. Oxford: Blackwell, pp. 1–20.

Jennings, J.E. and Brush, C.G. (2013). Research on women entrepreneurs: challenges to (and from) the broader entrepreneurship literature? *Academy of Management Annals*, 7(1), 663–715.

Jones, S. (2015). 'You would expect the successful person to be the man': gendered symbolic violence in UK HE entrepreneurship education. *International Journal of Gender and Entrepreneurship*, 7(3), 303–320.

Katz, J.A. (2008). Fully mature but not fully legitimate: a different perspective on the state of entrepreneurship education. *Journal of Small Business Management*, 46(4), 550–566.

Kelley, D.J., Bosmas, N. and Amorós, J.E. (2011). The global entrepreneurship monitor: 2010 global report. Wellesley, MA: Babson College.

Knight, J. and Pritchard, S. (1994). Women's development programs: 'No, we're not colour consultants!' In M. Tanton (ed.), *Women in Management: A Developing Presence*. London: Routledge, pp. 42–62.

Krais, B. (1993). Gender and symbolic violence. In C. Calhoun, E. Lipuma and M. Postone (eds), *Bourdieu: Critical Perspectives*. Cambridge, UK: Polity Press, pp. 156–177.

Kuratko, D.F. (2005). The emergence of entrepreneurship education: development, trends, and challenges. *Entrepreneurship Theory and Practice*, 29(5), 577–598.

Laviolette, E.M., Radu Lefebvre, M. and Brunel, O. (2012). The impact of story bound entrepreneurial role models on self-efficacy and entrepreneurial intention. *International Journal of Entrepreneurial Behavior and Research*, 18(6), 720–742.

Lawler, S. (2000). *Mothering the Self: Mothers, Daughters, Subjects*. London: Routledge.

Limerick, B., Heywood, E. and Ehrich, L.C. (1995). Women-only management courses: are they appropriate in the 1990s? *Asia Pacific Journal of Human Resources*, 33(2), 81–92.

Lovell, T. (2000). Thinking feminism with and against Bourdieu. *Feminist Theory* 1(1), 11–32.

Marlow, S. and McAdam, M. (2012). Analyzing the influence of gender upon high-technology venturing within the context of business incubation. *Entrepreneurship Theory and Practice*, 36(4), 655–676.

Marlow, S., Henry, C. and Carter, S. (2009). Exploring the impact of gender upon women's business ownership: introduction. *International Small Business Journal*, 27(2), 139–148.

Matlay, H. (2005). Entrepreneurship education in UK business schools: conceptual, contextual and policy considerations. *Journal of Small Business and Enterprise Development*, 12(4), 627–643.

McNay, L. (1999). Gender, habitus and the field: Pierre Bourdieu and the limits of reflexivity. *Theory, Culture and Society*, 16(1), 95–117.

Neck, H.M. and Greene, P.G. (2011). Entrepreneurship education: known worlds and new frontiers. *Journal of Small Business Management*, 49(1), 55–70.

Nixdorff, J. and Rosen, T. (2010). The glass ceiling women face: an examination and proposals for development of future women entrepreneurs. *New England Journal of Entrepreneurship*, October, 71–86.

Pettersson, K. (2012). Support for women's entrepreneurship: a Nordic spectrum. *International Journal of Gender and Entrepreneurship*, 4(1), 4–19.

Ruderman, M. and Hughes-James, M. (1998). Leadership development across race and gender. In C. McCauley, R. Moxley and E. Van Velsor (eds), *The Center for Creative Leadership Handbook of Leadership Development*. San Francisco, CA: Jossey-Bass, pp. 271–303.

Skeggs, B. (1997). *Formations of Class and Gender*. London: Sage.

Skeggs, B. (2004). Context and background: Pierre Bourdieu's analysis of class, gender and sexuality. In L. Adkins and B. Skeggs (eds), *Feminism after Bourdieu*. Oxford: Blackwell, pp. 19–34.

Solomon, G. (2007). An examination of entrepreneurship education in the United States. *Journal of Small Business and Enterprise Development*, 14(2), 168–182.

Steyaert, C. and Katz, J. (2004). Reclaiming the space of entrepreneurship in society: geographical, discursive and social dimensions. *Entrepreneurship and Regional Development*, 16(3), 179–196.

Strauss, A. and Corbin, J. (1998). *Basics of Qualitative Research: Techniques and Procedures for Developing Grounded Theory*. London: Sage.

Tegtmeier, S. and Mitra, J. (2015). Gender perspectives on university education and entrepreneurship: a conceptual overview. *International Journal of Gender and Entrepreneurship*, 7(3), 254–271.

Vanevenhoven, J. and Liguori, E. (2013). The impact of entrepreneurship education: introducing the entrepreneurship education project. *Journal of Small Business Management*, 51(3), 315–328.

Vinnicombe, S. and Singh, V. (2003). Women-only management training : an essential part of women's leadership development. *Journal of Change Management*, 3(4), 294–306.

Wengraf, T. (2001). *Qualitative Research Interviewing: Biographic Narrative and Semi-Structured Methods*. Thousand Oaks, CA: Sage.

Willis, L. and Daisley, J. (2008). Women's reactions to women-only training. *Women in Management Review*, 12(2), 56–60.

Wilson, F., Kickul, J. and Marlino, D. (2007). Gender, entrepreneurial self-efficacy, and entrepreneurial career intentions: implications for entrepreneurship. *Entrepreneurship Theory and Practice*, 31(3), 387–406.

Zhao, H., Siebert, S.E. and Hills, G.E. (2005). The mediating role of self-efficacy in the development of entrepreneurial intentions. *Journal of Applied Psychology*, 90(6), 1265–1272.

10. Bridging the entrepreneurial gender gap through social protection among women small-scale traders in Kenya

Anne Kamau, Paul Kamau, Daniel Muia, Harun Baiya and Jane Ndung'u

Past research on female entrepreneurship has largely focused on financial performance and growth of women's businesses (Hughes et al., 2012). Consequently, there have been efforts to enhance women's businesses through micro-credit and micro-financing support (ILO, 2008) with the expectation that this would increase women's visibility and business growth. This chapter argues that investment in social protection is necessary for advancement and growth of women's enterprises. Thus, entrepreneurship is not just about the 'economic act of wealth creation', but a broader aspect of economic and social development.

The literature on entrepreneurship depicts women's businesses as being less successful than men's business. According to Blomqvist et al. (2014), women start and own fewer businesses than men. They also have smaller and largely informal businesses which have lower sales turnover and lower success rate (Minniti and Naude, 2010). Although this may be true, the lack of comparable international data on men and women owned and controlled businesses means that women's entrepreneurship is not fully understood (OECD, 2012). This is especially the case for women small-scale traders whose businesses are small, not registered, and operate in temporary or semi-permanent premises. The lack of data is even more glaring when the women operate businesses in the informal settlements which are considered illegal and are often left out in urban planning. Thus, a woman small-scale trader operating in an urban informal settlement is likely to remain invisible, marginalized and excluded from mainstream national services, including social protection coverage.

Many women start businesses out of necessity with the need to survive being the primary motivator (Naituli et al., 2006; Minniti and Naude,

2010; OECD, 2012). Thus, although wealth creation is important in entrepreneurship (Rindova et al., 2009), business growth and profit maximization are often not the primary motives for women's engagement in business (Kamau et al., 2015b). In spite of this, women-owned businesses have higher exit rates compared to those of men (Minniti and Naude, 2010), partly due to the social set-up in which women operate (Maina and Mwiti, 2016) and the different industrial and geographic contexts that provide varying opportunities and constraints for women's businesses (Kalnins and Williams, 2014). The imbalances between men's and women's businesses are complex and include human, financial and social capital (Blomqvist et al., 2014). Hence, efforts to promote women's enterprises should address these imbalances and ensure that businesses started and run by women survive. Providing social assistance to women, particularly health insurance, can lead to improved productivity of women's businesses (Tenkorang, 2001; OECD, 2012) as well as cushion women from an involuntary exit from the businesses.

In this chapter we demonstrate that increasing women's entrepreneurial performance requires a focus beyond financial inclusion and profit maximization. Women entrepreneurs require access to affordable social protection services to cushion their businesses against unexpected economic and social shocks. The chapter focuses on women small-scale traders in Nairobi's urban informal settlements and explores the role that women's social networks can play in promoting their access to social protection.

URBAN INFORMAL SETTLEMENTS

Urban informal settlements (also known as slums) are considered 'informal' because they are built outside the legal planning framework (Bassett et al., 2003). There is no clear definition of what constitutes an informal settlement (Kinyanjui, 2010; RoK, 2012). They are, however, increasingly the norm in Africa and in many other developing countries where the need for urban housing for the poor cannot be matched with delivery of formal housing (NUSP, 2016). Informal settlements are characterized by high and uncontrolled population densities; limited or poor access to basic urban services such as water, sanitation, electricity and good transport; inadequate infrastructure and dwellings; and unsuitable environments (Bassett et al., 2003; RoK, 2012). They also have poor access to health and education facilities (Bassett et al., 2003).

In the mid 2010s, more than half of the world's population lived in towns and cities, and many people ended up living in the informal areas due to lack of affordable housing and problems in urban governance

(Ohlsson, 2013). In most countries in sub-Saharan Africa, over half of the urban population (61.7 per cent) lives in 'informal' settlements (Oxfam, 2009a; UN-Habitat, 2015). In Kenya, about 15 per cent of the urban population (1 801 699 people) live in informal settlements, mostly in Nairobi. More than one-third of Nairobi's population live in informal settlements (RoK, 2012). The informal settlements covered in our study (Kibera, Mukuru, Mathare, Korogocho and Kawangware) are among the largest in Kenya and Africa (Mutisya and Yarime, 2011; Desgroppes and Taupin, 2012).

Slums are seen as reflections of urban poverty and urban informality (Gulyani et al., 2014) and as places of disease and criminality (Bassett et al., 2003). Nonetheless, informal settlements are home to many ordinary citizens (Kinyanjui, 2012) who are placed there due to their low socio-economic conditions and who genuinely earn a living in these settlements (McAdam, 2013). Kinyanjui (2016) observes that a large subaltern population is emerging in countries in the global South that lives in slums and ekes out its livelihood in the informal economy. Living in urban informal settlements is gendered. In several sub-Saharan countries, men outnumber women in urban areas due to the gender-selective rural–urban migration, with Kenya having highly unbalanced sex ratios (Tacoli, 2012).

Female Entrepreneurs in Urban Informal Settlements' Informal Economy

In sub-Saharan Africa, the informal economy occupies about 66 per cent of the labour force, particularly in micro and small enterprises. In Kenya, the informal economy is the largest employer and makes up about 80 per cent of Kenya's workforce (Taddese, 2014). Employment in the sector increased by 6 per cent from 11 846 persons in 2014 to 12 560 persons in 2015 (RoK, 2016). However, the actual number of men and women employed in the informal sector is not available, partly because national government statistics often do not capture the activities of women working in economic informality and such data are not disaggregated by gender (Kinyanjui, 2016) and/or by region. Women constitute an important constituency of the urban population and the majority are in the informal economy (*ibid*). They outnumber men in the informal sector (Charmes, 2012) and make up the largest proportion of vulnerable informal workers (Rockefeller Foundation, 2013). In Kenya, women-owned micro enterprises account for over 48 per cent of all small and microenterprises and contribute to about 20 per cent of Kenya's gross domestic product (Maina and Mwiti, 2016). Women in the slums are more likely than men to be unemployed (Oxfam, 2009b), hence the increased feminization of poverty in the urban informal settlements (Kamau et al., 2015a). Furthermore, women's businesses in the informal areas are likely to be smaller and to have lower success rates compared to those in the formal urban areas.

Holmes and Scott (2016) observe that individuals in informal employment include employers and employees in informal enterprises, the self-employed (who own informal businesses), and those supporting family businesses. The informal sector includes seasonal workers and workers on short-term contracts who often may not qualify for formal social security coverage (MacKellar, 2009). Women small-scale traders (WSSTs) are part of the informal economy's workers and some have one or more employees (Kamau et al., 2015a), but many businesses are owner-operated. Many of the small-scale businesses are not registered and are operated in temporary or semi-permanent places like those in open-air markets, in front of residential houses or on the streets. The businesses that are registered are mainly those which are operated in permanent premises. Hence, most small-scale businesses lack legal recognition and they are thus considered risky by many financial institutions. As noted, informal-sector workers are mobile, scattered and difficult to reach with social protection coverage (MacKellar, 2009).

The urban informal economy is diverse and includes a wide range of activities like street vending, domestic work, home-based enterprises and waste collection (Brown and McGranahan, 2016). Other activities include hawking, market trade, craftsmanship, manufacturing and repairs (Kinyanjui, 2016). These types of entrepreneurial activities are characteristic of those performed by women in our study. Globally, women are largely in service and retail trade, a factor attributed to flexibility preferences and prioritization of household production (McAdam, 2013). This pattern is common in informal settlements and women tend to concentrate on 'gendered female-businesses' that are home-based or operated close to their homes. Ohlsson (2013) observes that women are likely to work within their communities and to combine income generation with domestic work. This, according to Moser (1993), is tied to the triple roles of reproduction, production and community engagement that women in poor areas perform. Given that African cities are increasingly becoming urban, it should be expected that informal businesses will increase and that the number of women engaged in informal work in the informal settlements will rise. Hence, their access to formal social protection should be a major area of concern.

The Social Protection Gap

In most developing countries, informal workers are excluded from social protection schemes (Hu and Stewart, 2009) like formal social security and pension arrangements (Njuguna, 2012). In Kenya, only 25 per cent of the population have access to health insurance (Mwaura et al., 2015) and about 15 per cent of the Kenyan workforce is covered by some form of retirement benefits schemes (Keizi, 2006). Consequently, most Kenyans depend on out-of-pocket payments to meet their health (KHF & TFHC, 2016) and social security needs. The situation in Kenya reflects that of other African countries where most individuals are not insured and where the functional health insurance schemes are associated with the formal sector which requires regular contributions (Tenkorang, 2001). In Kenya, only 16 per cent of informal sector workers have health insurance compared to the formal sector with coverage of 98 per cent. The gap is even wider in the informal settlements where only 11 per cent of the residents have health insurance (Kimani et al., 2012).

However, there is increased focus on informal workers' social protection (Hu and Stewart, 2009) and on the need to expand universal health coverage to overcome the existing gaps (De Allegri and Sauerborn, 2007; Muiya and Kamau, 2013). Consequently, several African countries have enrolled low-income individuals in social protection by providing them with subsidized insurance (Banerjee et al., 2014). Countries like Ghana, Rwanda and Ethiopia have tailor-made informal workers' social protection schemes like the community-based health insurance (Carrin et al., 2005; Donfouet and Mahieu, 2012; Holst and Schmidt, 2014). Kenya has also rolled out health insurance and pension schemes targeted at informal-sector workers. However, the coverage is still low.

METHODOLOGY

This chapter is based on empirical data from a mixed-method cross-sectional study conducted between July and November 2015 as part of a four-year *Wezesha Jamii* project.[1] The study covered five informal settlements in Nairobi, Kenya, which had an estimated population of 620 749 residents (RoK, 2012). These settlements have a mix of 'formality' and 'informality' as not all areas are informal. Whereas Korogocho is wholly an informal settlement, Kibera, Mukuru, Mathare and Kawangware have over three-quarters of their population living in informal areas and the remaining quarter in formal areas (ibid.). There were no complete records on the actual number of women employed in the informal sector or even those operating in informal settlements. Consequently, we used the population of the 20 000 *Wezesha Jamii* targeted beneficiaries to determine the sample size. A sample size of 390 women was arrived at using a predetermined sample-size calculation table for ±5 per cent precision levels, with a confidence level of 95 per cent and $P = 0.5$ (Israel, 1992). The sample size of 390 was adjusted upward by adding 50 respondents to take care of attrition, and incomplete and spoilt samples, thus giving a sample of 440. The sample was distributed in the different sectors (that is, trade, service, production and wholesale). In the absence of a complete sampling frame of informal-sector workers in the study areas, each sector was treated as a quota. Hence, convenient sampling method was used to identify 440 WSSTs who were interviewed until all the quotas were filled. After data cleaning, 31 interviews were removed from the analysis, leaving 398 WSSTs. In addition, eight focus group discussions were conducted with selected WSSTs as well as 34 key informant interviews with representatives of state and non-state agencies. Qualitative data were analysed thematically using content analysis.

RESULTS

WSSTs' Socio-demographic and Financial Characteristics

The WSSTs were aged between 20 and 56 years, with an average age of 35 years. Most of them had attained primary education (84 per cent) and had dependents aged 18 years and below (83 per cent) with an average household size of 3.7 members. Most (72 per cent) were married. Many WSSTs (55 per cent) ran retail trade businesses (cereals and green groceries and retail shops) and 31 per cent offered services (food kiosks, hotels and food vending; hair salons and barber shops or sold cosmetics; or ran ICT businesses like M-Pesa[2] shops, cyber cafés and photocopying). Another 13 per cent were in production, mainly tailoring and dressmaking, and 1 per cent had wholesale businesses where they sold new and used clothes, shoes and bags. These businesses were the main sources of income for 95 per cent of WSSTs. The daily profits from WSSTs' businesses were low, ranging from Kshs 20 to Kshs 2000[3] with a mean of Kshs 535.

WSSTs' Social Protection Coverage

Only 28.4 per cent of WSSTs had enrolled in at least one formal social protection scheme. Specifically, 26 per cent of WSSTs had enrolled in National Hospital Insurance Fund (NHIF), 4.3 per cent with the National Social Security Fund (NSSF) and 1 per cent with a private pension scheme (the *Mbao Pension Plan*). There were variations in enrolment between the married and the non-married WSSTs, with married women having higher enrolment through their spouses. Despite this low enrolment, about a third of WSSTs (33.2 per cent) expressed the desire to enrol in social protection schemes and therefore access an untapped opportunity.

WSSTs' Membership in Social Networks

Most women (70 per cent) belonged to informal groups such as merry-go-rounds or women's groups commonly known as *'chamas'* (or *vyama* in plural) (Kinyanjui, 2012). Membership of these groups is voluntary and most women join them to show solidarity and belongingness. In return, they get social and emotional support from the members. Through the *chamas*, the women pooled and accumulated savings from their businesses through daily, weekly or monthly contributions. They were then able to access quick, low interest and unsecured loans which had minimal or no administrative requirements. These included loans to cater for school fees, medical emergencies and funeral expenses. In spite of this, the *chamas* had not been used to address the social protection gaps of WSSTs. Consequently, the accumulated savings and businesses' profits would be consumed whenever health and related needs arose, yet such expenses could easily be covered through formal social protection services. The potential role of *chamas* to accumulate savings which can be used in accessing social protection services for WSSTs, especially health insurance and social security, needs to be explored and tapped.

DISCUSSION

Social Protection among WSSTs in Informal Settlements

The gap in social protection coverage witnessed in our study reflects the general situation in Kenya and most developing countries where informal workers have low social protection coverage (Hu and Stewart, 2009). According to Ulrichs (2016), low contributory capacity, low awareness about the benefits value, administrative procedures and socio-cultural norms are barriers to accessing social protection. Equally, distance to health services, social and educational deprivations and structure of the schemes are other contributing factors (De Allegri and Sauerborn, 2007). These imbalances should be addressed to protect women small-scale traders and cushion their businesses. Keizi (2006, p. 8), in arguing for greater involvement of informal-sector workers in social protection, observes that, if left to choose on their own, informal sector workers 'are likely to save inadequately or inappropriately, through risky investment products'. Nonetheless, examples from Rwanda Community Based Health Insurance

(CBHI) (MSH, 2016) and the India Self Employed Women Association (SEWA) show that it is possible to provide social protection and social security to informal-sector workers if the right structures, systems and investments are made, including tapping into the social networks (Holmes and Scott, 2016).

Household Structure and WSSTs' Social Protection Enrolment

The WSST households' structure has implications for social protection enrolment. In our study, a higher number of WSSTs who had health insurance had enrolled through their spouses. Thus the single WSSTs and those who are the primary income earners are less likely to belong to formal social protection schemes than their married counterparts. Hence, efforts to promote women's enrolment in social protection should take cognizance of this fact. In the informal settlements, family structures that are female-maintained and female-led (Moser, 1993; Buvinić and Gupta, 1997) exist even where the women are not the heads of households. The *de jure* female-headed households in which the male partner is permanently absent due to separation or death exist, as well as the *de facto* households where women head households in which the male partner is 'temporarily' absent. The *de facto* women-headed households were also common in our study, where male partners were simply 'guest husbands'. Although the literature suggests that female headship does not always correlate with poverty (Buvinić and Gupta, 1997), the women living in informal settlements have greater disadvantages. In some cases, the spouses and male heads stop providing for their families when WSSTs start businesses. This scenario was reported severally in the focus group discussions in our study. Several women indicated that 'our spouses stopped providing for us and some even stopped paying fees for our children when we started businesses, yet these businesses may not even have stabilized'. In such situations, the WSSTs have to use their profits to meet the additional responsibilities and may therefore not have excess money to invest in social protection.

The Role of Social Networks in Bridging the Entrepreneurial Gap

The low investment in WSSTs' social protection remains a concern as it affects their overall advancement. Nonetheless, as seen in our study, women have social capital which can be used to increase their social protection coverage. Maina and Mwiti (2016) also observe that many women entrepreneurs belong to social networks like merry-go-rounds, women's groups and micro-finance institution networks. Solidarity and trust between members of such groups can be used to stir them into pooling resources for common use (Donfouet and Mahieu, 2012), including accessing social protection benefits. We note that the flexible nature of *chamas* makes them appealing to WSSTs and women are unlikely to abandon them in favour of formal systems. Thus, it is important to tap the potential of these informal groups to pool contributions to cover and access social protection benefits for the women. The structure of these networks is such that the women know each other and are able to follow one another in case of default. Arguably, the *chama* system has provided a support system for the economic empowerment of women, and, if well tapped, it can be used to extend social protection coverage to women in small-scale businesses.

Potential Challenges of Enrolling WSSTs in Social Protection Schemes

Enrolling WSSTs in social protection schemes has potential challenges (Jeong, 2010). This is true of countries where the informal sector forms a large part of the economy (Banerjee et al., 2014). The greatest challenge emanates from the lack of reliable databases of informal-sector workers (UN-Habitat, 2015) and verifiable records of their earnings (Alatas et al., 2012). This makes it difficult for any government and social protection schemes to determine, assess and reach most informal-sector workers. Jeong (2010) observes that locating informal-sector workers can be a challenge. Thus even when the government provides subsidized social protection schemes, many of these hidden informal workers, like the WSSTs in the Nairobi informal settlements, may not benefit.

The perception among WSSTs that social protection contribution rates are high presents enrolment challenges. In Kenya, informal-economy workers pay Kshs 500 per month for NHIF and about Kshs 480 per month for NSSF, totalling to Kshs 980 (approximately US$ 10) per month. This amount is high for small-scale traders whose average daily sales turnover is about Kshs 235 (Kamau and Kamau, 2016). Thus, as noted by Jeong (2010), it is necessary for governments to establish a reasonable contribution rate for informal sector workers, taking into account that it is difficult to assess the incomes of self-employed workers (Jeong, 2010).

CONCLUSIONS

This chapter concludes that bridging the social protection entrepreneurship gap among WSSTs in informal settlements requires greater focus on the opportunities that are within the WSSTs. There is a need to establish an integrated informal-economy workers' social protection scheme to ease the financial, social and psychological burden that WSSTs and other such workers experience during shocks. The potential role of WSSTs' informal social networks should be recognized and tapped. There is also a need for accurate and regularly updated data on WSSTs in the informal economy and in informal settlements for purposes of informing policy formulation. Furthermore, organizations providing social protection should increase their presence in informal settlements and in areas where WSSTs operate to increase enrolment. The lessons from successful initiatives like the Rwanda CBHI and SEWA should be used to inform this process.

ACKNOWLEDGEMENTS

The authors are grateful to SITE Enterprise Promotion (SITE EP), Oxfam GB and the National Organization of Peer Educators (NOPE) for supporting this study through the European Union-funded *Wezesha Jamii* project. We thank the study participants for their support and participation in the study. We also thank the research team members for their contribution. Nonetheless, the authors take responsibility for any errors and omissions in the chapter.

NOTES

1. *Wezesha Jamii* Project is implemented by a consortium comprising four organizations: SITE Enterprise Promotion (SITE EP), National Organization of Peer Educators (NOPE), Youth Alive! Kenya (YAK), and Oxfam Kenya. See https://kenya.oxfam.org/press_release/launch-eu-funded-wezesha-jamii-project.
2. M-Pesa is a money transfer service and a joint venture between mobile Vodafone and Kenya's Safaricom. Retrieved from http://www.vodafone.com/content/index/about/about-us/money_transfer.html.
3. These were outliers and were mainly from women traders who operated chemists businesses.

REFERENCES

Alatas, V., Banerjee, A., Hanna, R., Olken, B. and Tobias, J. (2012). Targeting the poor: evidence from a field experiment in Indonesia. *American Economic Review*, 102(4), 1206–1240, doi:10.1257/aer.102.4.1206.
Banerjee, A., Finkelstein, A., Hanna, R., Olken, B., Ornaghi, A. and Sumarto, S. (2014). *Enrolling informal sector workers in national health insurance in Indonesia.* Abdul Latif Jameel Poverty Action Lab (J-PAL). Project brief. Retrieved from https://www.povertyactionlab.org/evaluation/enrolling-informal-sector-workers-national-health-insurance-indonesia.

Bassett, M.E., Gulyani, S., Vitkovik, C. and Debomy, S. (2003). Informal settlement upgrading in sub-Saharan Africa: retrospective and lessons learned. Report prepared for Africa Urban and Water Section, Africa Technical Unit 1, World Bank.

Blomqvist, M., Chastain, E., Thickett, B., Unnikrishnan, S. and Woods, W. (2014). *Bridging the Entrepreneurship Gender Gap: The Power of Networks.* Boston: The Boston Consulting Group (BCG).

Brown, D. and McGranahan, G. (2016). The urban informal economy, local inclusion and achieving a global green transformation. *Habitat International,* 53, 97–105.

Buvinić, M. and Gupta, R. (1997). Female-headed households and female-maintained families: are they worth targeting to reduce poverty in developing countries? *Economic Development and Cultural Change,* 45(2), 259–280.

Carrin, G., Waelkens, M. and Criel, B. (2005). Community-based health insurance in developing countries: a study of its contribution to the performance of health financing systems. *Tropical Medicine and International Health,* 10(8), 799–811.

Charmes, J. (2012). The informal economy worldwide: trends and characteristics. *Journal of Applied Economic Research,* 6(2), 103–132.

De Allegri, M. and Sauerborn, R. (2007). Community based health insurance in developing countries: removing financial barriers is only the first step towards better access to care. *British Medical Journal,* 334, 1282–1283.

Desgroppes, A. and Taupin, S. (2012). Kibera: the biggest slum in Africa. *Les Cahiers de l'Afrique de l'Est,* 44, 23–34.

Donfouet, P. and Mahieu, A. (2012). Community-based health insurance and social capital: a review. *Health Economics Review,* 2(5), 1–5.

Gulyani, S., Bassett, E. and Talukdar, D. (2014). A tale of two cities: a multidimensional portrait of poverty and living conditions in the slums of Dakar and Nairobi. *Habitat International,* 43, 98–107.

Holmes, R. and Scott, L. (2016). Extending social insurance to informal workers: a gender analysis. ODI Working Paper, London.

Holst, J. and Schmidt, O. (eds) (2014). *Global Health: Special Issue Global Health.* Gesundheit und Gesellschaf, the AOK Forum for Health Politics, Practice and Research in Cooperation with GIZ.

Hu, Y. and Stewart, F. (2009). Pension coverage and informal sector workers: international experiences. *OECD Working Papers on Insurance and Private Pensions,* 31, OECD Publishing.

Hughes, D.K., Jennings, J., Brush, C., Carter, S. and Welter, F. (2012). Extending women's entrepreneurship research in new directions. *Entrepreneurship Theory and Practice,* Baylor University, doi: 10.1111/j.1540–6520.2012.00504.x.

ILO (2008). Women entrepreneurs in Kenya and factors affecting women entrepreneurs in micro and small enterprises in Kenya. Primary research report. International Labour Office (ILO), Programme on Boosting Employment through Small Enterprise Development, Job Creation and Enterprise Development Department, Skills and Employability Department. Geneva: ILO, Regional Office for Africa.

Israel, G. (1992). Determining sample size. Fact Sheet PEOD 6. Retrieved from www.sut.ac.th/im/data/read6.pdf.

Jeong, H.-S. (2010). Expanding insurance coverage to informal sector populations: experience from republic of Korea. World Health Report, Background Paper, 38.

Kalnins, A. and Williams, M. (2014). When do female-owned businesses out-survive male-owned businesses? A disaggregated approach by industry and geography. Retrieved from http://scholarship.sha.cornell.edu/articles/654.

Kamau, A. and Kamau, P. (2016). Policy briefs on NHIF Health Scheme and NSSF and MPP Pension Schemes. Oxfam GB Urban Policy Briefs Development. Retrieved from https://kenya.oxfam.org/sites/kenya.oxfam.org/files/file_attachme nts/Analysis%20of%20Public%20Social%20Protection%20Schemes%20in%20Ke nya.pdf.

Kamau, A., Kamau, P. and Muia, D. (2015a). Women small scale traders' baseline report: promoting livelihoods and inclusion of vulnerable women small scale traders. Oxfam GB Policy Paper. Retrieved from https://kenya.oxfam.org/ policy_paper/women-small-scale-traders-baseline-report.

Kamau, P., Kamau, A., Muia, D., Baiya, H., and Ndung'u, J. (2015b). Women small scale traders businesses in informal economy in Nairobi: is profit making a primary goal? Paper presented at the IDS@50 Conference on 'Rethinking Development and Development Studies in the Post-2015 Era', University of Nairobi, Nairobi.

Keizi, L. (2006). Barriers to pension scheme participation by workers in the informal economy: Retirement Benefits Authority. Research paper. Research and Policy Analysis Department. Retrieved from http://www.rba.go.ke/index.php/ en/statistics/category/27-research-reports-2005-2006?download=31:barriers-to-pension-scheme-participation-by-workers-in-infor.

KHF & TFHC (2016). Kenyan healthcare: sector market study report – opportunities for the Dutch Life Sciences and Health Sector. Embassy of the Kingdom of the Netherlands in Nairobi, Kenya Healthcare Federation (KHF) and Task Force Health Care (TFHC). Retrieved from https://www.rvo.nl/sites/default/ files/2016/10/2016_Kenyan_Healthcare_Sector_Report_Compleet.pdf.

Kimani, J.K., Ettarh, R., Kyobutungi, C., Mberu, B. and Muindi, K. (2012). Determinants for participation in a public health insurance program among residents of urban slums in Nairobi, Kenya – results from a cross-sectional survey. *Health Services Research*, 12(66), 1–11.

Kinyanjui, M. (2010). Social relations and associations in the informal sector in Kenya. Social Policy and Development Programme Paper, 43. United Nations Research Institute for Social Development, UNRISD.

Kinyanjui, M. (2012). *Vyama: Institutions of Hope: Ordinary People's Market Coordination and Society Organization Alternatives – A Kenyan Case Study.* Oakville, ON: Nsema Publishers.

Kinyanjui M. (2016). *Women and the Informal Economy in Urban Africa: From the Margins to the Centre.* London: Zed Books.

MacKellar, L. (2009). Pension systems for the informal sector in Asia: social protection and labour. SP Discussion Paper, 0903. *Human Development Network.* Washington, DC: World Bank.

Maina, J.N. and Mwiti, J. (2016). Drivers of growth of women-owned micro enterprises in Meru municipality, Kenya. *Saudi Journal of Business and Management Studies*, 1(4), 208–215, doi: 10.21276/sjbms.2016.1.4.7.

McAdam, M. (2013). *Female Entrepreneurship.* London and New York: Routledge.

Minniti, M. and Naude, W. (2010). What do we know about the patterns and determinants of female entrepreneurship across countries? *European Journal of Development Research*, 22(3), 277–293, doi:10.1057/ejdr.2010.17.

Moser, C. (1993). *Gender Planning and Development, Theory, Practice and Training.* London and New York, NY: Routledge.

MSH (2016). The development of community-based health insurance in Rwanda: experiences and lessons. Technical Brief, Management Science for Health (MSH), UR-CMHS-SPH and Rwanda's Ministry of Health (MOH).

Muiya, B.M. and Kamau, A. (2013). Universal health care in Kenya: opportunities and challenges for the informal sector workers. *International Journal of Education and Research*, 1(11), 1–10.

Mutisya, E. and Yarime, M. (2011). Understanding the grassroots dynamics of slums in Nairobi: the dilemma of Kibera informal settlements. *International Transaction Journal of Engineering, Management and Applied Sciences and Technologies*, 2(2), 197–213.

Mwaura, R., Barasa, E., Ramana, G., Coarasa, J. and Rogo, K. (2015). The path to universal health coverage in Kenya: repositioning the role of the national hospital insurance fund. *Smart Lessons* (sharing forum), International Finance Corporation (IFC), World Bank Group. Retrieved from https://openknowledge.worldbank. org/bitstream/handle/10986/23485/The0path0to0un0pital0insurance0fund.pdf? sequence=1&isAllowed=y.

Naituli, G., Wegulo, F. and Kaimenyi, B. (2006). Entrepreneurial characteristics among micro and small-scale women owned enterprises in north and central Meru districts, Kenya. In C. Creighton and F. Yiek (eds), *Gender Inequalities in Kenya*. UNESCO, pp. 7–23.

Njuguna, A. (2012). Critical success factors for a micro-pension plan: an exploratory study. *International Journal of Financial Research*, 3(4), 82–97.

NUSP (2016). National upgrading support programme toolkit: part 1 – understanding your informal settlements. Department of Human Settlements, South Africa. Retrieved from http://www.upgradingsupport.org/content/page/ part-1-understanding-your-informal-settlements.

OECD (2012). Gender equality in entrepreneurship. In *Closing the Gender Gap: Act Now*. Paris: OECD Publishing, pp. 271–343. Retrieved from http://dx.doi. org.10/1789/9789264179370-en.

Ohlsson, H. (2013). *Gendered Spaces: A Socio-Spatial Study in the Informal Settlement Dharavi in Mumbai*. Karlskrona, Sweden: Institute of Technology.

Oxfam (2009a). Urban poverty and vulnerability in Kenya: background analysis for the preparation of an Oxfam GB urban programme focused on Nairobi. Research report. Retrieved from https://urbanhealthupdates.files.wordpress. com/2009/09/urban_poverty_and_vulnerability_in_kenya1.pdf.

Oxfam (2009b). Urban poverty and vulnerability in Kenya: the urgent need for co-ordinated action to reduce urban poverty. Oxfam GB Briefing Note. Retrieved from http://policy-practice.oxfam.org.uk/publications/urban-poverty- and-vulnerability-in-kenya-the-urgent-need-for-co-ordinated-actio-123932.

Rindova, V., Barry, D. and Ketchen, D. (2009). Introduction to special topic forum: entrepreneuring as emancipation. *Academy of Management Review*, 34(3), 477–491.

Rockefeller Foundation (2013). Health vulnerabilities of informal workers. Report. Retrieved from https://www.rockefellerfoundation.org/app/uploads/Health-Vul nerabilities-of-Informal-Workers.pdf.

RoK (2012). *2009 Kenya Population and Housing Census: Counting our People for Implementation of Vision 2030 – Analytical Report on Urbanization, VIII*. Republic of Kenya, National Bureau of Statistics (KNBS), Ministry of State for Planning, National Development and Vision 2030.

RoK (2016). *Kenya National Bureau of Statistics, KNBS, Economic Survey 2016.* Republic of Kenya, National Bureau of Statistics (KNBS).

Tacoli, C. (2012). Urbanization, gender and urban poverty: paid work and unpaid care work in the city. Urbanization and Emerging Population Issues Working Paper 7. London and New York: International Institute for Environment and Development (IIED) and United Nations Population Fund (UNFPA).

Taddese, A. (2014). Case study: Kenya national hospital insurance fund premium collection for the informal sector. Brief. USAID, Health Finance and Governance. Retrieved from https://www.hfgproject.org/wp-content/uploads/2014/06/14-1022-HFG-Mobile-Money-Case-Study-NHIF-mpesa.pdf.

Tenkorang, A. (2001). Health insurance for the informal sector in Africa: design features, risk protection, and resource mobilization. Health, Nutrition, and Population (HNP), Discussion Paper.

Ulrichs, M. (2016). Informality, women and social protection: identifying barriers to provide effective coverage. ODI Working Paper. London: ODI.

UN-Habitat (2015). Habitat III issue papers 22: informal settlements. United Nations Task Team on Habitat III, New York. Retrieved from http://unhabitat.org/wp-content/uploads/2015/04/Habitat-III-Issue-Paper-22_Informal-Settlements-2.0.pdf.

11. Challenges to the formalization of Palestinian female-owned home-based businesses

Grace Khoury, Wojdan Farraj and Suhail Sultan

In recent years, women entrepreneurs have been increasingly acknowledged as a prominent force in the economic standing of developing countries. However, in addition to typical entrepreneurship obstacles such as inability to access financial services, a shortage of capital and inadequate infrastructure, women entrepreneurs in developing countries suffer from other challenges such as weak institutions, whose role is to create an incentive structure for women's enterprises (Jones and Lefort, 2014). Institutional and social contexts are important in presenting opportunities and constraints that influence women's entrepreneurship (Naguib and Jamali, 2015). In particular, females in developing countries face gender-specific discrimination such as restrictions on mobility and interaction, and working outside their homes (Jones and Lefort, 2014). In post-conflict economies, necessity tends to drive women to launch their enterprises in the informal sector, hence the establishment of home-based businesses (HBBs), which usually operate from the entrepreneur's residence; the owner is self-employed and uses his/her residence to generate income (Sayers and Monin, 2005).

HBBs in Palestine are common among both men and women. They are part of the informal economy which represents an important yet unrecognized source of socio-economic development. The majority of Palestinian informal entrepreneurs are hesitant about joining the formal sector, due in part to a lack of awareness of tax exemptions and other benefits of formalizing their business (Fallah, 2014a). However, as a result of remaining informal, HBBs would be overlooked in business-oriented policies (Bennett and Robson, 2003).

Previous research confirms that female-owned businesses are hastily judged as underperforming and women are portrayed as flawed entrepreneurs despite the lack of any solid proof to support these notions and the generalizing of differences between the performance of male and female entrepreneurs (Marlow and McAdam, 2013). However, the term *underperformance* is quite often used in reference to small female-owned businesses, assuming that size constitutes success. As such, we may infer that these claims of underperformance by female-owned firms are more representative of unfair gender biases rather than well-observed facts. A more comprehensive description of women's performance would include the challenges women face. These challenges may be socio-cultural; they could be the lack of gender-sensitive policies to support women's entrepreneurship in legal, financial or other aspects. This, of course, does not justify use of the term 'underperformance' to classify female-owned businesses.

Despite the lack of research and recognition regarding the Palestinian woman entrepreneur *per se*, the concept of the working woman is nothing new to Palestinian society. In fact, a woman's contribution to providing for her family dates far back in Palestinian culture and can be larger than that of her spouse, or indeed any male family member. This is due in part to the exclusive circumstances of Palestinian life. For instance, a common scenario is where a father is imprisoned or martyred, leaving the sole responsibility of the family's survival to the mother. As stated in Palestine, 'a pebble can support the largest rock', in reference to the spirit and value of family collaboration, regardless of the nature or size of the actual contribution, as long as it is conducive to the well-being (financial and otherwise) of the family. Nevertheless, the decision to work from home is heavily influenced by socio-cultural factors, such that having women leave home is frowned upon (most often the case in rural areas) as well as the difficulty in finding a practical work–life balance, considering household responsibilities. It is common knowledge that scores of Palestinian women have been making significant financial gain by providing products and services, such as catering and embroidery, right from the convenience of their homes. However, this study demonstrates that women's HBBs are not confined to these areas of business and that the performance of these HBBs has led to expansion and, in some cases, formalization of their business.

Assisting the formalization of informal entrepreneurship is a practical policy approach through which governments should make simpler conformity to regulations as well as initiate incentives and amnesty to encourage informal entrepreneurs to enter the legitimate sphere (Williams and Nadin, 2012). Current research has not given ample attention to the types, characteristics and motives of informal entrepreneurship; as such, the barriers to formalization and the hidden culture of informal entrepreneurship have yet to be explored further (ibid.). Moreover, HBBs are under-researched and consequently not well understood, especially in the context of women's entrepreneurship (Breen, 2010). This paucity of research has led to the ignoring of HBBs in the economic development strategies of governments (Mason et al., 2011). Accordingly, it is crucial to understand the barriers to formalization as they vary across different countries. Investigating these issues allows for the introduction of gender-sensitive tailored policies to protect these female-owned HBBs and encourage their formalization in Palestine. Moreover, it is important for policy-makers and practitioners to identify the influence of gender ownership on the growth of micro-businesses (Clark and Douglas, 2014). However, the initiative towards formalization of female-owned HBBs has not been studied in the Palestinian context.

The aim of this study is to extend the literature on female-owned HBBs in Palestine and to dispel the assumption of underperformance. To this end, the researchers investigate the challenges faced by female-owned HBBs, particularly when attempting to formalize and highlight the initiatives provided by the various institutions to encourage these women to persist in their endeavours, and possibly, to formalize.

WOMEN'S ENTREPRENEURSHIP IN THE PALESTINIAN CONTEXT

Political instability, due to occupation and unresolved conflict has imposed major restrictions on movement and access in the Palestinian investment climate, resulting in uncertainty, risk, increased costs for businesses and investors, and the fragmentation of Palestinian economic space and markets (World Bank, 2014a). The Global Entrepreneurship Monitor (GEM) Palestine Country Report (2012) identifies the top three limitations for entrepreneurs in Palestine to include the political, institutional and social contexts, lack of financial support, and government policies. Although women in Palestine form half of the society (of a population of around five million in Gaza and the West Bank), their participation rate in the labour force is 19.4 per cent (PCBS, 2014). In 2012, female early-stage entrepreneurial activity in Palestine was among the lowest, ranking 58th out of 67 countries. Nonetheless, this modest rate of female entrepreneurship contributed to a remarkable employment rate of 5.6 per cent of the total Palestinian employed population (Abdullah and Hattawy, 2014). While women entrepreneurs increasingly run their own enterprises, their socio-economic contributions and entrepreneurial potential remain largely untapped. The majority are concentrated in the informal sector. Data from the World Bank's (2003) enterprise survey shows that more female entrepreneurs operate in the informal sector, with a share of 15 per cent relative to nearly 3 per cent in the formal sector. In general, 60 per cent of women in developing countries work in the informal sector (World Bank, 2014b).

The GEM Palestine Country Report (2010) called for policies to promote women's entrepreneurship and the continuous reform of institutions recommending that the key decision-makers in the relevant sectors and agencies work to promote women's cooperatives to improve productivity and reduce the cost of procurement and marketing. In reference to the role of government agencies in particular, several recommendations were given, such as ensuring women equality of currently enforced economic legislations in matters pertaining to the entry and operation of all business activities, the preparation of national plans and policies to promote female entrepreneurship, tax exemptions and incentives for micro and small enterprises, and systematic government programmes to support female entrepreneurs. Their recommendations also included giving favourable treatment and direct credit to productive female-run projects and developing training programmes for women to increase their potential for entrepreneurial activities.

In the Palestinian context, studies on women's entrepreneurship haven't focused on initiatives, policies and strategies targeting female-owned HBBs. Gender-responsive policies, support services and enabling business environments are crucial in stimulating the upgrade of women's HBBs. This would ultimately contribute to generating decent and productive work, achieving gender equality, reducing poverty, and ensuring stronger economies and societies. A mechanism for legitimizing, supporting and giving due community recognition for the growing female-owned HBBs is needed.

Women's Entrepreneurship and Institutional Theory

Institutional theory encompasses the formal and informal elements existing in business environments, acknowledging the role of regulatory institutions, socio-cultural norms, and their impact on entrepreneurial activity (Yousafzai et al., 2015). The institutional theory is important in explaining the intricacies of female entrepreneurship (Baughn et al., 2006). This, in turn, could be valuable in acknowledging the constraints impacting the performance of female-owned HBBs, as well as the policies needed to either protect their current informal status, or to support those women who choose to formalize. Previous research has shown that cultural and institutional barriers can constrain the performance of female-owned businesses (Orser and Elliott, 2015). In fact, more female than male entrepreneurs have shown interest in expanding their business beyond the home, yet they face barriers to growth, such as family commitments, negative perceptions of their business, and lack of access to financial resources and formal networks (Breen, 2010). In particular, women in developing countries face gender-specific discrimination such as restrictions on mobility and interaction, which would directly impede any efforts to work outside the home (Jones and Lefort, 2014). Thus the influence of institutional and social contexts on women's entrepreneurship, in presenting both opportunities and constraints, cannot be ignored (Naguib and Jamali, 2015). The growth and sustainability of female-owned businesses can be facilitated by enablers such as business and governmental support (Breen, 2010). For instance, in the United States, public policy considers any costs allocated to operating business from home as tax deductible; such policies provide the support and incentive needed to encourage home-based entrepreneurial activity (Shane, 2009). As such, developing countries are in need of incentive structures, particularly for women's enterprises, in order to alleviate the challenges they face due to weak institutions (Jones and Lefort, 2014). In terms of socio-cultural norms, family support plays a positive role in the performance and growth of female-owned business, and in facilitating family and household responsibilities (Jamali, 2009).

Performance: Fact and Fiction

Inferior gender-based preconceptions impact both actual and perceived performance and growth of female-owned businesses, resulting in the category of 'underperformance' (Ehlers and Main, 1998; Jamali, 2009; Loscocco and Smith-Hunter, 2004; Marlow and McAdam, 2013). However, Johnsen and McMahon (2005) shed light on performance criteria, demonstrating how performance results differ depending on how it is actually measured. Hence, when control variables are accounted for in measuring performance, there is no statistical evidence to support growth and performance differences among men and women. When adjusted for several elements such as size, risk propensity and demographic variables, gender has not proven to have a significant impact on performance (Robb and Watson, 2012). Similarly, studies have confirmed that female-owned firms do not necessarily underperform compared to male-owned firms (Zolin et al., 2013). When performance was explored according to various measures, while men outperform women in terms of sales, gender does not prove to be directly related to profitability (Du Rietz and Henrekson, 2000). Marlow and McAdam (2013) tackle the myth of underperformance of female-owned businesses, concluding that their performance is rather 'constrained' as a result of inferior stereotypical expectations. Thus the term 'constrained performance' is somewhat more reasonable to use, as demonstrated in a study by Jamali (2009) where the majority of women entrepreneurs who were studied indicated satisfaction with their performance, despite the challenges that they face. In fact, women are evidenced to shine through during times of peril, as Al-Dajani and Marlow (2010) identify the critical contributions made to family incomes by female-owned HBBs of displaced Palestinians located in Jordan.

Performance: A Matter of Perspective

Interpretations of what actually constitutes performance may vary depending on the individual. Thus, growth and performance goals may tend to differ for women; failure to acknowledge this contributes to the disadvantageous results due to rudimentary performance comparisons among men and women (Fairlie and Robb, 2009). For instance, women may derive satisfaction with performance of their business from rather intrinsic sources, such as joy and excitement; this, in turn, may motivate these women to expand their ventures (Bulanova et al., 2016). For some women, control over work arrangements in terms of time frames and choice of colleagues afforded via entrepreneurship equate with success (Davies-Netzley, 2013).

In the context of HBB owners in particular, while satisfaction with income is moderate, greater contentment is realized in terms of quality of life and control over life (Gritzmacher, 1993). Furthermore, Mason et al. (2011) draw attention to the marginalization of the economic significance of HBBs, assuming substandard performance due to their small size. HBBs, particularly those run by women, are known to be many things, such as small-sized, part-time, craft-like businesses with little economic impact and no intention to grow (Mason et al., 2011; Walker, 2003). Nevertheless, counter to these assumptions, Singh and Lucas (2005) point out the profitability of HBBs despite their relatively lower sales levels, as they don't incur the same costs as their formally established, distinct-location counterparts. Furthermore, both the social and economic contribution of HBBs to society has also been acknowledged (Walker, 2003).

Perspectives on Formalization

Boyle and Joham (2013) suggest the support and recognition of more fair linkages between the informal (such as HBBs) and the formal economy through a properly inclusive policy and regulatory environment. The authors stress the importance of the informal economy and the measurement of its value and its contribution to the economic performance of a country. Nevertheless, the informal economy in many countries, which consists of women working from HBBs, remains outside the legal and social protection of governments (Chen, 2012). Thus, supporting women in the informal economy is a solution to reducing poverty and achieving gender equality (Chen et al., 2004, 2005).

The four prevailing schools of thought on how formal and informal sectors are linked have different perspectives (Boyle and Joham, 2013; Chen, 2012). While the dualists consider few linkages between the two sectors, they suggest that governments should provide credit, business development services, basic infrastructure and social services to operators in the informal sector (Sethuraman, 1976). On the other hand, the structuralists see both sectors as fundamentally linked where the government should regulate the commercial and employment relationship between the two sectors (Moser, 1978). Yet, the legalists argue that entrepreneurs in the informal sector intentionally choose to operate in the informal economy to evade rules and regulations as a result of a hostile legal system which leads some people to self-employment via the informal economy. Accordingly, legalists recommend that governments should simplify bureaucratic procedures to promote informal enterprises to register and become formal (De Soto, 2000). Finally, the voluntarists suggest that entrepreneurs choose to operate in the informal economy to avoid fees and other costs such as taxes, and should therefore be brought under the formal regulatory environment to increase their tax base and reduce unfair competition to formal businesses (Chen, 2012; Maloney, 2004). Furthermore, some studies infer that because the formal sector does not cater to household responsibilities, women are forced into the informal sector (Benaria and Roldan, 1987; Moser, 1978). As such, HBBs seem to be the optimal solution to meeting their needs while at the same time avoiding these obstacles.

METHODOLOGY

The researchers had the intention for a multi-phase research design starting with a qualitative research phase. This phase adopted an exploratory design (that is, semi-structured interviews and focus groups) to investigate the phenomenon of HBBs in depth and to measure the prevalence of its dimensions in the Palestinian context. Semi-structured interviews were held with 28 female entrepreneurs and 10 respondents representing the policy-makers, representatives, and officials in ministries and related NGOs. Two focus groups were conducted: the first with three representatives of women's cooperatives that provide support to female-owned HBBs in Palestine, and the second with eight (of the 28) previously interviewed female entrepreneurs who recently registered and formalized their businesses for an in-depth investigation as to the challenges they faced.

First, 28 semi-structured interviews were held with female entrepreneurs working from home in three main districts of the West Bank area, that is, Ramallah, Bethlehem and Hebron. These districts were considered the most active areas for women's entrepreneurship according to an interview with a representative from the Federation of Palestinian Chambers. Sampling issues present a noteworthy limitation for researchers in Palestine, as accessing a reliable database of female-owned HBBs (most of which are not registered formally) was not possible. Therefore, a non-probability convenience or opportunity sample was selected based on availability from various lists received from organizations that have dealt with those women. Although non-probability sampling is suitable for interviewing definite groups (Fink, 1995), the information obtained can't be generalized back to the population (Bhattacherjee, 2012), especially since our sample is limited and selected from only three Palestinian districts.

The second sample, which consisted of ten respondents, was important to gather data from the perspective of institutions that shape women's entrepreneurship policies. These included representatives from Palestinian ministries and local NGOs working in the area of advocacy, training and economic empowerment of women's entrepreneurship. All interviews were semi-structured, personal and face-to-face, which allowed the researchers to ask probing and follow-up questions to clarify issues raised by respondents (Bhattacherjee, 2012).

FINDINGS AND DISCUSSION

Formalization Attempts and Enablers

It can be concluded from the responses provided that the intent and desire to formalize was in fact present amongst the female-owned HBBs. Eighty-six per cent indicated that their HBB experienced growth since its establishment and 53 per cent claimed that the premises from which they operate was not sufficient for expansion. Seventy-one per cent of the women studied have either hired or contracted help; 32 per cent of which have 1–3 people working for them, including family members. Thirty per cent have recently registered their HBB in one or more of the ministries required for formalization, the majority of which are educated at a level above high school (bachelor's degree or two-year diploma) and have received training in either managerial or technical skills. Furthermore, 82 per cent of the women HBB owners have established an online presence to market their products. Overall deduction of this information can support the notion of the interviewees' intent to expand and formalize. In fact, an embroidery-based HBB owner from Bethlehem district has grown to a level where she began applying modern design for traditional Palestinian embroidery on cloths, souvenirs, bags, home accessories, and most recently designing embroidered corporate gifts.

> The capacity building I received through the women's forum has developed my design and marketing skills. They brought an international designer to help us design new pieces with different colours and formats to meet consumer needs in other countries. Private companies and banks are now buying my products. (FP26)[1]

Another woman explained how the quality and design of her jewellery improved as a result of capacity building sessions.

> I was able to enhance the quality of my pieces by using various types of raw materials and unconventional methods of design, which encouraged me to start my own social media page. (FP17)

Similarly, another interviewee moved from home production of olive oil soap for family and friends to the establishment of a factory with 20 employees (upon receiving a sizable bank loan) to produce soap and natural beauty products.

> Without the loan, I could not have expanded my business nor provide employment opportunities, for which I am satisfied. (FP20)

These examples testify to the need of these women for support provided by various institutions and for enablers such as capacity building, access to financial resources, and formal networks in order to grow and expand (Breen, 2010).

Performance and Challenges

In line with previous research, our sample expressed satisfaction with their current situation, contentment with the income they generate from their projects, with no plans to expand their businesses. From their perspectives, they were satisfied with their business performance (Bulanova et al., 2016).

> As long as my children have completed their higher education there will be no need for me to continue supporting the family. (FP24)

This was also supported by a focus group held with cooperatives who work with female-owned HBBs suggesting the impact of gender-specific discrimination such as restrictions on mobility and interaction (Jones and Lefort, 2014).

> The women working from home informally who don't know the benefits [of registering] are not likely to go through the trouble of finding out, especially for as long as they feel they are meeting the needs of their families. Nevertheless, once discovered, knowledge of the process hasn't shown to make things any different. As the concept of work outside the home in and of itself is taboo (in some areas more than others), travelling from city to city to fulfil the requirement of registration presents an even greater turn-off. (Women Cooperative Representative, Focus Group 1)

As for the factors considered to be challenges in formalizing their HBB, cultural and social barriers were among the most frequently mentioned by 39 per cent of interviewed women. This agrees with another participant from Focus Group 1 held with cooperatives who work with female-owned HBBs, who commented, 'Culture and harsh judgement of society strongly discourage women from doing what they need to do to register their business', referring to socio-cultural factors which overwhelmingly attributed to women's apprehension to leave home altogether, let alone leave to work or register their HBB.

From the perspective of an official in this respect:

> Formalization is, in effect, a confirmation that woman-owned businesses are profitable; in a culture where women are held accountable to be transparent to husbands or other family members with financial and other business-related activity. (O3)[2]

This was found to be the case more often in rural than in urban areas, as cooperatives work with women in rural areas.

> Such pressures are far more prevalent for women living in villages and small towns. (Women Cooperative Representative, Focus Group 1)

Other factors reported as challenges to these women include fear of taxation (36 per cent) and lack of support services (29 per cent).

> Why would I register my business and pay taxes while working in such a small village with a limited number of customers? What would I be getting in exchange? (FP25)

> I'm working from home and providing for my family; why should I move to a commercial premises and leave the convenience of working from my home and pay taxes? I'm satisfied with the business as it is. (FP27)

I would love someone to help me exhibit my products or provide training in design and export. Would registration provide such benefits? (FP6, FP12, FP17)

As confirmed by interviewed officials:

There are those with the intent to expand yet are frightened and unaware of taxation laws; they think registering their HBB at the Ministry of National Economy will obligate them with tax payments to the Ministry of Finance. They are unaware of supportive policies to encourage formalization of HBBs. (O2)

Of equal concern among interviewees (18 per cent) were access to finance, complexity of registration processes, regulations, political instability, and ease of movement (as a result of roadblocks, checkpoints, separation wall, etc.).

Women who attempted formalization faced difficulties in obtaining a rent contract or proof of ownership in their name, as such documents are usually in the husband's name, or that of a close male relative; such documentation is mandatory in registering a business. Moreover, depriving women of real-estate inheritance rights is also a socio-cultural barrier to receiving bank collateral needed for business loans. (O6)

Benefits of Formalization

The majority of women interviewed were not familiar with the benefits of formalization, which include:

Better marketing opportunities and recognition in local and international trade exhibitions. (O1)

Evidence of business practice to obtain business travel visas and participate in specialized training programmes. (O2)

Computer bar codes to display their products in larger supermarkets. (O2)

and

A VAT number to allow participation in bidding and contracts, and higher profit margins as a result of direct sales. (O9)

Institutional Initiatives and Needed Policies

One of the findings of this research is that 70 per cent of the women interviewed did not attempt to formalize their businesses. This can be accredited in great part to the lack of awareness of the benefits discussed above. This result indicates a need for protecting these HBBs and encouraging those who intend to formalize. According to an interviewee responsible for the gender unit in one of the Palestinian ministries:

> There are no policies to protect women's HBBs, enabling owners of large businesses to take advantage of them by buying their products at low cost and selling to customers at large margins. (O6)

Although at a disadvantage in this situation, many of the interviewed women found this arrangement to be convenient; to them, selling to a few larger businesses or cooperatives that help them in marketing and promoting their products frees them from dealing with many customers, which they don't have the time, skills, nor access to markets to handle. A Ministry representative stated:

> Forcing these women to formalize could lead to the fatal outcome of their businesses. The government is responsible for providing the support and encouragement needed to sustain their businesses in their current informal state. (O3)

Many of these women are neither aware of how to register with the Ministry of National Economy for a trade record nor of the importance of having such a record.

> Formalization allows them to label and sell their products directly in the market, participate in local and foreign exhibitions, and receive an export code to sell their products in other countries. (O1)

One of the challenges that affect the impact of women's entrepreneurship in Palestine is the lack of genuine partnership, organization and coordination of a business model that supports the integration of programmes provided by donors, governmental agencies and NGOs. A major theme mentioned by the interviewed representatives is the redundancy of capacity building training programmes offered by the different organizations and the competition among these organizations on receiving donor funds allocated to women's economic empowerment. A director of a women's association NGO stated:

> The various stakeholders in the country should work in a complementary manner where the government attracts donors and identifies needed support, while some NGOs deliver the capacity building and others provide the economic empowerment. (O4)

Instead, institutions play similar roles where some ministries participate in delivering capacity-building programmes, competing with NGOs, as mentioned by focus group participants. Moreover, a common observation among some ministry officials is the diversion of focus of existing NGOs, as they have been getting involved in programmes funded by donors regardless of the NGO's original mission. For instance, it is common to find an NGO known to support health projects suddenly begin work in capacity building for women's entrepreneurship if such projects are demanded and funded.

This situation reinforces redundancy of programmes and limits the impact on the economy and society at large. (O10)

O2 and O6 both discussed Initiative 1 (Table 11.1), a donor-funded initiative aimed at establishing ten gender units in the Chambers of Commerce in ten districts throughout Palestine. This initiative has set six classification schemes for business registration in cooperation with the Ministry of National Economy and an economic empowerment NGO. For instance, Grade Four registration allows businesses with investment capital of $5000 or less to formalize their business in exchange for a small annual registration fee of 20 JD; this is meant to encourage informal female-owned HBBs to register their businesses. Women registered for at least three years can nominate themselves to join the Federation membership board and become involved in setting the policies of the Chamber in their district. As a result, more than 1500 women were motivated to register. However the following statement indicated a lack of interest in business growth:

Women tend to renew their registration only before receiving a specific service they need from the Federation such as participating in an exhibition out of the country. (O2)

Moreover, Initiative 2 (another example of incentive) is provided through a partnership agreement between a women's forum, a major national bank and a donor to select 20 active female-owned HBBs and allow them to participate in a mini MBA programme for six months aimed to help participants prepare a viable business plan, open a bank account and obtain zero-interest business loans without a need for a guarantor. As a result of this initiative, eight female-owned HBBs were encouraged to register.

Banks do not trust women, and accessing loans without collateral is not easy, so going through this programme made me have a better relationship with the bank to get a loan and expand my business beyond the Palestinian territories through exporting. (FP18)

The Ministry signed an MOU [memorandum of understanding] with a national bank to provide zero-interest loans to 15 projects with a total capital investment of $150 000; a quota of one-third of these projects is dedicated to women's enterprises with capital investment of less than $10 000. (O3 on Initiative 3)

Table 11.1 Initiatives

Initiative number	Purpose	Partners	Benefits	Results	
				Pros	Cons
1	Encourage HBBs to register	Government, donor, NGO	Federation board membership, involvement in setting Federation policies	1500 women entrepreneurs registered	Pursuit of renewal upon need for service
2	Empowerment and capacity building (mini MBA)	Women's forum, national bank, donor	Assistance in preparing business plans, opening bank accounts, obtaining zero-interest loans without guarantor	8 female HBBs registered	
3	Financing	Ministry, national bank	Zero-interest loans	Quota set aside for women's enterprises with minimal capital	
4	Provision of services and information needed to formalize (One Stop Shop)	NGO, donor	Convenience in registration procedures	Facilitation of registration process in one place	

The 'One Stop Shop' (Initiative 4) is a donor-funded initiative implemented by a local NGO in order to provide women with all the services and information they need for formalizing their business in one place. Feedback received from beneficiaries that participated in the study indicated that this initiative was instrumental in facilitating registration procedures. This agrees with the recommendations of Williams and Nadin (2012) to simplify regulatory compliance and initiate incentives.

> The One Stop Shop provided me with information about how to register without the need to go back and forth to different ministries. (FP19)

A combination of dualist and legalist perspectives on formalization might be needed to support Palestinian female-owned owned HBBs (De Soto, 2000; Sethuraman, 1976).

> For greater impact and sustainability, there should be organized collaboration among relevant Palestinian stakeholders, rather than the current *ad hoc* initiatives being implemented. (O7)

IMPLICATIONS FOR POLICY, PRACTICE AND RESEARCH

After conducting the qualitative (content and thematic) analysis of the data gathered through the various interviews and focus groups, the researchers have arrived at several inferences. To begin, policy-makers contend that the limited logistical, human and financial resources provided by government bodies have made them dependent on donor funds. This, in addition to the lack of a clear vision on how to address women entrepreneurs in general (and female-owned HBBs in particular) has allowed for random, redundant efforts, which have not contributed productively to this matter. Instead, the various stakeholders involved should cooperate by taking on complementary roles in addressing female-owned HBBs and entrepreneurship. Participatory efforts should be coordinated among public and private sectors, relevant ministries, municipalities, chambers of commerce, NGOs and donors.

For instance, the public sector would be best suited to assess needs, attract funds, instate policies and build awareness, leaving implementation to other groups of interest in the equation. It would play a major role by instating gender-sensitive policies, incentives and quotas to ensure that women entrepreneurs are provided ample opportunities. As part of their social responsibility, the private sector (including banks) can provide mentoring, access to financial resources, networking opportunities and marketing support. The private sector can also sponsor exhibitions and trade shows to facilitate outreach. NGOs have been said to chase after heavily funded, trending issues instead of focusing on their mandate. In the context of their involvement in women entrepreneurs, their efforts should be organized and integrated, rather than competitive and imitative. Educated women may find support in formalizing (that is, the registration process) from NGOs like businesswomen's forums, while other NGOs may target craft-based entrepreneurship, specialized IT projects, capacity building, and so on. Chambers of commerce and municipalities may concentrate on promoting certain projects by area in order to utilize resources available in each district, such as agriculture, tourism, traditional crafts enterprises, etc. Furthermore, municipalities can encourage cooperatives that work with these female-owned HBBs by holding local exhibitions and festivals to help them market their products and services. The Federation of Palestinian Chambers can contribute by building capacities and by easing the registration process.

Moreover, benefits to female-owned HBBs can increase exponentially through joint efforts among these stakeholders. For example, Palestinian chambers of commerce can work with governmental bodies in facilitating access to the international market through the cooperative NGOs that work with these women. Donors can guarantee efficient and effective use of the funds they provide by working closely with government bodies. Funding of local NGOs would be in line with a national strategic plan where needs and priorities are clearly outlined; funds would be allocated according to these NGOs' mandate and area of expertise. This approach would create an organized framework where each body involved in women's entrepreneurship would have a clear role in regard to what capacity they would contribute. These implications consider the recommendations of the structuralist, dualist and legalist schools of thought which suggest that there should be a linkage between the formal and informal sector, as well as providing incentives and easing the formalization process (De Soto, 2000; Moser, 1978).

Although this research studied Palestinian female-owned HBBs and the challenges for growth and formalization, future research may survey a larger sample, allowing for further investigation, hence generalization of the results. Researching other informal types of businesses and assessments of any support they receive by cooperatives, governmental institutions and other stakeholders would also be rather insightful.

CONCLUSIONS

This study is one of the few researches that studied female-owned HBBs in Palestine, drawing attention to the support and policies needed to help this sector overcome the myth of underperformance. This study can form a solid base for further research in this field. The findings of this study indicate that a number of women did, in fact, formalize, while others had the intention to do so. However, the majority studied did not show such interest. Policies, incentives and other forms of support are necessary from various stakeholders. It is recommended that a cooperative framework is developed, delineating roles for joint efforts from all relevant stakeholders in order to empower these women and help them overcome the barriers they face.

NOTES

1. 'FP' = female participant. Twenty-eight female participants were interviewed during the course of the study.
2. 'O' = officials and representatives.

REFERENCES

Abdullah, S. and Hattawy, M. (2014). Policies for scaling up female entrepreneurship in the State of Palestine. Report. Palestine Economic Policy Research Institute (MAS), Palestine.

Al-Dajani, H. and Marlow, S. (2010). Impact of women's home-based enterprise on family dynamics: evidence from Jordan. *International Small Business Journal*, 28(3), 470–486.

Baughn, C.C., Chua, B.L. and Neupert, K.E. (2006). The normative context for women's participation in entrepreneurship: a multicountry study. *Entrepreneurship Theory and Practice*, 30(5), 687–708.

Benaria, L. and Roldan, M. (1987). *The Crossroads of Class and Gender*. Chicago: University of Chicago Press.

Bennett, R. and Robson, P. (2003). Changing use of external business advice and government supports by SMEs in the 1990s. *Regional Studies*, 37(8), 795–811.

Bhattacherjee, A. (2012). *Social Science Research: Principles, Methods, and Practices*. Tampa: Global Text Project.

Boyle, S. and Joham, C. (2013). The informal economy and the arts: a two-country perspective. *The Journal of Arts Management, Law, and Society*, 43(3), 153–166.

Breen, J. (2010). Gender differences in home-based business ownership. *Small Enterprise Research*, 17(2), 124–136.

Bulanova, O., Isaksen, E.J. and Kolvereid, L. (2016). Growth aspirations among women entrepreneurs in high growth firms. *Baltic Journal of Management*, 11(2), 187–206.

Chen, M.A. (2012), The informal economy: definitions, theories and policies. Report, Women in Informal Economy Globalizing and Organizing, WIEGO No 1. Harvard Kennedy School.

Chen, M.A., Vanek, J. and Carr, M. (2004). *Mainstreaming Informal Employment and Gender in Poverty Reduction: A Handbook for Policy-Makers and Other Stakeholders*. London: Commonwealth Secretariat.

Chen, M., Vanek, J., Lund, F., Heintz, J., Jhabvala, R. and Bonner, C. (2005). Progress of the World's Women 2005. Report. Women, Work and Poverty, United Nations Development Fund for Women (UNIFEM), New York.

Clark, D.N. and Douglas, H. (2014). Micro-enterprise growth: lessons from home-based business in New Zealand. *Small Enterprise Research*, 21(1), 82–98.

Davies-Netzley, S.A. (2013). *Gendered Capital: Entrepreneurial Women in American Enterprise*. New York: Routledge.

De Soto, H. (2000). *The Mystery of Capital: Why Capitalism Triumphs in the West and Fails Everywhere Else*. New York: Basic Books.

Du Rietz, A. and Henrekson, M. (2000). Testing the female underperformance hypothesis. *Small Business Economics*, 14(1), 1–10.

Ehlers, T.B. and Main, K. (1998). Women and the false promise of microenterprise. *Gender and Society*, 12(4), 424–440.

Fairlie, R.W. and Robb, A.M. (2009). Gender differences in business performance: evidence from the characteristics of business owners survey. *Small Business Economics*, 33(4), 375–395.

Fallah, B. (2014a). The informal sector in the Palestinian territories. Report, Palestine Economic Policy Research Institute (MAS).

Fink, A. (1995). *How to Sample in Surveys: The Survey Kit, 6*. California: Sage.

Gritzmacher, J.E. (1993). Satisfaction with home-based employment. *Journal of Family and Economic Issues*, 14(2), 145–161.

Jamali, D. (2009). Constraints and opportunities facing women entrepreneurs in developing countries: a relational perspective. *Gender in Management: An International Journal*, 24(4), 232–251.

Johnsen, G.J. and McMahon, R.G. (2005). Owner–manager gender, financial performance and business growth amongst SMEs from Australia's business longitudinal survey. *International Small Business Journal*, 23(2), 115–142.

Jones, G. and Lefort, A. (2014). Female entrepreneurship in developing countries. Case study, Harvard Business School.

Loscocco, K. and Smith-Hunter, A. (2004). Women home-based business owners: insights from comparative analyses. *Women in Management Review*, 19(3), 164–173.

Maloney, W.F. (2004). Informality revisited. *World Development*, 32(7), 1159–1178.

Marlow, S. and McAdam, M. (2013). Gender and entrepreneurship: advancing debate and challenging myths; exploring the mystery of the under-performing female entrepreneur. *International Journal of Entrepreneurial Behavior and Research*, 19(1), 114–124.

Mason, C.M., Carter, S. and Tagg, S. (2011). Invisible businesses: the characteristics of home-based businesses in the United Kingdom. *Regional Studies*, 45(5), 625–639.

Moser, C.O. (1978). Informal sector or petty commodity production: dualism or dependence in urban development? *World Development*, 6(10), 1041–1064.

Naguib, R. and Jamali, D. (2015). Female entrepreneurship in the UAE: a multi-level integrative lens. *Gender in Management: An International Journal*, 30(2), 135–161.

Orser, B. and Elliott, C. (2015). *Feminine Capital: Unlocking the Power of Women Entrepreneurs*. Cambridge, MA: Stanford University Press.

PCBS (Palestinian Central Bureau of Statistics) (2014). *Labour Force Survey Results: Second Quarter*.

Palestine Country Report (2010). The Global Entrepreneurship Monitor (GEM). Ramallah: Economic Policy Research Institute (MAS).

Palestine Country Report (2012). The Global Entrepreneurship Monitor (GEM). Ramallah: Economic Policy Research Institute (MAS).

Robb, A.M. and Watson, J. (2012). Gender differences in firm performance: evidence from new ventures in the United States. *Journal of Business Venturing*, 27(5), 544–558.

Sayers, J. and Monin, N. (2005). *The Global Garage: Home-Based Business in New Zealand*. Southbank, Australia: Dunmore Press.

Sethuraman, S.V. (1976). The urban informal sector: concept, measurement and policy. *International Labour Review*, 114(1), 69–81.

Shane, S. (2009). Why encouraging more people to become entrepreneurs is bad public policy. *Small Business Economics*, 33(2), 141–149.

Singh, R.P. and Lucas, L.M. (2005). Not just domestic engineers: an exploratory study of homemaker entrepreneurs. *Entrepreneurship Theory and Practice*, 29(1), 79–90.

Walker, E. (2003). Home-based businesses: setting straight the urban myths. *Small Enterprise Research*, 11(2), 35–48.

Williams, C.C. and Nadin, S.J. (2012). Tackling entrepreneurship in the informal economy: evaluating the policy options. *Journal of Entrepreneurship and Public Policy*, 1(2), 111–124.

World Bank (2003). Urban development, program and project options: what is the informal economy? Internet document, accessed 10 June 2016 at www.worldbank.org.

World Bank (2014a). West Bank and Gaza investment climate assessment: fragmentation and uncertainty. Report. Washington, DC: World Bank, accessed 10 June 2016 at http://documents.worldbank.org/curated/en/249591468142766989/West-Bank-and-Gaza-Investment-climate-assessment-fragmentation-and-uncertainty.

World Bank (2014b). Informal economy and the World Bank. Policy Research Working Paper. Washington, DC: World Bank.

Yousafzai, S.Y., Saeed, S. and Muffatto, M. (2015). Institutional theory and contextual embeddedness of women's entrepreneurial leadership: evidence from 92 countries. *Journal of Small Business Management*, 53(3), 587–604.

Zolin, R., Stuetzer, M. and Watson, J. (2013). Challenging the female underperformance hypothesis. *International Journal of Gender and Entrepreneurship*, 5(2), 116–129.

FURTHER READING

Beck, S.E. and Manuel, K. (2008). *Practical Research Methods for Librarians and Information Professionals*. New York: Neal–Schuman Publishers.

Creswell, J.W. and Piano, V.L. (2011). *Designing and Conducting Mixed Methods: Research*, 2nd edn. Thousand Oaks, CA: Sage.

Fallah, B. (2014b). The pros and cons of formalizing informal MSEs in the Palestinian economy. Economic Research Forum working paper.

Guest, G., MacQueen, K.M. and Namey, E.E. (2012). *Applied Thematic Analysis*. Thousand Oaks, CA: Sage.

Marshall, C. and Rossman, G. (1999). *Designing Qualitative Research*, 3rd edn. London: Sage.

12. The influence of gender on social orientation and family-friendly policies in community-based enterprises in Brazil

Luisa Delgado-Márquez, Rachida Justo and Julio O. De Castro

The recent expansion of scholarship on women's entrepreneurship has highlighted the relevance of context: when, how, and why entrepreneurship occurs, and who becomes involved (Ettl and Welter, 2010; Gartner et al., 2006). In particular, community-based enterprises (CBEs), which are mainly characterized by the pursuit of both economic and social goals, have garnered great attention as an alternative to traditional enterprises owned and founded by one or a few entrepreneurs (Daskalaki et al., 2015; Haugh, 2007; Johannisson, 1990; Peredo and Chrisman, 2006; Somerville and McElwee, 2011). CBEs can become instruments of women's empowerment. In many developing countries women work individually, often isolated, in the informal economy, operating at a low level of activity and reaping marginal income. Joining forces in small CBEs can provide them with the economic, social, moral, and political advantages they need.

Despite substantial progress in research on women entrepreneurs, some important gaps remain. With few exceptions, studies on female entrepreneurship have focused on individuals, neglecting gender dynamics in entrepreneurial teams (Yang and Aldrich, 2014) or CBEs (Datta and Gailey, 2012) – even though those form a sizeable proportion of new ventures (Ruef, 2010; Ruef et al., 2003). Yang and Aldrich (2014) found that gender logic extends to the entrepreneurial domain, despite strong meritocratic pressures in this highly competitive context. Their results showed that gender stereotypes of leaders pervasively constrain women's access to power within co-founding teams. Some studies suggest that even in collective businesses such as CBEs gender differences still prevail, particularly in the distribution of rewards and leadership roles (Ridgeway, 2011). Nevertheless, we posit that in CBEs, which are naturally oriented towards participative decision-making and therefore should be more gender-egalitarian than traditional businesses, female co-founders should be much more able to influence business decisions. The question then becomes, how does their presence affect CBEs' initial motivations, ongoing achievements, and challenges?

Various studies of solo entrepreneurs have posited that women entrepreneurs are likelier than men to align with social as distinct from economic goals (Brush, 1992; Buttner and Moore, 1997; Davidson and Freudenburg, 1996; Hechavarria et al., 2016). The social science literature has demonstrated females' proclivity toward altruistic behavior in general (Calhoun, 2012; Gilligan, 1982; Jaffee and Hyde, 2000) and towards creating social businesses in particular (Hechavarria et al., 2016), and has shown that having women founders influences the goals of the business. Given the impact of team dynamics on business motivations in terms of goals and outcomes, gender influences on team dynamics are key (Milanov et al., 2015; Yang and Aldrich, 2014). But little is known about how women's inclination towards social concerns plays out within mixed entrepreneurial teams. Community-based enterprises represent an ideal setting to empirically test the assumption that, when given the opportunity to weigh in on business decisions, women entrepreneurs might favor different strategic orientations than those chosen by male-dominated teams (Ridgeway, 2011).

One specific potential consequence of female-dominant leadership is the adoption of family-friendly human resources policies. A number of scholars have emphasized women business owners' desire for work–family balance as a motivation for starting a business (Caputo and Dolinsky, 1998; Connelly, 1992; DeMartino et al., 2006; Parasuraman and Simmers, 2001). Work–family balance has a large impact on the type of business women create, and some choose to limit business growth to preserve the balance (Morris et al., 2006; Orser and Hogarth-Scott, 2002). Several studies have examined the work–family conflict experienced by women entrepreneurs (for example, Ufuk and Özgen, 2001). Adkins et al. (2013) have argued that the desire for better work–life balance may lead women entrepreneurs to create organizations with a more positive work–family culture and offer more family-friendly policies to employees. Accordingly, we expect that the presence of female leaders, coupled with the social nature of community-based enterprises, should result in increased family-friendly policies for their members.

However, given the limits on women's power mentioned above, we need to test this assumption empirically. This is important also because Cliff et al. (2005) find a disconnect between narrative and practice among both men and women business owners. Analyzing 229 businesses in Vancouver, they found that the owner's sex had no effect on the extent of a firm's bureaucracy or the femininity of its employment relationships. Even though the owners tended to talk as if they organized and managed their firms in gender-stereotypic ways, they did not do so in practice: both male and female owners managed their firms with a mix of masculine and feminine approaches. Heeding Cliff and colleagues' call for more systematic research on this topic, in this study we offer empirical evidence about how businesses' economic and social orientation changes depending on the presence of women.

Drawing on a large Brazilian database of community-based businesses, which exhibit great variety in gender composition, we examine (i) how the gender composition of founding teams influences the businesses' initial goals, ongoing achievements, and challenges, and whether they tend to emphasize the social or economic side; and (ii) how leaders' gender affects family-friendly policies. In what follows, we first present our theoretical framework and hypotheses. Next, we discuss our research methods, followed by our empirical results. We conclude with a discussion of these findings and their implications for theory, policy, and practice.

THEORETICAL FRAMEWORK AND HYPOTHESES

Gender and Attitudes Towards Social Versus Economic Initial Motivations, Ongoing Achievements, and Challenges

Extensive research has argued that women tend to be more aligned than men are with social as opposed to economic goals. For instance, Davidson and Freudenburg (1996) demonstrate that women have stronger environmental attitudes and behaviors. Gilligan (1982) maintains that there are fundamental differences between women's and men's framing of ethical issues.

Within the entrepreneurship literature, while scholars have tended to move beyond essential gender differences, they have acknowledged that gender socialization still influences the stated goals and strategic choices of entrepreneurs. Women entrepreneurs are found to be more likely than their male counterparts to emphasize non-monetary motivations such as environmental and social ones (Braun, 2010; Brush, 1992; Buttner and Moore, 1997; Hechavarria et al., 2016). Research has also examined gender differences in management characteristics, with traditionalists arguing that there are crucial differences, while other scholars assume that men and women are very similar in management styles and crucial business behaviors. Although Cliff et al. (2005) claim that these two perspectives are too extreme, a number of recent theoretical works describe in detail the characteristics that differentiate archetypically masculine and feminine approaches to organizing and managing. In general, the existing research in entrepreneurship is replete with extreme assumptions about gender issues (Gupta et al., 2009).

Most of those studies focus on gender differences in traditional businesses, and it is not clear how gender operates in community-based enterprises, which are expected to be naturally oriented towards gender equality (Nippierd, 1999). Community entrepreneurship moves away from the enterprising individual. It sees entrepreneurship as a collective event in a particular spatial context, the local environment, although some authors also identify national governments as actors in this process (Dupuis and de Bruin, 2003). A distinctive feature of these businesses is that they are collective entrepreneurial businesses from the beginning, and as such, they present idiosyncratic features that traditional entrepreneurship theories focusing on heroic individual founders can't explain (Datta and Gailey, 2012; Short et al., 2009). These businesses are 'the result of a process in which the community acts entrepreneurially to create and operate a new enterprise' (Peredo and Chrisman, 2006, p. 310). Well-known examples of CBEs are the Mondragon Corporation Cooperative in Spain, the Communal Enterprises of Salinacocha in Ecuador, and the village of Ralegan Sidhi in India.

Scholars analyzing community-based enterprises suggest that they tend to be structured as circles, networks, or webs rather than pyramids, ladders, or chains. In general, we know little about how the presence of women as owners affects CBEs' social versus economic initial goals, ongoing achievements, and challenges, given that most of these businesses do not follow rigid hierarchical structures and all members participate in decision-making. Collective businesses have been investigated in a few studies of social entrepreneurship, such as work on community-led social ventures in Scotland (Haugh, 2007), community-based ventures in Peru (Peredo and Chrisman, 2006), worker-owned cooperatives in the Basque region of Spain (Mair and Schoen, 2007), and a women's cooperative in India (Datta and Gailey, 2012).

This literature suggests that community-based enterprises should differ from traditional ventures in three main areas: social initial motivation, social achievement, and social challenge. While it is widely recognized that economic orientation focuses on profits and performance, it is less clear what issues the social perspective addresses. *Social motivation* is defined as an orientation toward helping people in the community. Actions that are intended to help or benefit an individual, group, or organization are discretionary and therefore not recognized by formal evaluation systems

(Osterloh and Frey, 2000). Examples of social motivations are: promoting interaction among all group members; promoting skills within a community; or strengthening an ethnic group. *Social achievement* depends on the resources and abilities to realize social changes and sustainable development through specific achievements (Salamzadeh et al., 2011). Examples of social achievements are: conquests for a local community; integration of group or collective; or self-management and democracy. Finally, *social challenges* are defined as those faced by the global community or, on a smaller scale, within local communities. These include addressing poverty, social exclusion, migration, and social conflicts (Konda et al., 2015). Examples of social challenges included in this study are: maintaining the unity of a group or collective; achieving more environmental awareness among members; and guaranteeing social protection in the future.

Based on this, we contend that significant presence of women in the management of the collective firm should positively influence its decision-making and its goals, outcomes, and challenges:

Hypothesis 1: The percentage of women in the founding team will be positively related to the social initial motivations to create a business.

Hypothesis 2: The percentage of women in the founding team will be positively related to the social achievements of the business.

Hypothesis 3: The percentage of women in the founding team will be positively related to the social challenges of the business.

Gender and Family-friendly Policies

Brush (1992) stresses that many, if not most, female entrepreneurs view their businesses not as separate economic entities but rather as endeavors entwined with other aspects of their lives, particularly their family relationships and responsibilities. She further emphasizes that female business owners tend to balance economic goals such as profit and growth with non-economic goals such as product quality, personal enjoyment, and helping others.

Scholars have espoused a 'family embeddedness perspective' (Aldrich and Cliff, 2003; Firkin et al., 2003; Heck and Trent, 1999), especially on women as entrepreneurs. So far, women's increasing involvement in entrepreneurial activity has been associated with the improved status of women, enhanced family and community well-being, and broader social gains (Haugh and Talwar, 2016). However, women have to face more conflicts than men do when they become entrepreneurs. For example, the literature on marriage and family indicates that women are more likely than men to have domestic responsibilities, making it hard for women to balance their business and family lives (Aldrich, 1989). Ufuk and Özgen (2001) examined the effect of being an entrepreneur on multiple roles (family, social, economic, and individual) and the conflict between the entrepreneur role and other roles in the family. They found that women believe that being an entrepreneur affects their roles in social, economic, and individual life but does not affect their participation in family decisions; that they suffer from conflicts between the role of entrepreneur and other roles (wife, mother, and housewife); and that the role of entrepreneur mostly conflicts with that of housewife. We argue that the presence of women in CBEs' management teams should increase the number of family-friendly policies provided by the business. Specifically,

Hypothesis 4: The percentage of women in the founding team will be positively related to the number of family-friendly policies provided by the business.

Brazil and Women Entrepreneurs

Brazil is the fifth largest and, with 162.6 million residents, the fifth most populous country in the world (Jones, 2000). It also has the world's fourth largest economy, with a gross domestic product (GDP) of $812 billion (Allen et al., 2007).

Brazil represents a good and interesting country to study entrepreneurship in general and female entrepreneurship in particular (Allen et al., 2007). Its total entrepreneurial activity (TEA) is said to involve approximately 14.3 percent of the population, with almost half (46 percent) of this fraction being women (ibid.). For comparison, an international study by Babson College shows that 19.95 percent of the women and 25.4 percent of the men in that population are business owners (Allen et al., 2008).

Since the 1970s there have been debates in Brazil about the relationship between the country's degree of economic growth and its social equity. The reported economic and social status of women in Brazil suggests that they have not been equitably incorporated into the economy. However, the contemporary milieu of Brazilian women is unlike the traditional one. The concept of freedom is becoming more prevalent in Brazilian culture, and, once clearly defined, gender roles are being challenged and women are raising their self-esteem and sense of identity.

METHODS

Database

For this study, we use data obtained from the Solidarity Economic Enterprise Database, created by the Brazilian government between 2009 and 2013 to gather information regarding the status of the solidarity economy in the country. The solidarity economy, an alternative economy driven by the principles of cooperation, self-management, and reciprocity (Miller, 2010), purports to fight inequality, social exclusion, and poverty. It has been identified as an innovative and effective alternative for creating jobs, generating income, and reducing poverty (Asseburg and Gaiger, 2005). In Brazil, it employed around 2 million people in 2013 (Nobrega, 2013). It has a very significant impact on women (Culti, 2004), and the database includes a specific appendix on women that includes various questions about work–family balance, social assistance programs, and charges such as director, coordinator, etc.

Sample

We focused our sample on businesses whose 'main economic activity' is production and commercialization. Other businesses within the database generally focus either on providing benefits to other businesses (for example, exchanging products or services, commercialization, or group savings) or on consumption by members. The final samples of businesses that provided answers to our questions include 1365 businesses for social initial motivations, 1035 for achievements, 1695 for challenges, and 12 146 for work–family policies. The variety in sample size is explained by data availability. As our database includes only cross-sectional information, having different sample sizes should not affect the implications of results, because we are mainly interested in examining the specific influence of the percentage of women in the founding team on the social side of the business.

Measures

Independent variable
Percentage of women in the founding team We calculate this variable as the number of women co-founders divided by the total number of members in the founding team. Given its distribution, we did a logarithmic transformation of the variable.

Dependent variables

Initial motivations to create the business   This variable takes the value 1 if the initial motivation was social; 0 if it was economic. The final variable is the sum of all social and economic initial motives for creating the business.

Achievements of the business   This variable takes the value 1 if the achievement was social; 0 if it was economic. The final variable is the sum of all social and economic achievements cited by the members.

Challenges of the business   This variable takes the value 1 if the challenge was social; 0 if it was economic. The final variable is the sum of all social and economic challenges cited by the members.

Family-friendly policies   This variable is a count variable. It covers the different work–family-balance policies that can be provided by the business: paid resting time, maternity leave, kindergarten, social and professional training safety equipment, risk prevention commission at work, social pension, insurance and/or dental insurance, education support, transport support, life insurance, and/or accident insurance. Thus, it ranges from 0 to 11.

Control variables

In accord with previous literature, we use a number of control variables to capture any additional phenomena that may affect the initial motivations to create the business, the ongoing achievements, and the challenges given the presence of women in the founding team. First, we control for the *role of income for members*. This variable is a dichotomous variable that takes the value 1 if the income from the business represents a main income source in the household and 0 otherwise.

Second, even though all the businesses included in our sample are community-based enterprises, so all members participate in decision-making, we control for those cases where women have a representative role in the business as either director or coordinator, in order to discover whether having more women in higher positions translates into a more social or economic orientation. For this purpose we use a count variable called *directors or coordinators*.

Third, we control for *profits*. This variable is calculated in thousands of reals as the logarithm of average monthly profits.

Fourth, we also control for *economic activity* with three dummy variables: production or production and commercialization, commercialization or the organization of commercialization, and services provision for third parties (the reference category).

Fifth, we control for *age profile* by differentiating among youth, adults, and elderly people (the reference category).

Sixth, we also control for the *business age*.

Seventh, extant research has provided evidence that race of organizational members may be related to performance. Businesses in our sample were asked which, if any, is the predominant race represented in the organization. Based on this, we control for *race* as a dummy variable that takes the value 1 if there is a predominant race among members and 0 otherwise.

Finally, we control for the *area* in which the business is located, with a dummy variable that takes the value 1 if the area is an urban area and 0 if it is a rural area.

Analyses

We conducted hierarchical ordinary least squares (OLS) regression analyses to estimate the relationship between the percentage of women in the founding teams and the motivations or initial goals, achievements achieved, and challenges of the business as well as the presence of family-friendly policies.

RESULTS

Tables 12.1 and 12.2 present the results of our analyses. Table 12.2 shows the results of our two models, model 1 being our baseline model, including only control variables as predictors, while model 2 tests the main predictions concerning the effects of the percentage of women in the founding team on the initial motivations, achievements achieved, and challenges of the business, as well as on the presence of family-friendly policies.

Hypothesis 1 predicted that the percentage of women in the founding team will be related positively to the presence of social initial motivations. As model 2 shows, the coefficient for the percentage of women is positive and significant ($\beta = 0.24$; $p < 0.010$). Thus, we find support for Hypothesis 1.

Hypothesis 2 predicted that the percentage of women in the founding team will be related positively to the social achievements of the business. Results from the OLS regression analysis are summarized in Table 12.2. Model 2 includes the effect of the percentage of women in the founding team, which was significantly and positively related to the social achievements of the business ($\beta = 0.28$; $p < 0.01$). This result supports Hypothesis 2.

Table 12.1   Correlation matrix

Variables	A	B	C	D	E	F	G	H	I	J	K	L	M	N	O
A. Initial goals in creating the business N = 1035															
B. Achievements of the business N = 1185	0.46**														
C. Challenges of the business N = 1695	0.47**	0.41**													
D. Work–family-balance policy N = 12146	0.07*	0.12**	0.07**												
E. Women in the founding team (logarithm)	0.07*	0.06*	0.02	−0.06**											
F. Role of income for members	−0.04	−0.05*	−0.08**	0.19**	−0.14**										
G. Women coordinators or directors	−0.06*	−0.02	0.02	0.09**	−0.51**	0.10**									
H. Profits (logarithm)	−0.03	0.02	0.01	0.25**	−0.38**	0.35**	0.35**								

Table 12.1 (continued)

Variables	A	B	C	D	E	F	G	H	I	J	K	L	M	N	O
I. Youth	-0.01	0.04	0.06**	-0.01	0.01	-0.02*	-0.02**	-0.06**							
J. Adults	0.03	-0.05	-0.06**	0.03**	-0.04**	0.07**	0.03**	0.09**	-0.60**						
K. Area	0.01	-0.01	-0.03	0.09**	0.34**	0.03**	-0.34**	-0.19**	0.02**	-0.04**					
L. Size	-0.04	0.07*	0.03	0.04**	-0.07**	0.03**	0.12**	0.11**	0.01	-0.02**	-0.05**				
M. Business age	0.02	-0.01	-0.01	0.01	-0.01	0.01	0.01	0.01	0.01	0.01	0.01	-0.01			
N. Production and production and commercialization	0.08**	0.01	0.05*	-0.12**	0.09**	-0.15**	-0.06**	-0.12**	-0.03**	0.01	-0.15**	0.01	0.01		
O. Commercialization or organization of commercialization	-0.04	-0.04	-0.05*	0.06**	-0.04**	0.14**	0.04**	0.11**	-0.07**	0.05**	0.07**	-0.03**	0.01	-0.77**	
P. Race	-0.04	0.02	-0.02	-0.11**	-0.02*	-0.01	-0.01	-0.04**	0.03**	0.06**	-0.10**	0.01	-0.01	0.12**	-0.12**

Notes: † $p < 0.10$; * $p < 0.05$; ** $p < 0.01$; *** $p < 0.001$.

Table 12.2 Effect of the percentage of women in the founding team on motivations, achievements, challenges, and work–family policies

	Motivations to create the business		Achievements		Challenges		Work–family-balance policies	
	Model 1	Model 2	Model 1	Model 2	Model 1	Model 2	Model 1	Model 2
Control variables								
Role of income for members	−0.07	−0.06	−0.41**	−0.40**	−0.23*	−0.21*	0.17***	0.17***
	(0.17)	(0.17)	(0.13)	(0.13)	(0.10)	(0.10)	(0.02)	(0.02)
Women coordinators or directors	−0.02	0.01	0.01	0.02	−0.01	0.02	0.01***	0.01***
	(0.02)	(0.02)	(0.01)	(0.02)	(0.01)	(0.02)	(0.01)	(0.01)
Age profile								
Youth	0.35	0.37	0.36	0.38	0.12	0.18	0.01	0.01
	(0.36)	(0.36)	(0.31)	(0.31)	(0.26)	(0.25)	(0.04)	(0.04)
Adults	0.25	0.27	−0.19	−0.18	−0.05	−0.03	0.07**	0.07**
	(0.23)	(0.23)	(0.18)	(0.18)	(0.15)	(0.15)	(0.03)	(0.03)
Profits	0.02	0.03	0.06†	0.07*	0.06†	0.06*	0.10***	0.10***
	(0.04)	(0.05)	(0.03)	(0.04)	(0.03)	(0.03)	(0.01)	(0.01)
Area	0.03	0.02	−0.07	−0.10	−0.04	−0.09	0.23***	0.22***
	(0.16)	(0.16)	(0.13)	(0.13)	(0.11)	(0.11)	(0.02)	(0.02)
Size	−0.01	−0.01	0.01*	0.01*	0.01*	0.01*	0.01†	0.01†
	(0.01)	(0.01)	(0.01)	(0.01)	(0.01)	(0.01)	(0.01)	(0.01)
Business age	−0.01	−0.01	−0.01	−0.01†	−0.01	−0.01	−0.01**	−0.01**
	(0.01)	(0.01)	(0.01)	(0.01)	(0.01)	(0.01)	(0.01)	(0.01)

Table 12.2 (continued)

	Motivations to create the business		Achievements		Challenges		Work–family-balance policies	
	Model 1	Model 2	Model 1	Model 2	Model 1	Model 2	Model 1	Model 2
Economic activity								
Production or production and commercialization	0.51*	0.48*	0.12*	0.09	−0.02*	−0.05	−0.33***	−0.34***
	(0.24)	(0.24)	(0.21)	(0.21)	(0.16)	(0.16)	(0.03)	(0.03)
Commercialization or organization of commercialization	0.31	0.27	−0.08	−0.11	−0.15	−0.17	−0.28***	−0.29***
	(0.27)	(0.27)	(0.23)	(0.23)	(0.18)	(0.18)	(0.03)	(0.03)
Race	−0.19	−0.18	−0.10	−0.09	0.04	0.04	−0.17***	−0.17***
	(0.16)	(0.16)	(0.12)	(0.12)	(0.10)	(0.10)	(0.02)	(0.02)
Independent variable								
% women in the founding team	–	0.24†	–	0.14	–	0.28**	–	0.04***
		(0.12)		(0.10)		(0.08)		(0.01)
R^2	0.011	0.015	0.016	0.017	0.011	0.019	0.116	0.117
Adj. R^2	0.001	0.003	0.010	0.010	0.003	0.010	0.115	0.117

Notes: † $p < 0.10$; * $p < 0.05$; ** $p < 0.01$; *** $p < 0.001$. $N = 1035$.

Hypothesis 3 predicted that the percentage of women in the founding teams will be related positively to the social challenges of the business. Examples of social challenges are 'Guaranteeing social protection, increasing members' environmental awareness, or maintaining the unity of a group or collective.' Among the control variables, the role of income for members was negatively and significantly associated with the social challenges of the business ($\beta = 0.14$). Model 2 includes the effect of the percentage of women in the founding team. We found no empirical evidence that the percentage of women in the founding team influenced the social challenges of the business. Thus, we do not find support for Hypothesis 3.

Finally, Hypothesis 4 predicted that the percentage of women in the founding team will be related positively to family-friendly policies of the business. The results in Table 12.2 support Hypothesis 4. We complement this analysis by running an OLS regression analysis to assess whether this effect remained for work–family-balance policies specifically affecting women (women-friendly policies): maternity leave and kindergarten assistance. We found strong empirical evidence that the percentage of women in the founding team influenced the presence of women-friendly policies ($\beta = 0.05$; $p < 0.001$).

In all models the R^2 is close to zero. This is especially relevant in the case of initial motivations to create the business. Even though the coefficient is significant, the value means that including the variable for the percentage of women in the founding team does not affect the model in a determinant way. This is very interesting, because according to our first model the percentage of women in the founding team explains why very few of the CBEs have more social motivations than economic motivations.

CONCLUSIONS

Our results show that while the percentage of women in the founding team positively influences the social motivations and achievements of the business, it does not appear to influence the social challenges of the business. We do find, however, that the presence of women in the founding team increases the presence of family-friendly policies, and this effect remains regardless of whether or not we take into account specifically gender-relevant policies such as maternity leave and kindergarten.

This research draws upon and seeks to contribute to the emerging literature on social entrepreneurship (Austin et al., 2006; Nicholls, 2006; Short et al., 2009) and community-based enterprises (Peredo and Chrisman, 2006). We focus on collective efforts to launch a social enterprise venture rather than on heroic individual social entrepreneurs (Short et al., 2009), and highlight the significance of Brazil as a site for exploration, given its large population base working in community-based enterprises and its growing global economic and political importance.

This study intends to make different contributions to the literature on community-based enterprises, entrepreneurial teams, and gender dynamics. In particular, we contribute to research on women entrepreneurs to the extent that women's influence on decision-making is different in community-based enterprises – specifically, showing how gender dynamics within entrepreneurial teams in those enterprises affect the economic and social dimensions of motives for business creation, goals achieved, and business challenges. This could help us better understand whether those supposedly more egalitarian businesses actually implement family-friendly policies equally for women and men, or whether they suffer from a gap between narrative and practice, as often happens in traditional businesses.

Implications

Despite all its difficulties, entrepreneurial activity is a path to self-realization and contribution to society. Women's sharing in this process is also important for the family economy and the national economy (Ufuk and Özgen, 2001). Effective involvement of women in economic life is important for both country development and improving families' quality of life. Understanding better how the presence of women in the founding team affects the social orientation of businesses that are naturally oriented toward the community, and also how it affects these firms' adoption of work–family-balance policies, can help us to place the role of women as entrepreneurs in economic life.

ACKNOWLEDGEMENTS

The authors are thankful for the funding received from the Ministerio de Economía y Competitividad de España through research project ECO2012-30932. In addition, Professor Justo acknowledges support received from the Ministerio de Economía y Competitividad de España through research project ECO2015-66146-R: El emprendimiento social desde un enfoque configuracional: Los determinantes individuales y contextuales de la acción estratégica y persistencia de los emprendedores sociales. Finally, the authors are also grateful to the Ministerio do Trabalho e Emprego-MTE from the Governo do Brasil (Brazilian Government) for its support and collaboration in providing the database utilized for this study.

REFERENCES

Adkins, C.L., Samaras, S.A., Gilfillan, S.W., and McWcc, W.E. (2013). The relationship between owner characteristics, company size, and the work–family culture and policies of women-owned businesses. *Journal of Small Business Management*, 51(2), 196–214.

Aldrich, H.E. (1989). Networking among women entrepreneurs. In O. Hagan, C. Rivchun, and D. Sexton (eds), *Women-Owned Businesses*. New York: Praeger, pp. 103–132.

Aldrich, H.E. and Cliff, J.E. (2003). The pervasive effects of family on entrepreneurship: toward a family embeddedness perspective. *Journal of Business Venturing*, 18, 573–596.

Allen, E., Langowitz, N., and Minniti, M. (2007). Global Entrepreneurship Monitor: 2006 report on women and entrepreneurship. The Center for Women's Leadership at Babson College, London Business School.

Allen, E., Langowitz, N., and Minniti, M. (2008). Global Entrepreneurship Monitor: 2007 report on women and entrepreneurship. The Center for Women's Leadership at Babson College, London Business School.

Asseburg, H.B. and Gaiger, L.I.G. (2005). The solidarity economy and the reduction of inequalities. *Annals of ANPEC–SUL*. Florianópolis: UFSC.

Austin, J., Stevenson, H., and Wei-Skillern, J. (2006). Social and commercial entrepreneurship: same, different or both? *Entrepreneurship Theory and Practice*, 30(1), 1–22.

Braun, P. (2010). Going green: women entrepreneurs and the environment. *International Journal of Gender and Entrepreneurship*, 2(3), 245–259.

Brush, C.G. (1992). Research on women business owners: past trends, a new perspective and future directions. *Entrepreneurship Theory and Practice*, 16(4), 5–31.

Buttner, E.H. and Moore, D.P. (1997). Women's organizational exodus to entrepreneurship: self-reported motivations and correlates with success. *Journal of Small Business Management Review*, 34(3), 552–569.

Calhoun, C. (2012). *Contemporary Sociological Theory*. Chichester, UK: Wiley.

Caputo, R.K. and Dolinsky, A. (1998). Women's choice to pursue self-employment: the role of financial and human capital of household members. *Journal of Small Business Management*, 36(3), 8–17.

Cliff, J.E., Langton, N., and Aldrich, H.E. (2005). Walking the talk? Gendered rhetoric vs. action in small firms. *Organization Studies*, 26(1), 63–91.

Connelly, R. (1992). The effect of child care costs on married women's labor force participation. *The Review of Economics and Statistics*, 74(1), 83–90.

Culti, M.Z. (2004). Mulheres na economia solidária: desafios sociais e políticos. Paper presented at 'IV Congreso Europeo CEISAL de Latinoamericanistas,' Bratislava, Slovakia.

Daskalaki, M., Hjorth, D., and Mair, J. (2015). Are entrepreneurship, communities, and social transformation related? *Journal of Management Inquiry*, 24(4), 419–423.

Datta, P.B. and Gailey, R. (2012). Empowering women through social entrepreneurship: case study of a women's cooperative in India. *Entrepreneurship Theory and Practice*, 36, 569–587.

Davidson, D.J. and Freudenburg, W.R. (1996). Gender and environmental risk concerns. *Environmental and Behavior*, 28(3), 302–339.

DeMartino, R., Barbato, R., and Jacques, P.H. (2006). Exploring the career/achievement and personal life orientation differences between entrepreneurs and nonentrepreneurs: the impact of sex and dependents. *Journal of Small Business Management*, 44(3), 350–368.

Dupuis, A. and de Bruin, A. (2003). Community entrepreneurship. In A. de Bruin and A. Dupuis (eds), *Entrepreneurship: New Perspectives in a Global Age*. Burlington, VT: Ashgate, pp. 109–127.

Ettl, K. and Welter, F. (2010). Gender, context and entrepreneurship learning. *International Journal of Gender Entrepreneurship*, 2(2), 108–129.

Firkin, P., Dupuis, A., and de Bruin, A. (2003). Familial entrepreneurship. In A. de Bruin and A. Dupuis (eds), *Entrepreneurship: New Perspectives in a Global Age*. Burlington, VT: Ashgate, pp. 92–108.

Gartner, W.B., Davidsson, P., and Zahra, S.A. (2006). Are you talking to me? The nature of community in entrepreneurship scholarship. *Entrepreneurship Theory and Practice*, 30(3), 321–331.

Gilligan, C. (1982). *In a Different Voice: Psychological Theory and Women's Development*. Cambridge, MA: Harvard University Press.

Gupta, V.K., Turban, D.B., Wasti, S.A., and Sikdar, A. (2009). The role of gender stereotypes in perceptions of entrepreneurs and intentions to become an entrepreneur. *Entrepreneurship Theory and Practice*, 33(2), 397–417.

Haugh, H. (2007). New strategies for a sustainable society: the growing contributions of social entrepreneurship. *Business Ethics Quarterly*, 17(4), 743–749.

Haugh, H.M. and Talwar, A. (2016). Linking social entrepreneurship and social change: the mediating role of empowerment. *Journal of Business Ethics*, 133(4), 643–658.

Hechavarria, D.M., Terjesen, S.A., Ingram, A.E., Renko, M., Justo, R., and Elam, A. (2016). Taking care of business: the impact of culture and gender on entrepreneurs' blended value creation goals. *Small Business Economics*, 48(1), 1–33.

Heck, C.A. and Trent, E.S. (1999). The prevalence of family business from a household sample. *Family Business Review*, 12, 209–224.

Jaffee, S. and Hyde, J.S. (2000). Gender differences in moral orientation: a meta-analysis. *Psychological Bulletin*, 126(5), 703–726.

Johannisson, B. (1990). Community entrepreneurship: cases and conceptualization. *Entrepreneurship and Regional Development*, 2(1), 71–88.

Jones, K. (2000). Psychodynamics, gender, and reactionary entrepreneurship in metropolitan Sao Paulo, Brazil. *Women in Management Review*, 15(4), 207–217.

Konda, I., Starc, J., and Rodica, B. (2015). Social challenges are opportunities for sustainable development: tracing impacts of social entrepreneurship through innovations and value creation. *Economic Themes*, 53(2), 211–229.

Mair, J. and Schoen, O. (2007). Successful social entrepreneurial business models in the context of developing economies: an explorative study. *International Journal of Emerging Markets*, 2(1), 54–68.

Milanov, H., Justo, R., and Bradley, S.W. (2015). Making the most of group relationships: the role of gender and boundary effects in microcredit groups. *Journal of Business Venturing*, 30(6), 822–838.

Miller, E. (2010). Solidarity economy: key concepts and issues. In E. Kawano, T.N. Masterson, and J. Teller-Elsberg (eds), *Solidarity Economy I: Building Alternatives for People and Planet*. Amherst, MA: Center for Popular Economics, pp. 25–42.

Morris, M.H., Miyasaki, N.N., Watters, C.E., and Combes, S.M. (2006). The dilemma of growth: understanding venture size choices of women entrepreneurs. *Journal of Small Business Management*, 44(2), 221–244.

Nicholls, A. (2006). *Social Entrepreneurship: New Models of Sustainable Social Change*. Oxford: Oxford University Press.

Nippierd, A.B. (1999). Gender issues in cooperatives. *Journal of Cooperative Studies*, 32(3), 175–181.

Nobrega, C. (2013). Solidarity economy: finding a new way out of poverty. *The Guardian*. Retrieved from https://www.theguardian.com/global-development-professionals-network/2013/oct/09/brazil-solidarity-economy-labour.

Orser, B. and Hogarth-Scott, S. (2002). Opting for growth: gender dimensions of choosing enterprise development. *Canadian Journal of Administrative Sciences*, 19(3), 284–300.

Osterloh, M. and Frey, B.S. (2000). Motivation, knowledge transfer and organizational forms. *Organization Science*, 11(5), 538–550.

Parasuraman, S. and Simmers, C.A. (2001). Type of employment, work–family conflict and well-being: a comparative study. *Journal of Organizational Behavior*, 22(5), 551–568.

Peredo, A.M. and Chrisman, J. (2006). Toward a theory of community-based enterprise. *Academy of Management Review*, 31(2), 309–328.

Ridgeway, C. (2011). *Framed by Gender: How Gender Inequality Persists in the Modern World*. Oxford: Oxford University Press.

Ruef, M. (2010). *The Entrepreneurial Group: Social Identities, Relations and Collective Action*. Princeton, NJ: Princeton University Press.

Ruef, M., Aldrich, H., and Carter, N. (2003). The structure of founding teams: homophily, strong ties and isolation among U.S. entrepreneurs. *American Sociological Review*, 68, 195–222.

Salamzadeh, A., Salamzadeh, Y., and Nejati, M. (2011). Social entrepreneurship: analyzing literature and proposing a comprehensive model. Paper presented at the 9th Asian Academy of Management International Conference, Penang, Malaysia.

Short, J.C., Moss, T.W., and Lumpkin, G.T. (2009). Research in social entrepreneurship: past contributions and future opportunities. *Strategic Entrepreneurship Journal*, 3, 161–194.

Somerville, P. and McElwee, G. (2011). Situating community enterprise: a theoretical exploration. *Entrepreneurship and Regional Development*, 23(5–6), 317–330.

Ufuk, H. and Özgen, O. (2001). Interaction between the business and family lives of women entrepreneurs in Turkey. *Journal of Business Ethics*, 31, 95–106.

Yang, T. and Aldrich, H.E. (2014). Who's the boss? Explaining gender inequality in entrepreneurial teams. *American Sociological Review*, 79(2), 303–327.

PART 4

Moving forward

13. Gender and business performance: the role of entrepreneurial segregation

Natalie Sappleton

Gender and entrepreneurship researchers have been investigating the relative performance of male-owned and female-owned enterprises for almost three decades. This corpus of research is at least partly responsible for fuelling the widely held yet controversial belief that the enterprises owned and operated by women are less successful than those controlled by their male counterparts in terms of economic aspects such as business size, global reach, sustainability and survivability, growth potential, sales and profitability (Zolin et al., 2013). However, in recent years, the so-called 'underperformance hypothesis' has begun to be challenged by researchers adopting a more sophisticated approach to empirical analysis, and particularly those who incorporate controls for sets of variables known to impact entrepreneurial performance and success (Justo et al., 2015; Robb and Watson, 2012; Watson, 2002b; Zolin et al., 2013). Such analyses are more vigilant in relating entrepreneurial inputs to outputs (for example, Watson, 2002a), adjusting for risk (for example, Watson and Robinson, 2003) or employing more nuanced definitions and understandings of key constructs such as 'failure' (for example, Justo et al., 2015) and 'success' (for example, Reavley and Lituchy, 2008).

One factor that has been identified as important is the industrial sector in which women- and men-owned firms are located (Robb and Watson, 2012). For instance, comparative studies that have matched samples of male and female entrepreneurs based on sector have revealed far fewer gender differences in business performance (Robb, 2002; Watson, 2002a, 2002b). In addition, the major industrial classification with the single greatest concentration of women-owned enterprises – personal services – is also the least profitable major industry sub-group in the US (US Census Bureau, 2011). In spite of these observations, published studies continue to overlook the impact that differences in business sector exert on firm size, survival, success and performance. This chapter represents a call to action to empiricists to make a more meaningful contribution to the literature by taking adequate account of business sector in future investigations into gender and entrepreneurial performance. Sector matters for a number of reasons. Of course, business characteristics differ from sector to sector, and these characteristics impact on myriad aspects relating to business activity, such as the degree and intensity of competitive rivalry between incumbents, level of replicability of the enterprise, the typical size and organization of firms, and their propensity for global reach (Caloghirou et al., 2004). Yet these sector characteristics would be extraneous to our understanding of gender and entrepreneurial performance if men- and women-owned enterprises were evenly distributed across sectors. This is far from the case. In fact, like the occupational arena, the realm of entrepreneurship is highly gender-segregated, with women-owned businesses overwhelmingly concentrated in the broad industry categories of retail and services (Sappleton, 2009). Moreover, the sectors in which women start businesses support small-scale, locally focused enterprises, and tend to be highly competitive in nature – aspects that exert a significant influence on the propensity for these firms to flourish and grow (Welter et al., 2014). Accordingly, in the discussion that follows, it is contended that the empirical existence of entrepreneurial segregation obliges investigators who do wish to examine gender and business performance to undertake analyses within narrowly delineated industry sub-categories.

The chapter is structured as follows. First, the concept of entrepreneurial segregation is defined and explicated. Second, the chapter contends that it is crucial that any comparative analysis takes adequate account of the role of the business sector, and, drawing upon a review of the pertinent literature, sets out an argument to support this assertion. Finally, the chapter sets forth arguments to explain the failure of researchers to account for industry in previous analyses and emphasises the need for researchers pursuing the gender–business-performance line of inquiry to undertake analyses within narrowly defined industry categories.

ENTREPRENEURIAL SEGREGATION

Occupational sex segregation is the term used to describe the unequal concentration of women and men into different segments of the labour market (Stockdale and Nadler, 2013). Occupational segregation consists of both vertical and horizontal elements. *Vertical segregation* refers to a pattern of segregation in which the lower levels of job hierarchies tend to be female-dominated, while senior management levels are primarily composed of men. This is the form of segregation that makes the most glaring contribution to social and economic inequalities (Martell et al., 2012; Stockdale and Nadler, 2013). In contrast, *horizontal segregation* is the dimension that refers to the concentration of women and men in different occupational classes and categories (Watts, 2005). For instance, the manual trades are dominated by male workers, while work in the caring professions tends to be undertaken by women (Huppatz, 2009; Sappleton, 2013).

Even a cursory observation of the organizational literature reveals that research has paid far greater attention to vertical segregation than to horizontal segregation (Evetts, 2014). One interpretation of this empirical imbalance is that, unlike the vertical element, horizontal segregation is believed to depict 'difference without inequality' (Jarman et al., 2012, p. 1006). This contention runs counter to the observation that the careers and occupations in which women tend to be concentrated, the so-called five Cs (cleaning, catering, caring, cash registering and clerical work), attract significantly lower pay and potential than the sectors of employment in which men work (Brynin and Perales, 2016).

That vertical and horizontal segregation both independently make a direct contribution to economic gender inequalities is evident from the research on self-employment (Eastough and Miller, 2004; Hundley, 2001; Lechmann and Schnabel, 2012). Elsewhere (Sappleton, 2009, 2014), the concentration of women- and men-owned businesses into separate segments of the economy has been termed *entrepreneurial segregation*. Entrepreneurial segregation embodies features that both distinguish it from segregation in employment, and deserve and necessitate distinct inquiry. Importantly, this form of segregation is characterized by *both* vertical and orthogonally horizontal qualities. From a horizontal perspective, the firms owned and operated by women and men are concentrated in very different sectors and industries. US Census Bureau data, for instance, shows that women-owned firms are over-represented in the Healthcare and Social Assistance and Educational Services sectors, and under-represented in Construction and the primary sectors. Men are under-represented in the sectors in which women are most commonly found, but in most industries, men form a majority (US Census Bureau, 2011).

The US Census Bureau and counterpart institutions outside the US generally report gender of owner at the two-digit industrial classification, a fact that masks considerable segregation (Sappleton, 2009). However, analyses of micro data sets reveal that segregation is even more extreme when examined at the six-digit industry classification. For instance, using US Statistics of Income data, Lowrey (2005) assessed the distribution of male- and female-owned sole traders across the business activities in which most sole proprietorships were engaged through the period 1985–2000. Of the top ten activities, most were heavily sex-segregated. Carpentering and floor contractors and miscellaneous special trade contractors were heavily male-dominated, while beauty shops and child day care were heavily female-dominated. In fact, 51.9 per cent of women-led sole proprietorships were concentrated in just ten activities including child day care, beauty shops, miscellaneous personal services and real-estate agents and brokers (in contrast, just 28.4 per cent of male sole proprietorships were concentrated in the top ten activities – largely carpentering and floor contractors, miscellaneous specialty trade contractors and door-to-door sales) (ibid.). In the UK, three in ten self-employed men work in the construction industry, whereas around a quarter of self-employed women are based in the service sector in areas such as the community, and social and personal services (Sappleton, 2009). The recent increase in rates of female self-employment that has been witnessed in that country has largely been driven by growth in two key sectors: administrative and support service activities (where there has been an overall growth in self-employment of 37 per cent) and human health and social work activities (20 per cent growth) (Hatfield, 2015).

At the same time, the businesses that are owned by women generate lower sales relative to male-owned firms; it is observed that these firms also tend to be smaller, to have lower growth rates, to employ fewer staff and to serve local markets (Sappleton, 2014). For instance, Mayer (2008) examined the horizontal and vertical dimensions of entrepreneurial segregation in her study of women-owned firms in the male-dominated high-tech industry in four US cities, including Silicon Valley. She found that even where women entrepreneurs break down gender barriers to establish enterprises in the high-tech industry, they were located outside of the high-tech core (that is, manufacturing) and tended to be concentrated in female-type segments of the sector, such as software publishing and research and consulting. Furthermore, these peripheral firms tended to have significantly fewer employees, a smaller sales volume and fewer sales per employee compared to firms within the high-tech core.

In the entrepreneurship literature, these observations have been attributed to women's underperformance (Zolin et al., 2013). However, it is contended here that this so-called underperformance is, in fact, merely reflective of the vertical aspect of entrepreneurial segregation. That women operate firms that are qualitatively different from those owned and operated by their male counterparts in terms of performance characteristics such as sales, revenues, profits and growth potential mirrors vertical segregation in occupations whereby women undertake jobs that are less well paid and offer fewer opportunities for promotion and progression. In other words, the so-called 'underperformance' of women-owned firms is nothing more than a manifestation of, and an outcome of, vertical gender segregation in entrepreneurship. For instance, although US Census Bureau (2011) data show that the receipts of all men-owned firms are more than three-and-a-half times the receipts of all women-owned firms, this disparity drops substantially when analysis is restricted to just one industry. In the construction industry, for example, the average sales of women-owned firms are comparable to the sales of men-owned firms (author's calculations, US Census Bureau, 2011). The next section comprises a short review of the literature in support of this assertion.

ENTREPRENEURIAL SEGREGATION AND THE 'UNDERPERFORMANCE' OF WOMEN-OWNED FIRMS

The number of studies that have taken the business sector into consideration when assessing the gender-performance link is relatively small. Nevertheless, research drawing on sector-matched samples has revealed far fewer gender differences in business performance than studies that have failed to account for this variable. Chell and Baines (1998) collected data from a sample of solely owned and jointly owned micro-sized ventures in the business services sector in two mid-sized British cities. Their analysis revealed significant gender differences in the turnover of these enterprises. Using a large random sample, du Rietz and Henrekson (2000) did find that female-headed firms underperform relative to male-headed firms on several measures (increases in sales, profits, employment and orders/commissions); however, gender of owner was no longer a significant determinant of performance when structural factors (firm size, industry and receiving sector) were controlled, and there were no differences in the performance of one-person enterprises.

Hokkanen and Autio (1998) restricted their sample to businesses over three years old in the business services sector and targeted male- and female-owned firms that were matched in terms of establishment year, legal status and geographical location. In their results, gender was uncorrelated with all measures of performance (sales, sales growth, number of employees, growth in number of employees and growth aspirations). In summing up, the authors suggested that earlier findings might have been skewed because male entrepreneurs are more common in manufacturing, a sector that enjoys greater levels of growth than typically female sectors.

In a longitudinal study of eating and drinking establishments, computer sales and software companies, and health-related firms in Indiana, USA, Kalleberg and Leicht (1991) found no gender differences in the rate of business dissolution, growth of earnings, confidence of owner or level of innovation. Only one factor generating survival was found to have differential effects on the success rates of men's and women's firms: involvement in a previous business venture. Using the same data set, Loscocco and Leicht (1993) found that men-owned enterprises tended to generate greater revenue than their female-owned counterparts, but the authors directly attributed the difference to the differential family responsibilities of men and women. Men have fewer domestic responsibilities, thus are able to devote more time to their firm, but single women with children (who have both the domestic responsibilities and the pressure to earn) generate more earnings than married women. Loscocco and Robinson (1991) also compared the receipts of men- and women-owned enterprises. They concluded that 'women approached an equivalent share of business when they operated in the major industry categories that capitalize on traditionally male-defined skills, such as construction, mining, and transportation and communication services' and that 'those women who operated retail or service businesses dealing with automobiles did particularly well relative to men' (ibid., p. 521).

Lowrey's (2005) examination of US sole proprietors supports this finding. He found that female sole traders were more competitive in the least segregated business activities. Compared to men, female real-estate agents and brokers reported similar net income as a percentage of gross profits; in janitorial and related services, women made more average annual net income than men. And, while the average woman-owned firm generated revenues of $186 000 in 2002, woman-owned Wholesale Trade firms averaged more than $1.9 million, woman-owned construction firms around $617 000 and woman-owned Manufacturing firms $956 000 (National Association of Women-Owned Businesses, 2013).

Examining four periods of data on almost 5000 Australian SMEs, Watson (2002a, 2002b) discovered that while the income and profit of firms owned by men were on average higher, data on return on assets and return on equity (which Watson argues are more useful measures of profitability than sales and profit because these do not pick up on the fact that women invest less in their firms) suggested that female-owned businesses outperformed male-owned businesses. Additionally, once industry, age of business and working hours were controlled, there was no significant variation in profitability that could be attributed to gender of owner; rather, industry was the more important factor in explaining the variance in business performance.

In another longitudinal analysis, Headd's (2003) examination of Census Bureau Data revealed that closure rates are lower amongst manufacturers (compared to service and retail trade firms), firms that start with more than $50 000 start-up capital, firms that employ others, and business owners with previous experience owning a firm. The conjecture is that the slightly higher-than-average closure rates for female owners is attributable to their tendency to start and stay small, to their limited experience in running other firms and to their being based in the retail and services sectors – domains in which competition is high because firms are easily identified and copied. Using the same data, Robb (2002) introduced ethnicity as a variable and found that Asian females have the highest firm survival rates of all groups. Finally, one study of small retailers reported that solo female operators demonstrated better performance (operationalized as sales per square foot) than their male counterparts, but that gender-mixed teams achieved superior performance than solo retailers of either sex or gender-balanced teams (Litz and Folker, 2002).

In sum, the dominant view is that women-owned enterprises underperform relative to those owned by men. However, this perspective is contested by empirical studies that compare women- and men-owned ventures within narrowly delineated industrial categories. Gender differences in a host of performance proxies – including closure rates, firm receipts, return on assets and return on equity – disappear when controls for the business sector are applied. The next section draws on the theoretical offerings of the strategic management literature to explicate this finding.

WHY THE BUSINESS SECTOR MATTERS

The strategic management literature has lent considerable conceptual and practical insight to entrepreneurship theory and practice (Hitt et al., 2002; Meyer et al., 2002). The chief concern of the strategic management discipline is how organizations can strive to achieve competitive advantage. In this pursuit, industry structure, firm resources and firm capabilities are thought to be key (Foss and Knudsen, 2013). Porter's (1980) competitive forces framework, for instance, derived from the Structure-Conduct-Performance (SCP) paradigm, contends that industry structure (including the relative power of buyers and suppliers, and the degree and intensity of rivalry between incumbents) is a key driver of competitive advantage and profitability. The Resource Based View (RBV) of the firm emphasises that a firm's stock resources must be valuable, rare, inimitable and non-substitutable (VRIN) if a firm is to generate economic rents (Foss and Knudsen, 2013). The dynamic capabilities literature, which draws heavily on Schumpeterian notions of competency, views firm performance as driven by 'the firm's ability to integrate, build, and reconfigure internal and external competencies to address rapidly changing environments' (Teece et al., 1997, p. 516). Thus, these three theoretical strands emphasise that the business ecosystem – the industry in which the firm operates, as well as its position within the industry and relationship towards it – shape and constrain firm performance. Importantly, industry characteristics exert a considerable impact on three areas of business activity: the ability to leverage finance, the degree of risk involved, and the propensity to expand and diversify beyond the local market.

Ability to Leverage Finance

The industry location of firms has consequences for the ability of the entrepreneur to leverage both start-up and ongoing finance (Sappleton, 2014). In making the decision about whether to invest in or extend a loan to a small business, financiers ostensibly make objective, generalized assessments of characteristics of the enterprise, such as its likely survivability, the riskiness of both the enterprise and the sector in which it is located and its growth potential (Nofsinger and Wang, 2011). Of course, these characteristics differ from industry to industry. For instance, the retail and services sectors, where women-owned businesses are predominately located, suffer from higher closure rates than other firms (Robb and Watson, 2012). Entrepreneurs operating in these risky sectors of the economy may therefore find it more challenging to raise funding and may have to rely on alternative funding sources, particularly bootstrapping (Brush et al., 2006; Hill et al., 2006; Manolova et al., 2006).

Venture capital investments, for instance, tend to be directed towards firms in industries that optimize risk/reward ratios (Vanacker and Manigart, 2010). In 2003, for instance, Greene et al. (2001) noted that 90 per cent of venture capital dollars were made in organizations in just nine industries – telecommunications, software, biotechnology, medial devices and equipment, semiconductors, media and entertainment, computers and peripherals, IT services and industrial energy – industries which continue to be extremely male-dominated. Indeed, up until 1998, no investments had yet been made in women-led firms in construction, public administration or finance, insurance and real estate (ibid.). While the authors observed that just 2.5 per cent of venture capital investments had been made in women-led firms since 1953, they did not ascribe this necessarily to overt discrimination, but to the empiric fact that 'the predominant industry choices of female entrepreneurs appear to be mismatched with the industry preferences of venture capitalists' (ibid., p. 68).

Furthermore, empirical research suggests that, due to gender stereotyping, women starting businesses in sectors that are deemed to be non-traditional for, or incongruent with, their gender, find it more difficult to leverage finance than women establishing enterprises in gender-congruent sectors (Sappleton, 2014). Women attempting to start businesses in male-dominated sectors speak of suffering heightened levels of discrimination and being perceived as less credible business owners when they approach external financiers for funding (Chesser, 1998; Coyle and Flannery, 2005; Verwey, 2005). Back in 1985, Gregg (1985, p. 12) was optimistic about the future in this respect:

> It would have been downright foolhardy for the restless housewife of the 1950s to suddenly get it into her head to start a pharmaceutical company. So, not surprisingly, the first generation woman entrepreneur started a baker or boutique or decorating firm – all low-overhead ventures that were extensions of the homemaking role and usually had women as their primary customers . . . but [the second generation woman entrepreneur] . . . will have the know-how, the professional contacts, and access to capital – the kind of credentials, in short, that male entrepreneurs accumulate before starting off on their own.

However, the available evidence suggests that even today, lack of appropriate capital restricts women entrepreneurs from establishing firms in male-dominated sectors, and where women do establish ventures in these sectors, they are undercapitalized. This is an important point, for undercapitalization is said to be the greatest cause of business failure amongst small firms (Blake, 2006). In addition, longitudinal analyses have shown that capital endowments at start-up are strongly associated with value of assets, number of employees and sales turnover many months or even years later (Alsos et al., 2005; Bird and Sapp, 2004; Carter and Rosa, 1998; Dahlqvist et al., 2000). Thus business sector, gender stereotyping and lack of capital work in tandem to make an industry-driven contribution to the relative 'underperformance' of women-owned firms.

Risk

Industries differ in terms of the market-driven and competitive risk incurred by their incumbents (Caloghirou et al., 2004). Empirical research undertaken in a range of geographical contexts repeatedly uncover systematic variations in market structure across industries (Segarra and Callejón, 2002). Market structure differences emerge from aspects such as the relative level of investment in R&D, the degree of product differentiation and the presence of economies of scale, which in turn give rise to specific patterns of firm behaviour, such as industry entry rates, growth rates and closure rates. These facts need to be considered alongside any examination of the gender-performance linkage. For instance, the retail industry, in which one-third of all US women-owned enterprises are located (US Census Bureau, 2011), is characterized by pro-cyclicality, so businesses in this sector are highly vulnerable to the economic climate (Koellinger and Roy Thurik, 2012).

Furthermore, competitive risk is industry-driven. Many locally focused, small-scale service-based firms, for instance, are highly imitable. Imitability is defined as the ease with which new and existing entrants in the industry can replicate or learn a firm's business model, technology or other resources (Autio et al., 2000). Degree of imitability differs according to business activity. In part, inimitability is caused by the ambiguity of organizational operations and routines, and in particular an inability of competitors to identify the causal drivers of performance outcomes (ibid.). In contrast, performance drivers that can be easily observed can also be replicated, preventing the focal firm from rapidly accumulating resources and exploiting opportunities.

Importantly, performance driver ambiguities are industry-driven (Foss and Knudsen, 2013). For instance, firms in sectors such as biotechnology and high technology draw heavily on the tacit components of their knowledge base for competitive advantage (Kim et al., 2013). Tacit knowledge is difficult for outsiders to comprehend, expropriate and imitate, and is thus a major source of competitive advantage (Meyer et al., 2002). In contrast, many small-scale firms in consumer-driven industries such as personal services tend to adhere to standardized business models that are easily replicated by others. This impacts performance outcomes because, according to the RBV, 'when a firm's key resources are imitable, the firm cannot realise its full rent-generating potential' (Autio et al., 2000, p. 914). Sustained revenue growth, for instance, is undermined in sectors where the barriers to entry are low and competitors can quickly attract sales from firms by imitating their outputs.

These aspects increase the hazards associated with establishing an enterprise in industries high in market-driven and competitive risk. Consequently, entrepreneurs establishing ventures in such sectors may find it more difficult to leverage initial and ongoing finance, and may find it more challenging to sustain and grow their enterprises. Given the degree of entrepreneurial segregation, the failure rates, sales growth and profitability of women-owned firms are likely to be disproportionately impacted in these respects. Paradoxically, research shows that women entrepreneurs make industry choices on the basis of careful appraisal of risk at the macro, micro and individual levels (Brindley, 2005). Women start service-based enterprises instead of, say, high-technology enterprises precisely *because* these are sectors with low barriers to entry, and firms in these sectors are commensurate with women's existing financial and social capital and need to accommodate domestic responsibilities, all of which are driven by gendered societal processes (O'Gorman and Aylward, 2007).

In other words, the choice of business can be seen in terms of 'high motivation to immediate independence tempered by economic rationality rather than a conscious desire to operate a "female-type" business' (Watkins and Watkins, 1983, p. 286). Thus, women entrepreneurs' risk assessments, undertaken within a gendered societal structure, induces them to start businesses in the riskiest business sectors.

Local Orientation

Small-scale firms in retail and service sectors tend to serve local markets. For instance, local high streets are replete with virtually identikit sole proprietorships that cater to narrowly delineated catchment areas (Mayer, 2008). This is important because local orientation constrains both the size of the venture, the size of the market that it serves, and the potential for international growth (Moen et al., 2016). In addition, broadening geographical horizons enables firms to gain access to specialized labour, crucial networks and other important resources that boost productivity and efficiency. These aspects are important because the industries in which women-owned enterprises are concentrated tend to be more locally oriented than those industries in which men-owned enterprises are more readily found (Mayer, 2008).

Curiously, very little research has examined the international orientation of women-owned enterprises. However, it is known that women's choice of workplace is location-driven due to the need to undertake domestic responsibilities (McGowan et al., 2012). For instance, many of the new generation of women entrepreneurs – the so-called *mumspreneurs* – operate their businesses from home to enable them to simultaneously care for their children (Duberley and Carrigan, 2013; Gimenez-Nadal et al., 2012). This issue is more salient where the firm is small and has few resources on which to draw – aspects that characterize many women-owned enterprises as a consequence of the residual effects of gendered socio-economic processes, including occupational segregation. Sex-role socialization (which draws females into female-type education and careers) and prescriptive gender stereotypes prepare women for roles that society deems to be appropriate for them (Jarman et al., 2012). These roles provide women with lower incomes than their male counterparts; and offer them fewer opportunities to acquire managerial experience and personal networks that sustain internationally oriented, high-growth enterprises. Faced with society's beliefs about their proper roles, encumbered with domestic responsibilities and lacking the appropriate infrastructural, financial and social support, where women decide to start a business, they often must do so in those sectors with the lowest barriers to entry, and drawing on limited resources.

These aspects act as a constraint on industry choice because certain types of enterprises, such as business services, are more congruent with a lack of premises (O'Gorman and Aylward, 2007). In contrast, men, who have had access to larger amounts of investment, relevant educational, management and employment experience, and the ability to attract many more crucial resources, have always had the ability to make broader choices in this regard. For instance, Mayer's (2008) examination of the spatial segmentation of women-owned high-tech firms finds that gendered spatial patterns are directly driven by the residual effects of occupational employment patterns by sex:

> Smaller firms – such as the female-typed high-tech firms in this sample – that operate with few employees and little financial resources will have a harder time finding premium office space in the commercial corridors and industrial centres of a region than their male counterparts. Women-owned firms may find it cost efficient to locate in cheaper space such as the home of the entrepreneur or office space that is outside the high-cost high-tech core of a region. (Mayer, 2008, p. 1374)

To summarize, due to the invidious and insidious residual effects of gendered societal and socio-economic processes, women entrepreneurs are channelled into those business sectors that are riskiest, attract limited external finance and focus on local markets. These three industry characteristics have consequences for the ability of incumbent firms to survive, thrive, grow and perform. Consequently, the 'underperformance' of women-owned firms should be understood, and treated by empiricists not as the consequence of competency deficiencies, growth avoidance, or the fear of attempting to raise external capital (the dominant explanations in the literature), but as both the manifestation and outcome of entrepreneurial segregation.

CONCLUDING REMARKS

Researchers have devoted considerable attention to comparing men- and women-owned enterprises on the basis of the performance and growth of their firms. It is likely that such attention is engendered by the upsurge in women's enterprise witnessed in recent years. This research often reports that the firms that women own and operate are smaller than those owned by men in terms of sales and employment; they have less potential for growth, lower levels of equity and capital and generate lower levels of sales and profits. In this chapter, the argument has been made that these conclusions are specious due to the existence of entrepreneurial segregation, and the failure of researchers to account for the industry location of women- and men-owned firms. Yet, just as the vast proportion of the gender pay gap can be explained by occupational segregation (Mandel and Semyonov, 2014), it is argued here that the 'performance gap' can be at least partly explained by entrepreneurial segregation. The concentration of women-owned enterprises in risky, locally serving industries that fail to attract outside investment helps to ensure that women-owned establishments underperform relative to those owned by men.

In spite of this, the majority of research on the gender-performance link-age has failed to control for industry. Where industry has been controlled, it has often been only broadly so, so that research has focused on owners in 'retail' or 'services', ignoring the considerable diversity of business types that are grouped into these vast categories and adding another layer of complexity to the relationship between business context and gendered business outcomes. It is therefore important that within-industry compari-sons take place in the narrowest defined categories, in order to ensure that like-for-like comparisons are made. Broad industrial classifications such as 'services' are unhelpful, for they mask considerable venture diversity (Sappleton, 2009). There is considerable difference in the size and scope of B2C and B2B service firms, for instance.

Just as the gender pay gap in employment is much smaller in narrowly delineated sectors than when aggregated across industries (for instance, the gender pay gap in the US construction industry is just 99.4 per cent (Bureau of Labor Statistics, 2010)), so these performance differentials disappear when goods controls are applied for industry. Why then, do researchers continue to ignore industry in their analyses of gender and business performance? Part of the problem is a lack of available published data that report both gender of business owner and industry sub-classifications. For instance, in the UK, there exists no gender disaggregated small business data set that reports businesses beyond the three-digit sector. The VAT register and Inter-Departmental Business Register provide detailed data on sector of business, but not on gender of business owner. The Labour Force Survey provides only sex disaggregated self-employment data and the Annual Small Business Survey is very small. Thus, in addition to making this call for action to researchers to take account of industry in the gender-performance analysis, the academic community are entreated to call for better national and private databases to enable them to achieve this objective.

REFERENCES

Alsos, G., Isaksen, E. and Ljunggren, E. (2005). Access to New Venture Financing and Subsequent Business Growth in Men- and Women-Led Ventures. The Twenty-Fifth Annual Research Conference, Wellesely, MA: Babson College.

Autio, E., Sapienza, H.J. and Almeida, J.G. (2000). Effects of Age at Entry, Knowledge Intensity, and Imitability on International Growth. *Academy of Management Journal*, 43(5), 909–924.

Bird, S.R. and Sapp, S.G. (2004). Understanding the Gender Gap in Small Business Success. *Gender & Society*, 18(1), 5–28.

Blake, M.K. (2006). Gendered Lending: Gender, Context and the Rules of Business Lending. *Venture Capital*, 8(2), 183–201.

Brindley, C. (2005). Barriers to Women Achieving their Entrepreneurial Potential: Women and Risk. *International Journal of Entrepreneurial Behaviour and Research*, 11(2), 144–161.

Brush, C.G., Carter, N.M., Gatewood, E.J., Greene, P.G. and Hart, M.M. (2006). The Use of Bootstrapping by Women Entrepreneurs in Positioning for Growth. *Venture Capital*, 8(1), 15–31.

Brynin, M. and Perales, F. (2016). Gender Wage Inequality: The De-Gendering of the Occupational Structure. *European Sociological Review*, 32(1), 162–174.

Bureau of Labor Statistics (2010). *Employment by Detailed Occupation, Sex, Race, and Hispanic Ethnicity, 2010 Annual Averages*. Retrieved from Washington, DC: Bureau of Labor Statistics.

Caloghirou, Y., Protogerou, A., Spanos, Y. and Papagiannakis, L. (2004). Industry- versus Firm-Specific Effects on Performance: Contrasting SMEs and Large-Sized Firms. *European Management Journal*, 22(2), 231–243.

Carter, S. and Rosa, P. (1998). The Financing of Male- and Female-Owned Businesses. *Entrepreneurship & Regional Development*, 10(3), 225–241.

Chell, E. and Baines, S. (1998). Does Gender Affect Business 'Performance'? A Study of Microbusinesses in Business Services in the UK. *Entrepreneurship and Regional Development*, 10(2), 117–135.

Chesser, M.L. (1998). Overcoming Structures of Inequality: A Study of the Personal Networks of Minority and Female Hi-Tech Business Owners. PhD Thesis. Austin, TX: The University of Texas at Austin.

Coyle, H.E. and Flannery, D.D. (2005). Gendered Contexts of Learning Female Entrepreneurs in Male-Dominated Industries within the United States. Summer Institute of the National Center for Curriculum Transformation Resources on Women, Turkey.

Dahlqvist, J., Davidsson, P. and Wiklund, J. (2000). Initial Conditions as Predictors of New Venture Performance: A Replication and Extension of the Cooper et al. Study. *Enterprise and Innovation Management Studies*, 1(1), 1–17.

Duberley, J. and Carrigan, M. (2013). The Career Identities of 'Mumpreneurs': Women's Experiences of Combining Enterprise and Motherhood. *International Small Business Journal*, 31(6), 629–651.

Du Rietz, A. and Henrekson, M. (2000). Testing the Female Underperformance Hypothesis. *Small Business Economics*, 14(1), 1–10.

Eastough, K. and Miller, P.W. (2004). The Gender Wage Gap in Paid- and Self-Employment in Australia. *Australian Economic Papers*, 43(3), 257–276.

Evetts, J. (2014). *Women and Career: Themes and Issues in Advanced Industrial Societies*. Abingdon, UK: Routledge.

Foss, N.J. and Knudsen, C. (2013). *Towards a Competence Theory of the Firm* (Vol. 2). London: Routledge.

Gimenez-Nadal, J.I., Molina, J.A. and Ortega, R. (2012). Self-Employed Mothers and the Work–Family Conflict. *Applied Economics*, 44(17), 2133–2147.

Greene, P.G., Brush, C.G., Hart, M.M. and Saparito, P. (2001). Patterns of Venture Capital Funding: Is Gender a Factor? *Venture Capital*, 3(1), 63–83.

Gregg, G. (1985). Women Entrepreneurs: The Second Generation. *Across the Board*, 22(1), 10–18.

Hatfield, I. (2015). Self-Employment in Europe. Report. London: Institute for Public Policy Research.

Headd, B. (2003). Redefining Business Success: Distinguishing Between Closure and Failure. *Small Business Economics*, 21(1), 51–61.

Hill, F.M., Leitch, C.M. and Harrison, R.T. (2006). 'Desperately Seeking Finance?' The Demand for Finance by Women-Owned and -Led Businesses. *Venture Capital*, 8(02), 159–182.

Hitt, M.A., Ireland, R.D., Camp, S.M. and Sexton, D.L. (2002). Strategic Entrepreneurship: Integrating Entrepreneurial and Strategic Management Perspectives. In M.A. Hitt, R.D. Ireland, S.M. Camp and D.L. Sexton (eds), *Strategic Entrepreneurship: Creating a New Mindset*. Oxford: Blackwell, pp. 1–16.

Hokkanen, P. and Autio, E. (1998). Growth Performance of Female Driven Firms. Paper presented at the Proceedings of 43rd ICSB World Congress: Entrepreneurship at the Threshold of the 21st Century, Singapore.

Hundley, G. (2001). Why Women Earn Less than Men in Self-Employment. *Journal of Labor Research*, 22(4), 818–828.

Huppatz, K. (2009). Reworking Bourdieu's 'Capital': Feminine and Female Capitals in the Field of Paid Caring Work. *Sociology*, 43(1), 45–66.

Jarman, J., Blackburn, R.M. and Racko, G. (2012). The Dimensions of Occupational Gender Segregation in Industrial Countries. *Sociology*, 46(6), 1003–1019.

Justo, R., DeTienne, D.R. and Sieger, P. (2015). Failure or Voluntary Exit? Reassessing the Female Underperformance Hypothesis. *Journal of Business Venturing*, 30(6), 775–792.

Kalleberg, A. and Leicht, K.T. (1991). Gender and Organizational Performance: Determinants of Small Business Survival and Success. *Academy of Management Journal*, 34(1), 136–161.

Kim, N., Im, S. and Slater, S.F. (2013). Impact of Knowledge Type and Strategic Orientation on New Product Creativity and Advantage in High-Technology Firms. *Journal of Product Innovation Management*, 30(1), 136–153.

Koellinger, P.D. and Roy Thurik, A. (2012). Entrepreneurship and the Business Cycle. *Review of Economics and Statistics*, 94(4), 1143–1156.

Lechmann, D.S. and Schnabel, C. (2012). What Explains the Gender Earnings Gap in Self-Employment? A Decomposition Analysis with German Data. Institute of Labor Economics IZA Discussion Paper No 6435. Retrieved from https://ssrn.com/abstract=2032003.

Litz, R.A. and Folker, C.A. (2002). When He and She Sell Seashells: Exploring the Relationship between Management Team Gender-Balance and Small Firm Performance. *Journal of Developmental Entrepreneurship*, 7(4), 341–359.

Loscocco, K.A. and Leicht, K.T. (1993). Gender, Work–Family Linkages and

Economic Success among Small Business Owners. *Journal of Marriage and the Family*, 55(4), 875–887.

Loscocco, K.A. and Robinson, J. (1991). Barriers to Women's Small-Business Success in the United States. *Gender and Society*, 5(4), 511–532.

Lowrey, Y. (2005). US Sole Propriertorships: A Gender Comparison 1985–2000. Government report. Washington, DC: Small Business Administration Office of Advocacy.

Mandel, H. and Semyonov, M. (2014). Gender Pay Gap and Employment Sector: Sources of Earnings Disparities in the United States, 1970–2010. *Demography*, 51(5), 1597–1618.

Manolova, T.S., Manev, I.M., Carter, N.M. and Gyoshev, B.S. (2006). Breaking the Family and Friends' Circle: Predictors of External Financing Usage Among Men and Women Entrepreneurs in a Transitional Economy. *Venture Capital*, 8(02), 109–132.

Martell, R.F., Emrich, C.G. and Robison-Cox, J. (2012). From Bias to Exclusion: A Multilevel Emergent Theory of Gender Segregation in Organizations. *Research in Organizational Behavior*, 32(1), 137–162, doi: http://dx.doi.org/10.1016/j.riob.2012.10.001.

Mayer, H. (2008). Segmentation and Segregation Patterns of Women-Owned High-Tech Firms in Four Metropolitan Regions in the United States. *Regional Studies*, 42(10), 1357–1383.

McGowan, P., Redeker, C.L., Cooper, S.Y. and Greenan, K. (2012). Female Entrepreneurship and the Management of Business and Domestic Roles: Motivations, Expectations and Realities. *Entrepreneurship and Regional Development*, 24(1/2), 53–72.

Meyer, G.D., Neck, H.M. and Meeks, M.D. (2002). The Entrepreneurship–Strategic Management Interface. In M.A. Hitt, R.D. Ireland, S.M. Camp and D.L. Sexton (eds), *Strategic Entrepreneurship: Creating a New Mindset*. Oxford: Blackwell, pp. 19–44.

Moen, Ø., Heggeseth, A.G. and Lome, O. (2016). The Positive Effect of Motivation and International Orientation on SME Growth. *Journal of Small Business Management*, 54(2), 659–678.

National Association of Women-Owned Businesses (2013). The State of Women-Owned Businesses, 2013. Washington, DC: National Association of Women-Owned Businesses.

Nofsinger, J.R. and Wang, W. (2011). Determinants of Start-Up Firm External Financing Worldwide. *Journal of Banking and Finance*, 35(9), 2282–2294.

O'Gorman, B. and Aylward, E. (2007). *An Insight into Why Women Start Service Enterprises versus High Technology Enterprises*. Paper presented at the 30th Institute for Small Business and Entrepreneurship Conference, Glasgow.

Porter, M.E. (1980). Industry Structure and Competitive Strategy: Keys to Profitability. *Financial Analysts Journal*, 36(4), 30–41.

Reavley, M.A. and Lituchy, T.R. (2008). Successful Women Entrepreneurs: A Six-Country Analysis of Self-Reported Determinants of Success? More Than Just Dollars and Cents. *International Journal of Entrepreneurship and Small Business*, 5(3–4), 272–296.

Robb, A.M. (2002). Entrepreneurial Performance by Women and Minorities: The Case of New Firms. *Journal of Developmental Entrepreneurship*, 7(4), 384–397.

Robb, A.M. and Watson, J. (2012). Gender Differences in Firm Performance:

Evidence from New Ventures in the United States. *Journal of Business Venturing*, 27(5), 544–558.

Sappleton, N. (2009). Women Non-Traditional Entrepreneurs and Social Capital. *International Journal of Gender and Entrepreneurship*, 1(3), 192–218.

Sappleton, N. (2013). Women in Men's Jobs. In J.G.G. Vicki Smith (ed.), *Sociology of Work*. Thousand Oaks, CA: Sage.

Sappleton, N. (2014). Gender Congruency Theory, Experience of Discrimination and Access to Finance. In K.V. Lewis, C. Henry, E.J. Gatewood and J. Watson (eds), *Women's Entrepreneurship in the 21st Century: An International Multi-Level Research Analysis*. Cheltenham, UK and Northampton, MA: Edward Elgar Publishing, pp. 50–73.

Segarra, A. and Callejón, M. (2002). New Firms' Survival and Market Turbulence: New Evidence from Spain. *Review of Industrial Organization*, 20(1), 1–14.

Stockdale, M.S. and Nadler, J.T. (2013). Paradigmatic Assumptions to Disciplinary Research on Gender Disparities: The Case of Occupational Sex Segregation. *Sex Roles*, 68(3/4), 207–215.

Teece, D., Pisano, G. and Shuen, A. (1997). Dynamic Capabilities and Strategic Management. *Strategic Management Journal*, 18(7), 509–533.

US Census Bureau (2011). *Survey of Business Owners – Women-Owned Firms: 2007. Summary of Findings*. Retrieved from Washington, DC: http://www.census.gov/econ/sbo/get07sof.html?12.

Vanacker, T.R. and Manigart, S. (2010). Incremental Financing Decisions in High Growth Companies: Pecking Order and Debt Capacity Considerations. *Small Business Economics*, 35(1), 53–69.

Verwey, I.V. (2005). A Comparative Analysis between South Africa and USA Women Entrepreneurs in Construction. PhD Thesis. Pretoria: University of Pretoria.

Watkins, J.M. and Watkins, D.S. (1983). The Female Entrepreneur: Her Background and Determinants of Business Choice – Some British Data. In J.A. Hornaday, J.A. Timmons and K.H. Vesper (eds), *Frontiers of Entrepreneurship Research*. Wellesley, MA: Babson College, pp. 271–288.

Watson, J. (2002a). Comparing the Performance of Male- and Female-Controlled Businesses: Relating Outputs to Inputs. *Entrepreneurship: Theory and Practice*, 26(3), 91–100.

Watson, J. (2002b). Revisiting the Female Under-Performance Hypothesis. Paper presented at the 22nd Annual Entrepreneurship Research Conference, Babson College, MA.

Watson, J. and Robinson, S. (2003). Adjusting for Risk in Comparing the Performances of Male- and Female-Controlled SMEs. *Journal of Business Venturing*, 18(6), 773–788.

Watts, M.J. (2005). On the Conceptualisation and Measurement of Horizontal and Vertical Occupational Gender Segregation. *European Sociological Review*, 21(5), 481–488.

Welter, F., Brush, C. and De Bruin, A. (2014). The Gendering of Entrepreneurship Context. Working paper, 1, 14, Institut für Mittelstandsforschung, Bonn.

Zolin, R., Stuetzer, M. and Watson, J. (2013). Challenging the Female Under-performance Hypothesis. *International Journal of Gender and Entrepreneurship*, 5(2), 116–129.

14. Still bringing up the rear: why women will always be 'Other' in entrepreneurship's masculine instrumental discourse

Joan Lockyer, Cherisse Hoyte and Sunita Dewitt

Recent years have witnessed emerging debates surrounding the study of female entrepreneurship, the roots of which rise from, amongst others, 'feminist' (Baines and Wheelock, 2000; Bourne and Calás, 2013) 'institutional' (Morris and Trotter, 1990) and 'structural' perspectives (EC, 2015). Furthermore, studies have started to highlight similarities in entrepreneurial potential between men and women, especially in terms of their contribution to wealth creation, employment (Malach-Pines and Schwartz, 2008; Women's Enterprise Policy Group, 2011) and recognition by global governments of women as an 'untapped source' of economic growth and development (Malach-Pines and Schwartz, 2008; Minniti and Naudé, 2010). Some studies have gone further to argue that women's contribution tends to be higher than that resulting from the entrepreneurial activity of men (de Bruin et al., 2006; Minniti and Naudé, 2010). Evidence of narrowing the gender gap through support programmes has provided strength to women entering and operating in diverse sectors (GEM, 2012, 2014). However, the majority of research on female entrepreneurship continues to single out women from the mainstream entrepreneurship arena (Minniti and Naudé, 2010). The aim and focus of enterprise and entrepreneurship within political discourse appears to be to drive forward an agenda that demands, rather than encourages, parity between the sexes in terms of entrepreneurial performance. The solutions offered, with little reflection, seem to be more of the same diet of business support programmes to get women up to speed on finance, networking and resource management. Despite many years of such support, the gender gap persists, regardless of the level of economic activity (Santos et al., 2016).

Much of the literature and research on female entrepreneurship focuses on this interplay of the need to engage more women into entrepreneurial activities and the problem of their underperformance when they do so. When we wrote the chapter title, it encapsulated the essence of our belief that women 'underperform' not because they are incapable of being entrepreneurial but because of the ways in which we define and then judge the performance of the entrepreneur. Given that the conceptualisation of an entrepreneur and entrepreneurship are male-gendered (Ahl, 2006; Santos et al., 2016), the rules of the game, so to speak, were not written to give women an equal chance of competing, let alone winning. So as the situation stands now and probably for the foreseeable future, no amount of support and special provision will enable women to match men in terms of the number of start-ups or performance ambitions that society has for them in entrepreneurship. When we argue that the rules of the game are stacked against women, what we actually mean is that the role of women is frequently more complex than the role of men in society. It was ever thus, and as a consequence women have developed different mechanisms for coping with and managing their lives. This approach is frequently presented as disorganised, chaotic and emotional. Men, on the other hand, are characterised as having more stable, focused and rational dispositions. The values of instrumental rationality, which underpin our understanding of what it means to be an entrepreneur, are strongly associated with men, while women are associated with that 'Other' world of chaos and disorder (Pringle, 1988, p. 88, cited in Putnam and Mumby, 1993).

Whilst neither caricature is entirely true in reality, they do represent a form of known understanding that, even at a subliminal level, is taken as reflecting the different approaches between men and women to all aspects of work, including entrepreneurship. The juxtaposition between these roles is frequently cited as the cause of the performance gap and this led us to want to explore further how the relationships between three concepts play out, those being: entrepreneurship, instrumentality and women as 'Other'. For us this reflects an unholy triad which conspires to perpetuate the structures, both social and institutional, that result in underperformance. We found the interplay between these concepts in some ways very hard to separate and equally as hard to reconcile. However, our aim has been to show how entrepreneurship and instrumentality create a barrier to entry for women in entrepreneurship. Instrumental reason, which is core to mainstream entrepreneurial thinking, marginalises women and in so doing reinforces their relegation to the position of 'Other'. This chapter is structured to start to explore what we have characterised as three tensions: the first between entrepreneurship and instrumentality, the second between women as 'Other' and entrepreneurship, and the third between a wider understanding of instrumentality and 'Other'. There are overlaps and interlinks between these tensions, which we hope further expose the need to reframe the ways in which we consider the performance of women in entrepreneurship and which may perhaps contribute to building an alternative theory on the women's underperformance narrative.

We draw upon a range of perspectives to support our argument, which are broadly: postmodernism, to explore the relationship between organisation and gender; feminist, to explore power and agency; and critical theory, to explore instrumentality. All perspectives challenge the nature of power and its influence on women's ability to enact their role as entrepreneurs. The focus is not on power *per se*, but rather the perception of agency and the implication of inferiority that is imbued within the instrumental narrative of entrepreneurship.

ENTREPRENEURSHIP AND INSTRUMENTALITY

There is scarcely a corner of the globe immune from the call for the population to be more entrepreneurial. When considering what that means in practice, it is a call for economic growth and development driven largely by business start-up and small business growth. Entrepreneurship is generally described as the process whereby individuals pursue opportunities by being active risk-takers, innovators and profit-seekers (Bird and Brush, 2002). These characterisations in essence bring together both the nature and the role of the entrepreneur as a vital part of social growth and progress, presenting them as inherently good and right (Berglund et al., 2012). The drive for entrepreneurial activity enshrines the implicit belief that sizable sections of the population, specifically women, can and will want to be entrepreneurial. It is also recognised that huge social, cultural and economic benefits can be realised from getting women to be more *economically* productive in this way (Malach-Pines and Schwartz, 2008; Minniti and Naudé, 2010). Part of the rationale driving the global imperative is the disparity between the performance of men and women in business start-ups and the belief that women are seeking equality in this regard.

Entrepreneurship and instrumentality are terms that are frequently used in tandem and are intended to show how the instrumental mind-set of the entrepreneurs creates entrepreneurial impact. The downside of linking entrepreneurship with instrumentality is that the latter is frequently built upon male-centred notions of the entrepreneur, which reinforce the masculinity and ethnocentricity found in Western society; it further creates the assumption that entrepreneurship is the domain of men as extraordinary or heroic individuals and not a role universally present in everyday human action (Ogbor, 2000; Bird and Brush, 2002; Shockley and Frank, 2011, p. 14; Berglund et al., 2012).

However, the tendency to eulogise and heroise the entrepreneur has the capacity to 'make each and every one of us turn into the "Other" in relation to the entrepreneur' (Berglund et al. 2012, p. 167; see also Jones and Spicer, 2005). The position of women is further exacerbated as 'women are just not men. Thus attempting to analyse their entrepreneurial activity from an essentially male biased stance is problematic, as it appears that women just do not measure up' (Henry and Marlow, 2014, p. 119).

From this perspective the definition of the entrepreneur appears alienating, especially (but not exclusively) for women. However, both Schumpeter and Kirzner (Shockley and Frank, 2011) argue that the function of entrepreneurship takes precedence over the definition of the entrepreneur. Schumpeter (1934 [2002], p. 74) clearly distinguishes between entrepreneurship and entrepreneurs when he defines enterprise and entrepreneurial activity as 'the carrying out of new combinations' and entrepreneurs as 'the individuals whose function it is to carry them out' (Shockley and Frank, 2011, p. 17). Shockley and Frank remind us that the process of entrepreneurship has a more substantive role in driving economic growth and development, which extends beyond the individual entrepreneur (ibid., pp. 17–18). Equally Kirzner's concern is not for the entrepreneur *per se*, but rather the effects that follow the process of entrepreneurship. While he recognises that the 'psychological and personal qualities of boldness and creativity, and self-confidence will doubtless be of help or even necessary . . . the analytical essence of the pure entrepreneurial role is itself independent of these specific qualities' (Kirzner, 1999, p. 12). As Shockley and Frank comment, 'it is the process of entrepreneurship, not the instrumentality of the individual, which is paramount in both Schumpeterian and Kirznerian entrepreneurship' (Shockley and Frank, 2011, p. 14). While they approach it in different ways, both Shockley and Frank (2011) and Berglund et al. (2012) discuss how the reconceptualisation of entrepreneurship along more egalitarian lines may open the door for wider engagement in the process of entrepreneurship by all marginalised groups. Both approaches shift the focus from the instrumental individual to the more universal concept, applicable to any person (Shockley and Frank, 2011, p. 14) and mobilised from the bottom up (Berglund et al., 2012, p. 3).

If the aim is to mass-produce entrepreneurs, rationalising and systematising the process is perhaps seen as a necessary evil. Instrumentality is seen as bureaucratic, systematic and rule-based, aimed at the efficient maximisation of self-interest. Entrepreneurship on the other hand requires creativity and innovation, 'in other words, far from the rational calculation of business planning or systematic market research, insights and "gut" feelings drive the Schumpeterian entrepreneur' (Shockley and Frank, 2011, p. 11).

The tension that is created as we push for societal entrepreneurship is based on how we present, train and therefore expect entrepreneurs to behave. People do not identify with the persona of the entrepreneur, women especially, and so it may be better to revert to more classical interpretations of the entrepreneurial process if we are to engage women effectively in entrepreneurship.

WOMEN AS 'OTHER' AND ENTREPRENEURSHIP

Many of the discussions on female entrepreneurship directly or indirectly refer to women as 'Other'. Terms such as 'hidden', 'outsiders' and 'invisible backbone' (Baker et al., 1997; Baines and Wheelock, 2000; Kerfoot and Miller, 2010) are also still often associated with studies and research on female entrepreneurship. Our discussion on the roots of women as 'Other' draws upon Simone de Beauvoir's (1949 [2010]) influential and pioneering book, *The Second Sex*. In essence, for anything to exist as 'Other', that from which it stands apart must be defined. The approach, which was not new to de Beauvoir, establishes the male as the standard human (the essential, the one), with women by default assuming the position of 'Other'. However, for the male to be 'the one', women must accept their inferiority and submit to male sovereignty.

With the essentialising of men as the norm there is no doubt that 'Other' is implicit of a weakness or a lack of something; a diminished position in need of rescue and rehabilitation (Fournier, 2002, p. 68). As discussed above, entrepreneurship essentialises male characteristics and behaviours, and, as women are not men, they are attributed 'Other' status in entrepreneurship research. It is taken as given that those who are 'less' must want to be more and it is also similarly assumed that this means aiming for parity through imitation.

The conversion from 'less' to 'more', from 'Other' to 'mainstream' in terms of entrepreneurship theory, is frequently manifest in the form of training and development, confidence-building and special support (ibid.; Ahl, 2002) which is made available to women to help them to overcome their limitations and natural failings. However, as Fournier argues, 'improvement' in these terms frequently comes at a cost. To be accommodated, she argues, it is necessary for 'Otherness to be flattened out and managed within a framework of various degrees of sameness' (Fournier, 2002, p. 68). Fournier suggests that women might alternatively be cast as 'not' as opposed to 'less', that is, women are not the same as men, as opposed to women are less than men. She also argues that the 'Other' can only be positioned as 'not' by withdrawing from the category of difference in which it is framed and moving somewhere else (ibid., p. 69). To become or remain a 'not' requires a different frame of reference, movement and versatility on the part of women entrepreneurs. So, rather than a flattening out of the differences, they should be acknowledged and a new frame of reference created, one that recognises the disposition not just of women, but of feminine characteristics (Putnam and Mumby, 1993; Bird and Brush, 2002; Henry and Marlow, 2014). Yet in some respects, highlighting the differences between men and women plays directly into the characterisation of women as irrational and emotional. Much of the *rehabilitation* of women aims to make them into entrepreneurial facsimiles of men by training them to overcome their natural emotional disposition and lack of confidence. The difference between men and women is at the heart of 'Otherness' and so women are in an eternal bind of acknowledging the difference and being plagued with the characterisations that accompany it, or trying to prove that they are the same as men and failing because they are not.

There are no redeeming features in the characterisation of women as 'Other' and many of the pejorative terms still used in the women-as-'Other' narrative originate from ancient classical and biblical texts. 'Legislators, priests, philosophers, writers, and scientists have striven to show that the subordinate position of women is willed in heaven and advantageous on earth' (Sterba, 2003, p. 10). Even before a woman was blamed for the original sin, she was cast down biblically and intended only for social union (ibid.). Horowitz (1976, p. 183) describes Aristotle's views on the inferiority of women and his arguments for the political subordination of women in the home and in society. It was Aristotle who defined women as 'mutilated males' and it was he who strongly advocated the need for patriarchy as the proper form of government for the home. His views were adopted and passed on by St Thomas Aquinas in his *Summa Theologica* (1266). Aquinas considered women to be 'defective', 'misbegotten' (Sterba, 2003, p. 122), 'incomplete man' and 'incidental' beings (de Beauvoir, 1949 [2010], p. 5). The *Summa Theologica* is still influencing the teachings of the church and is still in print today. Many of the theories that we draw upon within entrepreneurship and management teaching have links (directly and indirectly) to theory and doctrine derived from faith-based and/or gender-based studies or approaches (those of Max Weber, for example). The portrayal of entrepreneurial traits and characteristics are still, for some, predefined attributes of the sexes; men being predominantly rational and women being predominantly emotional. Even if we disagree with this notion of predefined attributes attached to sex, 'subordination [still] arises from a constructed gendered order articulated through the binary divisions of femininity and masculinity mapped onto biological sex' (Henry and Marlow, 2014, p. 119).

While gender is inherently a social construction, specific masculine and feminine characterisations are ascribed to men and women respectively (Oakley, 1972; Mills, 1988; Ahl, 2004). As Bradley argues, '[w]hilst gender is a fluid performance, transgressions or "gender threats" . . . risk sanctions, as social expectations, conventions, communications and norms are steeped within gendered order' (Bradley, 2007, cited in Henry and Marlow, 2014, p. 123). The assumptions that underpin these social constructs have been developed and refined in ways that privilege males and disadvantage females. Henry and Marlow (ibid., p. 119) argue that 'gender is institutionalised at the most fundamental level of human interaction and so pervades all forms of behaviour'. Yet despite this, they argue, there remains a lack of focus and development around the concepts of femininity and gender in entrepreneurship.

If we consider the arguments forwarded by Schumpeter and Kirzner discussed earlier, entrepreneurship (and not the entrepreneur) is the critical force in economic growth, so why is our gaze so firmly fixed on the concept of the entrepreneur as an individual? By focusing on the attributes of the entrepreneur, women reinforce their position as 'Other' and in effect contribute to maintenance of the status quo. Despite the progress that has been made in research on women and entrepreneurship, Henry and Marlow (2014, p. 121) argue that 'there remains a curious reluctance to develop a critical explanatory analysis for subordination through feminist theory'. Even within our own more enlightened research community, as female authors we witness a rolling of the eyes from our male colleagues when we discuss these issues in the shared office space. It is our own experience and one articulated by others (Ahl, 2004; Bradley, 2007; Bowden and Mummery, 2014) that taking a feminist perspective leads to accusations of 'men bashing', which, even when said in a light-hearted way, evidences a form of disagreement if not mild hostility. Yet all evidence supports the continued disadvantage of women in society, as gendered practices are embedded in organisational and cultural values and therefore reproduced as a familiar and natural landscape. Women are still disadvantaged in terms of pay and conditions. In fact, the American Association of University Women (AAUW, 2016) argue that, based on the decreasing rate of pay differentials between 1960 and 2015, it will take until 2059 for the pay gap to be closed.

The tension that we perceive between *entrepreneur* and '*Other*' is manifest in two ways. First, in the definition and presentation in literature of the entrepreneur; this focuses on the realisation of individual potential and the maximisation of self-interest through the conversion of opportunities into action. The characterisation of the entrepreneur in these terms reinforces 'the prevailing masculinized discourse . . . upon the normative gendered binary (that which is masculine is normal, natural and dominant, whilst that which is feminine is in opposition [Other])' (Henry and Marlow, 2014, p. 121). Second, if women are to be 'Other', they cannot also be 'entrepreneur' by this definition, without becoming more male-like in their approach to entrepreneurship. As Fournier (2002, and others: Henry and Marlow, 2014, p. 121), point out, the pursuit of 'sameness' in reality requires acquiescence and not equality and therefore does not in reality further the position of women. Women can be entrepreneurial, as Schumpeter and Kirzner define it, without being pigeonholed as entrepreneurs.

INSTRUMENTALITY AND 'OTHER'

In this section we return to instrumentality to explore organisational structures that support and sustain entrepreneurship masculine discourse and its links to rationality and emotionality; a distinction that is often presented as the binary positions of men and women within entrepreneurship and in society at large. While the structural challenges faced by many women considering entrepreneurship as a career are acknowledged, still the range and nature of support created by social institutions does not in reality meet with women's needs or expectations. Women remain structurally disadvantaged by institutional forms that neither reflect nor respond to their needs. Consequently, the entrepreneurial environment in which women operate casts them as entrepreneurial failures and so we hope that by exploring this tension we will contribute to the unmasking of the narrowness of the window through which underperformance is viewed and judged.

If the processes adopted in the creation of new ventures are 'inherently rational and instrumental' (Bird and Brush, 2002, p. 42) then the masculine character of organisations is hardly surprising as men have been (and continue to be) the predominant population involved in entrepreneurial activities (ibid., p. 42). The 'organisational discourse' (Helms-Mills, 2003, p. 134), that is, the perspective on how entrepreneurship is organised, gives us a way of looking at the world that provides a 'taken-for-granted, more or less unconscious meta-understanding about the way things are achieved in society' (ibid.). We still live in a world predominated by bureaucratic structures and it perpetuates the emphasis on 'rationality' over 'emotionality', the former being positive and masculine, the latter being negative and feminine; 'instrumental rationality . . . is defined by its opposition to emotionality as an alternative mode of experience' (Putnam and Mumby, 1993, p. 43).

The extensive literature on female entrepreneurship, which Carter et al. (2012) describe as emerging only as an identifiable and coherent field in the 1990s (cited in Henry and Marlow, 2014, p. 109), tells us that women continue to underperform globally when it comes to evidencing the attributes of an entrepreneur. More recent research (by Lewis, 2013; Santos et al., 2016, p. 49) restates the assertion. Women accounted for 'only 29% of the 40.6 million entrepreneurs in the EU in 2012' (EC, 2015). Women's activities are clustered in low-growth, low-skilled business sectors (Gupta et al., 2009; Naudé, 2011, 2013; EC, 2015; Santos et al., 2016). Low growth and business failure are often attributed to a lack of ambition, lack of commitment or a choice to operate lifestyle business with little aspiration for growth (Mirchandani, 1999; Malach-Pines and Schwartz, 2008; Shinnar et al., 2012, 2014). According to the EU (EC, 2015, p. 7), 'domestic circumstances often force women into periods of intermission; this hinders their ability to accumulate social, cultural and financial capital and constrains the generation of a respectable credit history'.

When women *do entrepreneurship well* it is often because they have deferred their aspirations until a stage in their life when they are less responsible for family and can focus on their careers or business venture (Davis and Shaver, 2012; Hughes et al., 2012). Alternatively, as Eddleston and Powell (2012, p. 2) suggest, it is because they satisfactorily merge entrepreneurship with work–life balance by developing higher levels of 'instrumental family-to-business enrichment' resulting in a more synergistic approach to family and work. Eddleston and Powell also point out that male entrepreneurs, by comparison, benefit from a more focused instrumental level of support from the family. Research by Carr and Hmieleski (2015) suggests that this detachment of home life and work life leads to far less tension and conflict. While this is welcome news, for many women family life is central, because it is where their status is located and also it is not possible for both partners in a relationship to be simultaneously detached from domestic routines. Some women may even distrust the rhetoric that challenges this affective investment in their daily lives and only when liberated from 'the social weight of caring roles' (ibid., p. 312) do they feel able to explore the potential of an alternative future for themselves and their family. More importantly, men and society need women to perform this role as it is fundamental to social cohesion (Durkheim, 1893 [2013]). An alternative approach adopted by Lewis (2013) looked at how women constructed their entrepreneurial identity through a process of combining a preferred feminine discourse to differentiate themselves from what they perceived to be the overtly hegemonic masculinity of entrepreneurship and complemented it with the masculine discourse of professionalism to create a new authentic identity. While eschewing entrepreneurialism, the women still felt the need to project a masculine persona which they elected to do through professionalism. The professionalism was used to counterbalance the femininity which they felt lacked credibility on its own.

The role of women in the home, with their duties as home-maker, care-giver and child-rearer, is a constant refrain in the discussion of women as entrepreneurs. There are clear links between these roles and marriage, patriarchy and the sexual division of labour. Durkheim (1893 [2013]) believed that the division of labour along sex lines had several meaningful impacts, not least that it embellishes and enhances society to such a degree that without it society would not function. He believed that if the division of labour between the sexes were to be diminished beyond a certain point, marital life would disappear, leaving only sexual partnerships that are predominantly ephemeral (ibid.). The domination of women therefore is vital for the maintenance of the status quo and for the effective running of society. Patriarchy is an effective means of control and discrimination, which as a culturally embedded practice has perpetuated. Heidi Hartmann (1979, p. 11) defined patriarchy as 'a set of social relations amongst men, which have a material base and which, through hierarchy, establish or create interdependence and solidarity amongst men that enable them to dominate women'. Her argument is that the material base upon which patriarchy rests is men's control over women's labour power and that this is done in two ways, first, by excluding women from access to essential productive resources, and, second, by restricting women's sexuality (ibid.) (specifically with respect to child bearing). The sexual division of labour means that men and women experience the labour market differently, both materially and psychologically. She argues that the capitalist system of labour produces places for a hierarchy of workers, but it does not determine who fills those places. Hartmann argues that it is a matter of gender and racial hierarchies that fill these places. By working in the home, women exonerate men from performing household tasks and from the lion's share of the child-rearing duties, thus perpetuating for the next generation their gendered place in the hierarchy. Outside the home, she argues, patriarchy is reinforced through the education system, churches and schools; more recently this is reinforced through the myriad of social media. While women don't have to be married to be subject to patriarchal control, the institution of marriage continues to create the social cement that Durkheim discussed as being the fabric of cohesion.

The third tension aims to draw out how women are still bound not just by the instrumentality of entrepreneurship, but also by the wider social and filial expectations that restrict freedom and opportunities. Structural restrictions limit not just freedom to act but the perception of opportunities to act. In their capacity of 'Other', women still subjugate their own needs and aspirations to those of others or defer them until they are released from other responsibilities.

DISCUSSION

Despite all we already know about female entrepreneurship, the gains made in recent years seem not to reflect the effort and investment made in helping women to become more entrepreneurially active, so as a consequence the underperformance narrative rolls on. Data from the European Commission support the faltering increase in women engaged in entrepreneurship.

It was evidenced in the article by Lewis (2013) that women want to engage in entrepreneurial activities, but they don't want to do so in the narrow instrumental ways that current practice dictates. For them to be authentic and effective (as women and business professionals) was paramount, but they firmly eschewed the notion of being classified as entrepreneurs. What the article demonstrates is that if these women wanted to be feminine in their approach and to be taken seriously as businesswomen, they needed to complement their femininity with a professional persona that still seemed to utilise a set of highly instrumental and masculine traits (self-control; efficiency; business acumen; and so on) to establish their credibility. While these might be regarded as simply evidencing good business practice, they also betray nervousness about moving too far from accepted practices. To be authentic and credible still poses a number of challenges. However, what Lewis (ibid., p. 263) argues is that by making use of the concept of authenticity women move away from the notion of failure to one of agency.

By exploring the tensions above through the three dimensions of entrepreneurship (the entrepreneur), instrumentality and 'Other', we hope to add a further voice to the call for research that firmly moves women away from the futile need to imitate the instrumental practices typically attributed to entrepreneurs. We claim above that women will never be successful utilising this strategy as it's not just about imitating behaviour but the wider social and cultural context in which women operate. Even if women successfully act the part of the entrepreneur, they are still women and therefore 'Other'. Being 'Other' and choosing to stand outside the conventions of entrepreneurship is not a comfortable place to be either. Women who take this path, as Lewis comments (ibid.) risk being labelled as 'trundlers' or 'lifestyle' businesses. Nevertheless, the pursuit of an authentic female entrepreneurial identity has to be worth the effort.

If we accept the legitimacy of the global imperative to increase the number of female entrepreneurs, simply using the 'rinse and recycle' approach of incentivising and supporting women along the journey must be reconsidered. Given that what has already been invested has resulted in a relatively modest increase in engagement, it seems like a stagnant – if not a failed – project. New approaches to engaging women in entrepreneurship should surely be considered. Women are 'Other' as they are not men; masculine discourse still predominates in both entrepreneurship theory and practice and we still live in a largely patriarchal society with structures and institutions that disadvantage women. Despite this, or probably because of this, there is a fear and distrust of the feminist perspective giving voice to the continued subordination of women. Ahl (2004) and many others cited above eloquently express the problem faced by feminist critique of the prevailing orthodoxy. We add our voice to the call for research that supports and empowers women to create an authentic female persona, which embraces 'Otherness' and supports their engagement in entrepreneurship as a process. In harking back to Kirzner and Schumpeter, we aim to draw out the distinction they made between the entrepreneur as a person and the entrepreneurial process. In drawing out this distinction, Shockley and Frank (2011, p. 12) comment that entrepreneurial discovery is a 'creative and innovative process, not an instrumental act; it is non-rational thinking [that] isolates the entrepreneurial moment'. The nature of women as exemplified in the 'Other' narrative may have unique and untapped advantages in this respect.

CONCLUSIONS

The discussion aims to highlight the continuing positioning of women as 'Other' in the conceptualisation of entrepreneurship. The roots of this problem, which run very deep, continue to be reconstructed and reinforced in society today. By looking at the tensions between entrepreneurship, 'Other' and instrumentality, we feel that we have highlighted the need to challenge the construction of all three concepts in the field of female entrepreneurship. The research has highlighted again just how limiting the concept of the entrepreneur is to women and by further exploring the 'Otherness' of women just how valuable it would be to do so through the lens of feminist theory. By shining a feminist light boldly on the field of entrepreneurship we should aim to build a new theory and develop a new understanding of the challenges faced by women entrepreneurs through both empirical and analytical approaches (Henry and Marlow, 2014).

Feminist arguments, however, have been subjected to heavy criticism as they seek to challenge the masculinised normativity upon which social order has been constructed (Ahl and Marlow, 2012). However, we do need the academic community to accept that entrepreneurship is a gendered practice. Although there is over 30 years of documented, peer-reviewed research on women's entrepreneurial activities, the influence of gender is still not acknowledged (Henry and Marlow, 2014). We also recognise that to be human is to articulate a gendered identity (Butler, 2004) and we stress the need for the research freedom to explore all gendered identities in the domain of entrepreneurship.

The issues over the division of labour often reinforce patriarchy and prompt us to ask, as Hartmann (1979) proposes, 'who is benefiting from women's labour'? In doing this it may raise awareness of the oppressive nature of many patriarchal relationships in which women find themselves. Our proposed research agenda highlighted above is nullified without the appropriate changes to government policy on entrepreneurship and to our academic practice. In terms of our academic practice, we must acknowledge that researchers do not control publications. To get published and to make any research valid, researchers must also play by the rules of the academic community, rules devolved from the structural, institutional, patriarchal subordination we aim to critique (Bradley, 2007; Ahl and Marlow, 2012).

Besides the academic community, governments have an important role to play in promoting entrepreneurship as a gendered practice. At present, policy on women's entrepreneurship that provides special assistance (for example, in terms of access to finance) has reinforced the myth that women are weak and disadvantaged. We do not suggest that entrepreneurial aid be removed; only that the discourse be changed. Government assistance, whether it is through funding, education or networking opportunities, should lean towards discourses associated with the benefits of entrepreneurship irrespective of the individual entrepreneur in question. This does require a challenge to the nature and range of services provided to women specifically and a deeper understanding of the contextual issues and challenges that confront them.

REFERENCES

AAUW (The American Association of University Women) (2016). The simple truth about the gender pay gap. Available at: http://www.aauw.org/aauw_check/ pdf_download/show_pdf.php?file=The-Simple-Truth.

Ahl, H. (2002). The construction of the female entrepreneur as the Other. In B. Czarniawska and H. Hopfl (eds), *Casting the Other: The Production and Maintenance of Inequalities in Work Organizations*. London: Routledge, pp. 52–67.

Ahl, H. (2004). *The Scientific Reproduction of Gender Inequality: A Discourse of Research Texts on Women's Entrepreneurship.* Copenhagen: Copenhagen Business School Press.

Ahl, H. (2006). Why research on women entrepreneurs needs new directions. *Entrepreneurship Theory and Practice*, 30(5), 595–621.

Ahl, H. and Marlow, S. (2012). Exploring the dynamics of gender, feminism and entrepreneurship: advancing debate to escape a dead end? *Organization*, 19(5), 543–562.

Baines, S. and Wheelock, J. (2000). Work and employment in small businesses: perpetuating and challenging gender traditions. *Gender, Work and Organization*, 7(1), 45–56, doi.wiley.com/10.1111/1468-0432.00092.

Baker, T.A., Aldrich, H.E and Liou, N. (1997). Invisible entrepreneurs: the neglect of women business owners by mass media and scholarly journals in the USA. *Entrepreneurship and Regional Development*, 9(3), 221–238.

Berglund, K., Johannisson, B. and Schwartz, B. (2012). *Societal Entrepreneurship: Positioning, Penetrating and Promoting.* Cheltenham, UK and Northampton, MA: Edward Elgar Publishing.

Bird, B. and Brush, C. (2002). A gendered perspective on organizational creation. *Entrepreneurship Theory and Practice*, 26(3), 41–66.

Bourne, K.A. and Calás, M.B. (2013). Becoming 'real' entrepreneurs: women and the gendered normalization of work. *Gender, Work and Organization*, 20(4), 425–438.

Bowden, P. and Mummery, J. (2014). *Understanding Feminism.* Abingdon, UK: Routledge.

Bradley, H. (2007). *Gender.* London: Polity Press.

Butler, J. (2004). *Undoing Gender.* New York and London: Psychology Press.

Carr, J.C. and Hmieleski, K.M. (2015). Differences in the outcomes of work and family conflict between family and nonfamily businesses: an examination of business founders. *Entrepreneurship Theory and Practice*, 39(6), 1413–1432. Available at: http://doi.wiley.com/10.1111/etap.12174.

Carter, S., Marlow, S. and Bennett, D. (2012). Gender and entrepreneurship. In S. Carter and D. Jones-Evans (eds), *Enterprise and Small Business.* London: Prentice Hall, pp. 218–231.

Davis, A.E. and Shaver, K.G. (2012). Understanding gender variations in business growth intentions across the lifecourse. *Entrepreneurship Theory and Practice*, 36(3), 495–512.

De Beauvoir, S. (1949 [2010]). *The Second Sex: Women as Other.* New York: Vintage Paperbacks.

De Bruin, A., Brush, C.G. and Welter, F. (2006). Introduction to the special issue: towards building cumulative knowledge on women's entrepreneurship. *Entrepreneurship Theory and Practice*, 30(5), 585–593.

Durkheim, E. (1893 [2013]). *The Division of Labour in Society.* 2nd edn of English translation, W.D. Halls (trans.). Basingstoke, UK: Palgrave Macmillan.

Eddleston, K. and Powell, G. (2012). Nurturing entrepreneurs' work–family balance: a gendered perspective. *Entrepreneurship Theory and Practice*, 36(5), 513–541.

EC (European Commission) (2015). Women's entrepreneurship: closing the gender gap in access to financial and other services and in social entrepreneurship. Available at: http://www.europarl.europa.eu/RegData/etudes/STUD/2015/519230/IPOL_STU(2015)519230_EN.pdf.

Fournier, V. (2002). Practising disconnection. In B. Czarniawska and H. Hopfl (eds), *Casting the Other: The Production and Maintenance of Inequalities in Work Organizations*. London: Routledge, pp. 68–88.

GEM (Global Entrepreneurship Monitor) (2012). Available at: http://www.gemcon sortium.org/.

GEM (Global Entrepreneurship Monitor) (2014). Available at: http://www.gemcon sortium.org/.

Gupta, V.K., Tuban, D.B., Wasti, S.A. and Sidkar, A. (2009). The role of gender sterotypes in perceptions of entrepreneurs and intentions to become an entrepreneur. *Entrepreneurship Theory and Practice*, 33(2), 397–417.

Hartmann, H.J. (1979). The unhappy marriage of Marxism and feminism: towards a more progressive union. *Capital and Class*, 3(2), 1–33.

Helms-Mills, J. (2003). *Making Sense of Organizational Change*. London: Routledge.

Henry, C. and Marlow, S. (2014). Exploring the intersection of gender, feminism and entrepreneurship. In Fayolle, A. (ed.), *Handbook of Research on Entrepreneurship: What We Know and What We Need to Know*. Cheltenham, UK and Northampton, MA: Edward Elgar Publishing, pp. 109–126.

Horowitz, M.C. (1976). Aristole and women. *Journal of the History of Biology*, 9(2), 183–213.

Hughes, K.D., Jennings, J.E., Brush, C. and Welter, F. (2012). Extending women's entrepreneurship research in new directions. *Entrepreneurship Theory and Practice*, 36(3), 429–442.

Jones, C. and Spicer, A. (2005). The sublime object of entrepreneurship. *Organisation*, 12(2), 223–246.

Kerfoot, D. and Miller, C. (2010). Organizing entrepreneurship? Women's invisibility in self-employment. In P. Lewis and R. Simpson (eds), *Revealing and Concealing Gender: Issues of Visibility in Organisations*. London: Palgrave, pp. 100–124.

Kirzner, I.M. (1999). Creativity and/or alertness: a reconsideration of the Schumpeterian entrepreneur. *Review of Austrian Economics*, 11, 5–17.

Lewis, P. (2013). The search for an authentic entrepreneurial identity: difference and professionalism among women business owners. *Gender, Work and Organization,* 20(3), 252–266. Available at: http://doi.org/10.1111/j.1468–0432.2011.00568.x.

Malach-Pines, A. and Schwartz, D. (2008). Now you see them, now you don't: gender differences in entrepreneurship. *Journal of Managerial Psychology*, 23(7), 811–832.

Mills, A.J. (1988). Organisation, gender and culture. *Organisation Studies*, 9(3), 351–369.

Minniti, M. and Naudé, W. (2010). Introduction: what do we know about the patterns and determinants of female entrepreneurship across countries? *European Journal of Development Research*, 22(3), 277–293. Available at: http://www.palgrave–journals.com/doifinder/10.1057/ejdr.2010.17.

Mirchandani, K. (1999). Feminist insight on gendered work: new directions in research on women and entrepreneurship. *Gender, Work & Organization*, 6(4), 224–235.

Morris, M.H. and Trotter, J.D. (1990). Institutionalizing entrepreneurship in a large company: a case study at AT&T. *Industrial Marketing Management*, 19(2), 131–139. Available at: http://www.sciencedirect.com/science/article/pii/001985019090037V (accessed 21 June 2015).

Naudé, W. (2011). Entrepreneurship is not a binding constraint on growth and development in the poorest countries. *World Development*, 39(1), 33–44. Available at:

http://www.sciencedirect.com/science/article/pii/S0305750X10001208 (accessed 12 September 2015).

Naudé, W.W. (2013). Entrepreneurship and economic development: theory, evidence and policy. *IZA Discussion Paper*, 7507, pp. 1–20. Available at: http://www.econstor.eu/handle/10419/80532\nhttp://ftp.iza.org/dp7507.pdf.

Oakley, A. (1972). *Sex, Gender and Society*. London: Temple Smith.

Ogbor, J.O. (2000). Mythicizing and reification in entrepreneurial discourse: ideology–critique of entrepreneurial studies. *Journal of Management Studies*, 37(5), 605–635.

Pringle, R. (1988). *Secretaries Talk*. London: Verso.

Putnam, L.L. and Mumby, D.K. (1993). Organizations, emotion and the myth of rationality. In S. Fineman (ed.), *Emotion in Organizations*. Thousand Oaks, CA: Sage, pp. 36–57.

Santos, J.F., Roomi, M.Z. and Liñán, F. (2016). About gender differences and social environments in the development of entrepreneurial intentions. *Journal of Small Business Management*, 54(1), 49–66.

Schumpeter, J.A. (1934 [2002]). *The Theory of Economic Development: An Inquiry into Profit, Capital, Credit, Interest, and the Business Cycle*. New Brunswick, NJ: Transaction Publishers.

Shinnar, R.S., Giacomin, O. and Janssen, F. (2012). Entrepreneurial perceptions and intentions: the role of gender and culture. *Entrepreneurship Theory and Practice*, 36(3), 465–493. Available at: http://doi.wiley.com/10.1111/j.1540–6520.2012.00509.x.

Shinnar, R.S., Hsu, D.K. and Powell, B.C. (2014). Self-efficacy, entrepreneurial intentions, and gender: assessing the impact of entrepreneurship education longitudinally. *The International Journal of Management Education*, 12(3), 561–570. Available at: http://www.sciencedirect.com/science/article/pii/S1472811714000512 (accessed 11 February 2015).

Shockley, G.E. and Frank, P.M. (2011). Schumpeter, Kirzner and the field of social entrepreneurship. *Journal of Social Entrepreneurship*, 2(1), 6–26, doi: 10.1080/19420676.2010.544924.

Sterba, J.P. (2003). *Social and Political Philosophy: Classical Western Texts in Feminist and Multicultural Perspectives*, 3rd edn. Belmont, CA: Wadsworth CENGAGE Learning.

Women's Enterprise Policy Group (2011). A multi billion £ opportunity: the untapped growth potential of UK women entrepreneurs. Briefing Paper. Women's Enterprise Policy Group, October.

FURTHER READING

Bartky, S.L. (1988). Foucault, femininity and the modernisation of patriarchal power. In I. Diamond and L. Quinby (eds), *Femininity and Foucault: Reflections and Resistance*. Boston: Northern University Press, pp. 93–111. Available at: http://faculty.uml.edu/kluis/42.101/Bartky_FoucaultFeminityandtheModernization.pdf.

Bem, S. (1993). *The Lenses of Gender: Transforming the Debate on Sexual Inequality*. New Haven, CT: Yale University Press.

Brush, C.G. (2006). Women entrepreneurs: a research overview. In M. Casson, B.

Yeung, A. Basu and N. Wadeson (eds), *The Oxford Handbook of Entrepreneurship*. Oxford: Oxford University Press, pp. 611–628.

De Bruin, A., Brush, C.G. and Welter, F. (2007). Advancing a framework for coherent research on women's entrepreneurship. *Entrepreneurship Theory and Practice*, 31(3), 323–339.

Dy, A.M., Martin, L. and Marlow, S. (2015). Unmasking the internet: deconstructing the discourse of digital entrepreneurship. Paper presented at the 'Critical Management Studies Conference', University of Leicester, July.

García, M.C.D. and Welter, F. (2011). Gender identities and practices: interpreting women entrepreneurs' narratives. *International Small Business Journal*, 31(4), 384–404.

Marlow, S. and McAdam, M. (2013). Gender and entrepreneurship: advancing debate and challenging myths; exploring the mystery of the under-performing female entrepreneur. *International Journal of Entrepreneurial Behaviour and Research*, 19(1), pp.114–124. Available at: http://www.emeraldinsight.com/doi/abs/10.1108/13552551311299288.

Perren, L. and Jennings, P.L. (2005). Government discourses on entrepreneurship: issues of legitimization, subjugation, and power. *Entrepreneurship Theory and Practice*, 29(2), 173–184.

Spicer, A. (2012). Critical theories of entrepreneurship. In K. Mole and M. Ram (eds), *Perspectives in Entrepreneurship: A Critical Approach*. London: Palgrave, pp. 149–160.

Index